Beyond the Last Inning

Also by Zak Ford
and from McFarland

Called Up: Ballplayers Remember Becoming Major Leaguers (2023)

Beyond the Last Inning

Life and Careers After Playing Professional Baseball

Zak Ford

McFarland & Company, Inc., Publishers
Jefferson, North Carolina

Library of Congress Cataloging-in-Publication Data

Names: Ford, Zak, 1978– author
Title: Beyond the last inning : life and careers after playing professional baseball / Zak Ford.
Other titles: Life & careers after playing professional baseball
Description: Jefferson, North Carolina : McFarland & Company, Inc., Publishers, 2026 | Includes index.
Identifiers: LCCN 2026018890 | ISBN 9781476699622 print ∞
ISBN 9798368601045 ebook
Subjects: LCSH: Baseball players—Psychology | Identity (Psychology) | Life change events | Stress (Psychology) | Adaptability (Psychology) | BISAC: SPORTS & RECREATION / Baseball / General | LCGFT: Biographies
Classification: LCC GV867.6 .F67 2026 | DDC 796.357019—dc23/eng/20260526
LC record available at https://lccn.loc.gov/2026018890

ISBN (print) 978-1-4766-9962-2
ISBN (ebook) 979-8-3686-0104-5

Printed in the United States of America

McFarland & Company, Inc., Publishers
Box 611, Jefferson, North Carolina 28640
www.mcfarlandpub.com

For my wife, Meredith, who has supported
all my career transitions since college.

Table of Contents

2000s 98

Since 2010 177

Preface

This is a collection of first-person, human-interest stories. While every story is told by a former professional baseball player, they are not traditional autobiographical baseball stories. These stories tell what players face when they hang up their cleats, through their post-playing career transitions.

While a comprehensive study of post-playing career transitions would be beneficial, the collection of adequate information to complete such a task would be overwhelming for any author. Much of the information available is incomplete and inconsistent. Additionally, a lot of obtainable information is anecdotal or provided voluntarily by players, which would eliminate much of the data for players unwilling to share difficult post-playing journeys. Understandable pride and confidentiality become challenging factors.

I am fortunate that 49 players shared their post-playing career transitions with me for this book. Of the 49 players, 45 were in my first book, *Called Up: Ballplayers Remember Becoming Major Leaguers* (McFarland, 2023). The other four are former minor leaguers I made connections with through *Called Up*. Having established relationships helped players speak more candidly about post-playing challenges and highlights. While I didn't shy away from sharing challenges and negative experiences, I kept an overall positive angle for stories.

My criteria for inclusion in this book were broad. I sent an informal note to all 109 players featured in *Called Up*, letting them know I'd like to include them if they were interested in sharing their post-playing career transitions. From that initial outreach, I received positive responses from nearly 25 percent of the players. After conducting that first round of outreach and interviews, I then targeted players based on both their likely willingness to participate and on the careers I knew they entered after playing. I wanted to ensure the book included a good mix of players who remained in baseball and who entered completely different careers.

Interviews were conducted between the spring of 2024 and summer of 2025. Many of these former players are still working; therefore, some have experienced career changes since their interviews with me.

Stories are organized by the year players last played in affiliated baseball, meaning the last year they were associated with a major league team. This order was chosen to show evolutions impacting rosters and resources beneficial for post-playing lives. Some players ended their careers at the major league level, and others ended their careers in the minors. While many players attempted to return to affiliated baseball through independent leagues, I did not use that as a factor in ordering stories unless they were later successful in finding a major league affiliate. The years players ended their careers in affiliated baseball range between 1973 and 2019.

The first-person narratives will read like spoken word. Stories have been edited only minimally from the interview transcripts. Text has been selected and rearranged, but these are the words of the players. Grammar may be inconsistent, and sometimes even incorrect, but the meaning should be clear. Some stories may fluctuate between past and present tense. Additionally, many stories include baseball terms that may require a basic understanding of the game.

Introduction

Professional baseball players are human. While this statement is obvious, fans often don't consider the human side of the players they watch perform. This disconnect frequently continues into the post-playing lives of players, as many fans have the misconception that players can retire after their playing days without the need to transition into other careers. This is far from true for most players.

My great-uncle, Larry Powell, pitched professionally for 14 seasons, between 1937 and 1954, and we were very close. As a teen and young adult, I had the opportunity to join him for many of his player reunions. Through this experience, I was blessed to become friends with many of his former teammates and opponents. While these men played long before I was born, the relationships gave me an appreciation for both their playing and post-playing lives. I got to know them as people with real-life struggles and challenges, just like everyone else.

After experiencing a few career transitions myself, I settled in the field of workforce development nearly 15 years ago. Through influencing public policy and providing support services on the issue, I find it intriguing how people select their chosen professions and journey through their career paths. Given my own indirect career path and devotion to baseball, I find the post-playing career transitions of players especially interesting. In what other field can you reach the pinnacle of your profession in your twenties only to then need to find a new line of work in your thirties (or sooner)? Not many.

Through working on my first book, *Called Up: Ballplayers Remember Becoming Major Leaguers,* I was exposed to the personal lives of many of the book's featured players. While exposure to the personal lives of former players wasn't new for me, given my early experiences connected to my great-uncle, the exposure was considerably different. Instead of men who were long retired from both playing and post-playing careers by the time I met them, numerous players featured in *Called Up* were men

I had the opportunity to watch play. Many were my age, or even younger. While I was obviously never a professional baseball player, I was still able to see parallels between their lives and mine, especially regarding career transitions.

In 2021, while I was still working on *Called Up*, one of the players I had interviewed for the book, Casper Wells, published a blog on his post-playing transition. He humbly addressed his challenges with identity, fulfillment, and finding a post-playing career, all while maintaining a positive angle. I didn't just find his story interesting. In a unique way, I also found it inspiring.

By the time *Called Up* was released during the fall of 2023, I had begun considering ideas for my next book project. I knew I wanted to complete another book of human-interest baseball stories but was unsure of the topic. Wells's blog kept surfacing during my brainstorms. However, I was unsure how I would expand on what Wells shared. Additionally, even if I could, would enough players be willing to speak with me candidly for a book? This time I wouldn't be asking about their big-league call-ups and debuts, often a highlight of their playing careers. Now, I would be asking about the darkest moments of their playing days and the challenges they faced while transitioning into post-playing careers.

In January of 2024, I vetted the post-playing career transition idea with seven former players I knew, including Wells. I reached out to players strategically, wanting to ensure I received input from players with varying experiences. The consensus was that the concept was interesting and unique, and something that should probably be done. However, players were also candid about the difficulties I could face regarding the readiness of other players to share such personal details. Ultimately, I decided I was willing to tackle the challenge.

While on a trip to spring training in Arizona in March of 2024, I connected with Wells for the first *Beyond the Last Inning* interview. Over the following 15 months, I was fortunate to interview 48 additional players who were willing to be part of the book. Understandably, some men shared more details about their post-playing career transitions than others. However, I was pleased with how much players shared.

Post-playing career transitions aren't as simple as just switching jobs for former players. Imagine excelling at something since you were a boy, having it become a profession, and reaching the pinnacle of that profession as a young adult. Then, often within just a few years, you realize that everything you've worked toward is over, and likely not on your terms. There's not just a challenge of finding a new profession. There's often a challenge of finding a new identity, and fulfillment within that new identity.

Give or take a few years, most players end their playing careers around the age of 30. At this age, many have additional family responsibilities, which may add another layer of complexity to the situation.

Although professional baseball can be a lucrative profession, few of the men in this book made enough money to sustain them much beyond their playing days. Those that did still needed to find something to occupy their time. Some took a few years off to find their next profession. Many had much shorter windows.

Players overwhelmingly mentioned camaraderie with teammates as the thing they missed most from their playing days. This was followed closely by missing the high level of competition. Although it is not possible to replicate either equally, some found substitutes in new hobbies and professions. Others returned to the game in varying capacities.

Post-playing career transitions include many complex human elements. I hope these stories give you an understanding of them.

1970s

Several evolutions in professional baseball during the 1970s impacted rosters of major league affiliated teams throughout the decade.

While there was major league expansion, the overall number of affiliated teams decreased, as many minor leagues disbanded. Labor relations evolved considerably, improving player conditions and salaries, and providing players the opportunity to explore free agency. International baseball grew in prominence, and some players left affiliated ball to play elsewhere, primarily Japan. Additionally, the number of Latin players in affiliated baseball grew.

These major changes undeniably impacted the journeys of the five players whose playing careers ended during the decade.

Mike Averill

Mike Averill played three seasons of affiliated baseball in the Red Sox system. His last year playing in affiliated baseball was 1973. He was a third-generation professional baseball player. His grandfather, Earl Averill, was elected to the National Baseball Hall of Fame in 1975, and his father, Earl Averill, Jr., spent many years in the major leagues. Following his baseball career, Mike entered the boat and marine industry and operated his own business for many years. At the time of the interview for this book, he was semi-retired and living in Washington state.

I grew up on the ball field. I used to go to the ballpark with my dad, hang out, and shag balls. I was always in the clubhouse, and sometimes managers would let me sit in the dugout.

I was never pressured to play. It was just in my heart to play baseball.

In 1974 I made the Double-A team. The day before joining the team, they wanted to send me back down because some guy came down from Triple-A. When they wanted to send me back down to A-Ball, I was devastated. I quit and asked for my release.

I wish I was more mature. I should have stayed with the Red Sox, but I didn't ask for any advice. That said, I don't know if I would have listened to any advice at the time. I was pretty upset.

I came back to Anaheim and was going to find a job. A scout, Joe Stephenson, called and asked, "What are you doing?" I said, "It's just not working out." He said, "Well, go try out for this team playing in the Northwest League. It's an independent team and they've having tryouts in Long Beach." I said, "Okay." I went there, did good, and they wanted me. The deal with that team was that if they sold you to a big league club, you would get half of that money.

I was doing really well until I fouled a ball off my foot. I played most of that year with a sore foot. Some days I could run and some days I couldn't. I was still having a good year until about the last week when I broke my wrist, which I finished playing the season with. I was discouraged. I was just about 22, and I was done.

I was upset with baseball for quite a while and was resentful. I missed playing. I loved everything about the physical part of baseball and playing the sport.

I had always liked working on mechanical stuff. When I was still playing, I actually got drafted into the Army. To stop from going into the war, I got into the National Guard. I went through basic training and Military Occupational Specialty (MOS) training. I learned to work on trucks, tanks, and stuff like that.

When I got out of baseball and was living in California, I knew I wanted to get back up to Washington state. I was looking for a vocation that could get me back to Washington, where my roots are. Somehow, boats just clicked, and I thought I'd learn how to work on boats. That's how it started.

I like everything about the water. I love fishing, water skiing, and all that.

I didn't have any conversations with my grandpa or dad about their transitions out of baseball. However, my dad did help me a little bit with figuring out how to get into the boat business. It was very hard to get into the boat business at that time, but he did a little research and let me know about some classes and opportunities.

I was able to take some basic classes at a community college and get a job at Riverside Boat and Marine. I made almost no money. Back then, you could get a laborer job for about five bucks an hour, but I went to work for them for about $2.50 an hour, basically just to have them train me.

In the summer of 1975, my grandpa was inducted into the Baseball Hall of Fame. I had gone with my grandpa to some old timers' games and had been to some dinners when there was a drive to get him in. But I didn't go to the ceremony because I had just entered the boat business, and the summertime is so busy.

I worked at Riverside Boat and Marine for a year and a half to get the training, and then I got a job up in Washington.

I had just got the job in Washington when the Italians wanted me to come and play. I literally got a call in the middle of the night about coming to play in Italy. I had a teammate in New Westminster who had gone over there and had a lot of fun. However, I was still devastated at the time and had just started the new job. I told them no.

Mike Averill was a third-generation professional baseball player. Following his baseball career, he entered the boat and marine industry (courtesy Mike Averill).

Eventually, I started a family-owned boat business in 1988. I started it with my in-laws, and my wife worked with me. We were in a small town, Gig Harbor, and right across the street from the water. It was a fantastic business. I knew all my customers and almost everybody in town. I grew it to a couple other locations.

I specialized in bass boats, which were just starting up here. We were a little ahead of the curve. While I sold some boats, it was pretty much repairs. We put on new outboards, would rig them with electronics, do any rewiring, or anything the boat would need.

I took on a partner, and he started to get ill, so we had to sell it. I wasn't ready to retire, but that's what I did.

When I retired, I went on a 4,000-mile catamaran ride to help a friend move his boat from Mexico to Florida. I had a lot of time to process things. When I got back, I told some guys in Auburn I was ready to come to work three or four days a week. Now, that's what I do. I often subcontract out to boat shops and mostly put on outboards and sterndrives. It keeps me busy.

All I ever wanted to do was play baseball. What helped with the transition was staying in something where I could use my physical skills for a release. I got into softball right away. I was quite a softball player, and that was a major relief for me, especially with being part of a team. That was a good release. Otherwise, I don't know what I would have done.

Bill Denehy

Bill Denehy played 10 seasons of affiliated baseball, including parts of three in the major leagues. His last year playing in affiliated baseball was 1973. Following his playing career, he worked in numerous industries, including real estate and radio. He also coached at the professional and collegiate levels. He passed away June 27, 2025, shortly after the interview for this book.

My fastball kept getting slower and slower every year. I was throwing breaking ball after breaking ball, and changeups, and using my fastball sparingly. I couldn't keep pitching like that. I'd get killed. I went to spring training with the Giants in 1974, didn't make the team, and that was the final straw.

Earlier that spring, I went to a dinner and ran into a former high school teacher that was in real estate. We talked a little bit, and he said, "If you ever decide to get out of baseball, give me a call and I'll start you up in real estate out here." I got released, gave him a call, and the next thing I knew, I moved out to Arizona. The only reason I took the job was because of money, as I had a brand-new daughter and a wife to support.

The company I was with went through Century 21. I got involved with doing some work with them, and then there was an opening up in Wisconsin. I interviewed for the job and eventually became the director of sales and management development for the Midwest region.

I had worked with one of the local stations in Milwaukee as a fill-in for Sal Bando when he couldn't make it. One day one of the producers said, "You should really think about doing this full-time. There's an all sports radio station getting started in Connecticut. You might want to give them a call and see if they might be interested in hiring you." That's what I did. I contacted them. It was Enterprise Radio at the time.

John Chanin, a former ABC executive, was the executive vice president of production. I flew into Connecticut and interviewed with him. It was funny. We talked for probably half an hour, and he said to me, "Well, obviously you know baseball and football, but I'm concerned about some other sports." I said I could handle myself with other sports. He said, "I'll tell you what. Answer this question for me. In 1960, Jerry Lucas was the All-American for the Ohio State Buckeyes basketball team. There was another player on the team that became very famous. Can you name him?" The player he was talking about was John Havlicek. However, I also knew Larry Siegfried was on that team, along with Joe Roberts, Mel Nowell, Bob Knight, and that the coach was Fred Taylor. He laughed and said, "How about if I pay you this much?" I said fine and the next thing I knew, I was on air with Enterprise Radio.

It only lasted about nine months until they ran out of money. The Rasmussens who started ESPN and sold to Getty thought they could do the same thing with Enterprise Radio. They just didn't have enough money bankrolled to do that.

Since it was in Connecticut and close to where the Red Sox had their Double-A team, I contacted the Red Sox and told them I had an interest in being their pitching coach. They said to come down and talk to the manager, Tony Torchia, and if it was okay with him, they'd give me a contract. That's what happened and I was with them for three years—'81, '82, and '83. The first year I had Brian Denman, second year I had Oil Can Boyd, and in '83, I had Roger Clemens. All three years we led the league in earned run average as a team.

Between the '82 and '83 seasons, I was looking for a way to make some extra money during the winter and contacted Middlesex Community College about teaching a course on baseball. They gave me a figure based on 25 students in the class. I said I thought I could get a lot more than that. I said, "If I only get 25 people, I'll accept your offer. But if I get more than 25 people, can we add on?" I forget what the figure was, but they said they'd give me X amount of money per student over 25. I had over 130 people sign up for the course. We had to move it to the cafeteria.

On the first day, I drew a diagram on the blackboard of the pitching mound and rubber, and then a line to home plate. I said, "You've got an index card in front of you. You'll get a passing grade today if you put your name on it and tell me how far the distance is from the pitching rubber to home plate." Everybody started to laugh and said, "That's easy." I said, "Well, let's see." Everyone signed their card and passed it in. Everyone had 60'6". I said, "Wrong. It's on the blackboard here. I said from the pitching rubber to home plate. It's 59'1". The extra 17 inches of the plate brings it to 60'6"." I still hear people on television say 60'6".

I only taught the course that one semester. After that and my last season coaching with the Red Sox, I went to my hometown bank, talked to the president, and asked if I could do some work for them. I thought I'd be best suited for some PR work, but they offered me a job in sales. I think I'm a good salesman if I believe in, and really know, what I'm selling. However, talking to people about stuff like better rates wasn't my forte. That bank job only lasted about a year.

I remember there was an article in the *Hartford Courant* about the University of Hartford going to Division I. The writer knew I was looking to get back into baseball and called me. He said, "You might want to call these people and see if there's a baseball position there." I went there, interviewed with the vice president, and looked at their facilities. Their facilities were so bad. It was like a grammar school softball field. It was brutal. They hadn't won a game the prior two seasons. There were two guys on the team who started all 28 games over those two seasons and didn't get a hit.

Well, my time there was not a happy time. They poured a lot of money into basketball, but we were lacking money. I needed new equipment, uniforms, and everything. The year before, the guy in charge of washing uniforms made a mistake and washed the red tops with white bottoms, and they turned out pink. I told the development people that we needed money and let them know I'd like to work on coordinating a dinner to raise funds. They asked, "Who are you thinking of bringing in?" I said, "Roger Clemens, Pete Rose, or George Steinbrenner." They laughed and said, "You're going to bring George Steinbrenner on campus? We've been trying to contact Mr. Steinbrenner for a couple years now and he won't even answer our calls." Well, I brought him in.

I got Nikki O'Neill, the governor's wife, to be a co-chair for the event. She asked, "What are my duties?" I said, "You have two duties—hold a cocktail party at the governor's residence before the dinner, and call George Steinbrenner." She laughed and said she could do both. I had a couple of people I knew who could get to George and tell him to expect her call. He accepted her call, she talked to him, and he came in.

Well, there were two depressing things about the event. First, security called me from the governor's residence and said we could only have a maximum of 125 people. Well, the president of the university invited all the department heads without me knowing, and we had over 140 show up, which created an issue. Also, we made $60,000, but only $15,000 went to our baseball program for a trip out west and our new uniforms. The rest of the money was put in the basketball account.

With the pressure of working my tail off, not seeing results, and bringing in money without being able to get it, I was drinking pretty heavily.

One night we played the University of Connecticut and got into two brawls on the field. I made some negative comments about the game, the umpires, and the University of Connecticut. They got printed in the paper, and I got fired.

After the Hartford job, the next work I got was in construction. It was an easy place to go, and I knew some people who were able to get me a job.

Then, I got a call from John Chanin, the guy who had hired me at Enterprise Radio. He was living in Florida and wanted me to be one of the analysts for the Senior Professional Baseball Association. I went down and did a winter of that. He was also working on doing a daily talk show out of Disney. He offered me that job, but things never worked out between the company and Disney.

That's when I got sober. On June 15, I will have 34 consecutive years of sobriety with no relapses. With another recovering person, I started the National Association of Recovering Professional Athletes. However, that didn't work out. From there the last two jobs I had were with Edwin Watts Golf doing shipping, and at Universal Studios as a greeter.

I started having problems with my eye. I lost the retina in my right eye and wasn't able to work on a regular basis. We could never prove it, but we think that the number of cortisone shots I got playing baseball caused the weakening of the retina. I had 57 shots in 26 months. I ended up getting Social Security Disability, and once I got to 62, I completely retired.

Sam McDowell

Sam McDowell played 16 seasons of affiliated baseball, including 15 in the major leagues. His last year playing in affiliated baseball was 1975. Following his playing career, he entered the real estate and insurance industries. His struggle with alcoholism is well known within the baseball community. Once he achieved sobriety, he worked for many years as a counselor and helped many baseball players through his work with Major League Baseball's Baseball Assistance Team (B.A.T.).

Throughout my entire baseball career, I knew something was wrong. I didn't know what it was. I knew that when I was standing on that mound, something was wrong, and I just couldn't figure it out. About halfway through my career, I decided it was something to do with sports psychology because I had probably read every self-help book on the market, sometimes over and over. I figured they would help me, but they didn't. I was an alcoholic, but I didn't realize it. During addiction, there's always this nagging deal going on inside of us that something isn't right. I thought it was sports psychology that could turn me around, but of course, it didn't.

I was a starter that pitched every fourth or fifth day. I did nothing but eat proper dinners, take vitamins, and drink lots of liquids two nights prior to my pitching. I would make sure I was healthy. But on the nights I pitched, after the game was my time to go crazy. I would drink myself into oblivion. Whether I won or lost, it didn't matter. Then, the next day, I would get to the clubhouse early and make sure I did extra workouts, thinking I could sweat it out. Then, that night I would go out after the game and drink into oblivion again. The next two nights I was a perfect health nut, so to speak, without realizing or understanding how it affected me psychologically and emotionally when pitching. That didn't come about until much later on.

My last year with Cleveland I was on the disabled list a couple different times. I didn't realize it at the time, but I had torn my rotator cuff. At first, as long as I got rest, I could pitch six or seven innings without the pain taking over. Eventually, I just couldn't anymore. Gabe Paul, the GM of the Indians, knew that and traded me to the Giants for Gaylord Perry anyhow.

When I got to the Giants, I knew my days were basically numbered. The pain was killing me. Previously to that, as referenced, I was an organized, functioning alcoholic, but I then tried to medicate myself with alcohol over and over. With drug addiction and alcoholism, it will always progress. I hate the word *progress* because it sounds positive. You keep getting worse.

Once I got to the Yankees, it was horrendous. I was in the bullpen and had no idea how to plan my drinking then. I was drunk half the time, and they released me.

When I was released by the Yankees in '74, I went down and talked to Joe L. Brown of the Pirates because I lived there in Pittsburgh. He let me know right then and there, he knew I had a drinking problem. I convinced him that it was all taken care of, and I didn't have the problem anymore. He said, "I'll make you a deal. We'll take you to spring training, but you've got to earn your way. If you do well, we'll sign you. But the very first time you have a drink, we will release you." I said, "Oh, yeah. No problem." But willpower only lasts so long with a drunk.

With the Pirates, there were three or four occasions I got drunk without him knowing about it. Then, we were in New York, and Bruce Kison started a game against the Mets. In the first inning, he got bombed. They replaced him and brought me in. I pitched well, and we ended up winning the game. It was a Saturday afternoon and after the game was over, I went out, had dinner, and got drunk out of my mind. The next day I showed up for the day game, and I was still drunk. I knew that was it. There was no hiding it.

After I was drunk in New York, we went to Philly for a few days. Danny Murtaugh put me in another game, but they knew they were going to release me, and I knew they were going to release me as well. I understood it.

On the plane flight home to Pittsburgh, halfway through the flight, Joe L. Brown goes by me, taps me on the shoulder, and says, "I want you in my office tomorrow at nine o'clock." I said, "Okay." I went in his office the next morning and he said, "Sam, there's no need to discuss anything. We made a deal. You're going to be released. We're not going to let anybody know why. We're just going to bring up a right-handed pitcher because we have so many left-handers in the bullpen." I said, "Okay. See you later, Joe." That was it.

During my last few years in baseball, I took some psychology and sociology classes during the wintertime. I was fortunate to live in a city where they had two colleges that were on the trimester system, so after baseball seasons, I would take a course here and there. I also got my licenses for real estate, insurance, stocks, bonds, and mutual funds. I had no idea what I was going to do, but I at least wanted to get the licenses, so I wasn't delayed a year or so while not making any money. I just wanted to prepare.

Even though I was released by the Pirates in the middle of the 1975 season, I still got paid through the end of the year. I knew January 1, 1976, was coming, so in October I took a job in real estate because a friend of the family owned the company. I found I hated just sitting there waiting for somebody to come to me to sell their house or buy a house. I just couldn't understand how you could sit there and wait for people to come to you. That wasn't me. It only lasted about a year.

I went into insurance and did extremely well. Many alcoholics are successful because they don't want people to point at their drinking. In fact, I still hold records with the insurance company.

Eventually, the progression of addiction took over. I had been a periodic drunk. I would go on binges for two or three days, drinking morning, noon, and night. Then, for the next month, I would not drink anything. I used the excuse that I couldn't be an alcoholic because I thought they drank every day. However, I reached the point where I was getting drunk almost all the time.

I was just out of control. My wife and family never knew when I'd come home drunk. I remember one day leaving the office when I knew my wife was upset with me. I said to myself while leaving, "I am not going to drink no matter what." Well, I got halfway home and pulled right into a bar without even thinking about it. I just automatically pulled in. Of course, I then told myself I'd have just one or two drinks. Well, that was it.

My wife ended up leaving me. She got her own apartment with the kids. I lost my wife, my kids, and my job. I had 35 cents in my pocket and debt of about $140,000. I ended up moving in with my parents.

About six months later while living with my parents, I went

downstairs and made a pot of coffee. While drinking coffee, I walked back and forth in the living room thinking, "You beat me. You beat me." I sat down, called an operator, and asked her to connect me to Gateway. She immediately connected me to the rehabilitation center.

The rest is history with my sobriety. I'm obsessive-compulsive, even to this day, so I wanted to find out how it could happen. That was the first time I found out it was a disease and not a mental illness or something psychological. I followed exactly, to the letter of the law, what I needed to do for my recovery. I went to 90 meetings in 90 days. Thereafter, I went to four meetings a week for the next 30 years. I went over the 12-step program three or four times. I found out you have to live them. You could read them all you want, but until you actually live them, you won't feel the change.

Fortunately, I had a mentor, Dr. Abraham Twerski, who to this day is considered the foremost authority in the world on alcoholism and drug addiction. He knew it was a disease long before anyone ever thought of it being that.

I was an amateur coach for my son's baseball teams, and later with other amateur teams. Kids started coming to me because they had heard of my recovery. They would come to me with all kinds of different problems, not necessarily addiction. I didn't feel qualified. I would take the kids down to St. Francis Hospital to see Dr. Twerski. After a year or year and a half, Twerski said, "Sam, you need to learn what's going on because the kids are going to you, not me. You need to learn how to help." I said, "I don't really want to be a counselor. They work 24 hours a day and don't get paid their just dues." However, I agreed I needed to learn something.

Twerski started taking me to different conventions throughout the country. He would have me attend workshops where they would bring in experts to teach and explain all the new findings, what the new data was on addiction, how to be a counselor, and so on. I loved that. During this period, I realized I could become a counselor because of my prior education credits. I also heard of employee assistance programming (EAP), researched that, and took the test to become an EAP counselor.

I started my own counseling and also went back to selling insurance. The counseling was always beyond substance abuse. There were kids that were troubled with bullying, parent issues, and other severe emotional and psychological problems. It wasn't just kids fooling around with drugs and alcohol. Eventually, I didn't have time for selling insurance because the counseling started to grow.

Then, out of the blue, I got a call from Commissioner Bowie Kuhn. He had heard about my recovery and asked me to help him because baseball had a serious drug problem, and they didn't know what to do about it. He asked if I would design a program for them. I designed the program for baseball, but he told me, "Thank you, but no thank you. It's too involved, and you also address alcohol. We don't have an alcohol problem. We have a drug problem." I went back to working with teenagers.

About six months later, I got a call from Mike Stone, the president of the Texas Rangers. He said, "We want your program. We want you to come down and talk to our team during spring training to see how it works." I actually tried to talk him out of it because I didn't want to waste my time or money. I wasn't going to pay for my own way to go. He kept insisting, and we made the deal that he would pay for my expenses plus a couple thousand dollars for the money I'd lose from my counseling if I'd go for 10 days. I went down and talked with individual players, and the team collectively. Seven or eight players came up to me right on the field and said they wanted help with some of their problems. I told them that since it was a confidential program, we wouldn't talk there. To this day, nobody knows of 90 percent of the players that I have worked with over the years because that was very sacred to me. I told the players what room I was in, and they would call me to set up an appointment, sit down, and talk. That's how I became the EAP counselor for Texas.

Eventually, the players from Texas were telling the players from Toronto how I was helping them, not just with drug and alcohol addiction, but with sports psychology. I got a call from Toronto saying they want to sit down and hire me. I had to get permission from Texas because nobody really works with two teams, especially when you're in a position to know all the secrets of players with problems. I called Texas, and they agreed it was okay as long as I shared my time equally.

Around this time, I got a call from Joe Garagiola with the Baseball Assistance Team (B.A.T.). He said, "Sam, you've got to work for us." I said, "I can't. I just agreed with Toronto to help them." He said, "Well, at least come and explain the program to our board of directors at the meeting next month in New York." I said, "I'll bring you a list of bona fide therapists that can help you and if you want me to train them, I will train them." I showed up to the meeting and handed Garagiola the list. He didn't even look at it. He tore it up in front of everybody and said, "You're working with us." I said I would volunteer for one year, train whoever he wanted, but that I just had too much going on. Well, after I got a check from him for the first month, I decided to end my volunteerism.

Baseball had the semblance of a program but was hoping to clarify the problems and get help for things that were going on because of the bad publicity. It wasn't just dealing with alcohol and drug addiction. They were dealing with many more problems. There were financial, emotional, psychological, family, marital, and other problems.

I helped design a program. The rule was for me to work with retired players only, both from the minor leagues and major leagues. Each team was supposed to have their own program, similar to the one we had for Major League Baseball. Occasionally, I would work with some current major league players, but it had to be on the hush because they didn't want to step on the EAPs of some teams.

I did that for many years, and we were able to help thousands of baseball players and family members with the program. It was so successful, we had the NFL, NBA, and NHL try to refine their programs to be something like ours.

Periodically, there were guys that needed orthopedic help and couldn't find it in their hometowns. Many didn't have insurance and needed an avenue for help. I befriended an orthopedic surgeon, Dr. Mike Ray, because I had a bad knee that he was taking care of. We formed a partnership with B.A.T. and in many instances for the indigent ballplayers, he would do everything free of charge. He would also get a hospital or physical therapist to discount their fees to help out. There were probably over 200 players to get orthopedic help through Dr. Ray before he died, just two years ago.

I've always had a wintertime house in Florida. I invested with 14 other baseball players and one football player to build a championship golf course in Clermont, Florida. Once it was built, our golf pro asked if any of us could come down and help with managing the golf course. I was still doing a lot of traveling with baseball, but I told him I would. As a management tool for free advertising, I would

Sam McDowell played in 15 major league seasons and was inducted into the Cleveland Indians Hall of Fame in 2006. After his playing career, and gaining sobriety, he helped many baseball players through his work with Major League Baseball's Baseball Assistance Team (B.A.T.) (courtesy Society for American Baseball Research-Rucker Archive).

pool together the former athletes in central Florida and let them play at the golf course free of charge, but with the condition that when we held charity events, they would come and play without payment and sign autographs. They agreed to it. Additionally, there were a couple developers in Clermont that wanted to build homes and make a village. One of the villages was around our golf course. I negotiated a deal where they would give a 10 percent discount off everything to former athletes—land, building of the house, and so on. They agreed, and that's how the City of Legends came about.

I've been able to help an awful amount of people and be at peace with myself, which I'm not sure I could have experienced if I didn't go through addiction and recovery. Because of my alcoholic personality, I never came close to enjoying baseball like a normal baseball player would. I could say unequivocally that I was in a depressed state my entire baseball career. There were times I enjoyed the camaraderie and fellowship, but I knew something was wrong. Something was missing, and I never truly enjoyed it because I was never at peace. However, I don't regret anything. I wouldn't have been able to help people like I did for over 40 years after playing if it didn't happen the way it did.

Roe Skidmore

Roe Skidmore played 10 seasons of affiliated baseball, including part of one in the major leagues. His last year playing in affiliated baseball was 1975. Following his playing career, he entered the life insurance and financial services industry. After retiring, he worked for many years as a part-time scout. At the time of the interview for this book, he was completely retired and living in Illinois.

In 1974, I spent most of the year in Denver with Houston's Triple-A club. There was a season ticket holder that was a regional manager for Equitable Life, which later became AXA Financial. He sat right behind the home dugout, and I got to know him a little bit. I got into a conversation with him one day, and he asked what my plans after playing were. I was almost 29 at the time.

I let him know I had talked with my wife a little bit about maybe retiring because our kids were school aged and I had to make the decision of either leaving them at home or bringing them and having them go in and out of schools. He asked if we were going back to my hometown of Decatur after the season. I said that we were. He said, "Well, I know a guy that's a district manager for Equitable that lives in Decatur." I said, "I don't know about selling insurance. That's what all old, retired baseball guys do." However, I said I wasn't afraid of talking to him.

I came home, the guy called me, and said, "I heard you wanted an interview." I ended up having several interviews with him that winter, and he got me interested. In fact, I thought about maybe quitting baseball then.

I got a call that winter letting me know Houston had traded me to the Boston Red Sox. I figured I couldn't quit then and decided to give it one more shot.

Well, I went to spring training with Boston, and they sent me to Pawtucket, Rhode Island, which was their Triple-A club. I was there for three or four weeks, and the leaves hadn't even gone green. It was still winter with cold gray days. I was sitting on the bench, and I'd been an everyday player every year I played. I didn't know them, and they didn't know me. It was pretty miserable. I thought, "I hung on one more year just for this?"

I called Joe Sparks, who was the manager of Des Moines, which was then Houston's Triple-A club. They had moved from Denver. I said, "Get me out of here. Who's playing first base for you?" I can't remember who it was, but he said whoever it was was hitting a buck and a half. He said, "Let me see what I can do."

About two days later, I got a call that I was going back to the Houston organization and going to Des Moines. I finished the rest of '75 in Des Moines.

My oldest daughter was in fourth or fifth grade at the time. She started school in Decatur. Then, when I went to spring training in Florida with the Red Sox, we put her in school there. Then, she went to school for those few weeks in Pawtucket. Then, when I went to Des Moines, we put her in school there, and that's where she finished her school year. That was when I started crying, "Uncle."

You're faced with either leaving your wife and kids at home and not seeing them until June or taking them with you and putting them in school. I told myself that it wasn't good. That was kind of the impetus for me to quit playing.

When I quit, I had three opportunities to stay in the game. Houston sent me a contract, and it probably would have ended up being another Triple-A gig. I also got a call from the Cincinnati organization, offering me a job to manage their Double-A club. Then, additionally, my really good friend Adrian Garrett called me about a chance to go to Japan.

I debated and prayed, but in the end told myself it's the same life. The main reason for my wanting to quit was my family.

I made the decision to quit and go to work for Equitable, which eventually became AXA Financial. They had stayed with me even after that winter of '74 when I talked to them several times but ultimately told them I was going back to play another year. They had kept in touch and let me know the job was still available if I wanted it. When I came back from playing in Des Moines, I went to work about a week later in Decatur.

I had a couple advantages starting off. First, my name is Roe Skidmore, and nobody else in the world has a name like that. Also, I came back to my hometown where I'd gone to high school and college, and even played a couple seasons of minor league ball in. I could get people to talk to me, and that part was a definite advantage. But I also had to show I knew what I was doing.

One thing I found very quickly after leaving baseball is that the life of a ballplayer is pretty laid back. There's structure, but when you're not at the ballpark, you're pretty much doing your own thing. In the financial business, there's a lot of organization you must learn and follow. I had to make my own list of things to do and stay on top of it every day. I don't want to say it was hard for me, but it was definitely one of the things in the transition I had to learn and deal with.

When I started, I was mostly selling life insurance. Then, it evolved into estate and financial planning, which became a better job. Most of my career was spent as a financial planner.

I worked for about three years before I took over as manager for the office, then I became the district manager. Eventually, I ended up having my own office here in Decatur, and it worked out well. I spent 33 years with them. It's a great company, and I had a really good experience over the years.

Our main company was AXA Financial, and we had them on the door. However, we brokered with a lot of other companies as well. I was really fortunate to have my son-in-law work with me for almost 17 years and then take over. Being in the business for over 30 years, I had established a lot of relationships that became more than just official business. You've got a client base that become friends. A lot of guys don't have somebody to take over their businesses, they just retire, and it goes into the wind. Again, I was really fortunate. It was a good transition for both him and me, as well as the clientele. It worked out very well.

About six months after I retired, a fellow named Scott Trcka called. He was a scout for the Phillies and asked if I'd be interested in scouting. I said I would be. To make a long story short, I ended up scouting for a decade and following Scott around with the Phillies, Mets, and Orioles. I was part-time, and about the lowest on the totem pole. However, it was very enjoyable.

It was mainly high school and college, but I did a little bit of professional baseball. They'd send me names, and I'd go around and give my opinions. When Covid came, I finally cut the cord when a lot of high schools, colleges, and minor leagues didn't play their seasons.

I know I made the right decision when I quit playing, but it was a tough transition. I can probably count on one hand the days I haven't thought about what if I'd stayed in baseball. It's all I ever wanted to do. From the time I was a little kid here in Decatur going to the playgrounds and playing ball, it was what I wanted to do my whole life. It basically becomes who you are. You identify yourself as being a ballplayer and play for 10 years, then all of a sudden, it just kind of stops.

Roe Skidmore entered the life insurance and financial services industry (courtesy Roe Skidmore).

It's not just the physical part; the mental part is most of it. You identify as a certain person and then you're not that anymore. I had to say I was an insurance person, and I didn't really like saying that at first.

Early on, I'd say the number one motivator that got me really involved in the insurance business was the competition. With playing ball, there's always somebody there to take your job. You go to the ballpark, and they have programs that list your batting average, RBIs, and all your statistics. You want to be high on the list. Well, the insurance and financial business is the same way. Every office is part of a region or district, and your production is listed in some publication that's sent to all the other offices and agents. Competition makes you want to stay at the top of the list. You want to look good, just like when you're playing baseball.

Nyls Nyman

Nyls Nyman played in eight seasons of affiliated baseball, including parts of four in the major leagues. His last year playing in affiliated baseball was 1979. Following his playing career, he entered collegiate-level education and spent many years in coaching and administration. At the time of the interview for this book, he was retired and living in California.

I saw the end of my career coming from a mile away, but it was hard to let go. The signs were there, flashing in front of my eyes. I had played sports for as long as I could remember, and it was my career. There was the thought that "I'm an athlete and I'm just going to keep going as long as I can."

I literally played half of my eight seasons in professional baseball injured. I went from being a rather well-thought-of centerfielder to a part-time first baseman and DH in Triple-A. I saw what was coming. When it was finally over with the Reds Triple-A in Indianapolis, I was really battered.

There was a sense of relief after my career was over. I was done with the hundreds of hours in the training room before and after games. That part was a relief, but I was still distraught. There's a sense of loss, there's anxiety, there's depression.

I went back to my parents' place, and it was a difficult time. I did a lot of thinking.

I was a professional athlete. That was my job. Imagine if you told an accountant or physician when they were 25 or 26 years old that they couldn't do that job anymore. That would be shocking. Well, in the sports world, that happens every day. Most of our careers end while we're young.

Most guys don't have lengthy professional careers, and even if you're one of the stars that makes it until you're 40 years old, you're still relatively young. Professional athletes can rarely duplicate what encompasses the playing experience post-playing career. I saw a story about Tom Brady considering a comeback again. He is set for life, yet he still has that urge and desire. One of the greatest examples is Michael Jordan. He is one of the greatest athletes of all time, but he could not resist the urge of trying to duplicate that experience when he signed to come back and play for Washington. It's just human nature.

I should have spent more time exploring my talent base, my likes, and dislikes. As a professional athlete, I was one-dimensional and hadn't given that much thought.

I decided to go back to school. I had managed to get a couple semesters of college credit during my playing career in the offseasons, so I had a head start there. I think I had 30 units, so that really helped. I was a little bit older so if I was going from scratch, having not done it, I don't know if I would have pulled that trigger and gone to college.

At first, I wondered if I could do it. I wasn't a really good student in high school. I had been a C student. However, I was more mature when I went back.

I thought I'd use my professional playing career to help get me through my education by getting an assistant coaching job while I finished up a degree. I was fortunate. I was camping at my parents in the St. Louis area, went across the river to Southern Illinois University–Edwardsville, and talked with Gary Collins, the head baseball coach. Since I didn't have a degree yet, he couldn't hire me as an assistant coach per se, but he found me a job on campus in the athletic equipment area.

Although I wasn't a paid assistant coach at the university, I worked as one of his assistant coaches. What I was getting paid to do was keeping inventory in the equipment room, taking equipment out to the recreation fields, lining the soccer fields, and stuff like that. I coached on the side.

I have to be honest. I wasn't real keen on the thought of coaching. I didn't know if I could pull it off. I had never seen myself as a student of the game. I was talented and could go out and play. It just happened.

Coaching is a totally different entity. I had to learn how to coach, and my first experience was working with talented young college baseball players. I figured there were things I could teach, and I could learn the rest. The head coach was really supportive. He knew I was learning on the fly too.

I was blessed to have some extraordinary coaches in the minor leagues, and I leaned on those experiences a lot. Like with anything, as I gained some experience, I gained some confidence.

I coached while I got my degree and then applied for a graduate assistantship at Illinois State. I was fortunate to get that graduate assistantship and receive a stipend, along with my tuition, in exchange for being the assistant baseball coach.

I was working on my master's when Al Pickering, the athletic director at Lincoln College, called. Lincoln College was down the road from Illinois State. Pickering remembered me from my playing career and practically offered me the head coaching job over the phone. At Lincoln, in addition to coaching, I taught health education, recreation administration, and physical education. It was a nice place to start a second career, and I was there for four years.

I applied for a bit of a bigger job at Kankakee Community College south of Chicago and got that job. That was a management position. I was head baseball coach, but I was also director of student activities, the college center, and shared some academic counseling responsibilities. I really liked it, but the problem was that it was more than one job. It was hard. I actually liked the other parts of the job more than the baseball part. I was getting a little burned out with baseball and coaching, and gravitating towards organizing student activities and special events.

I had a friend at Lassen Community College in Susanville who had been the wrestling coach at Lincoln College, my first job. He called one day and said they had a job opening for the director of student life, which involved student activities, special events, and managing the residence hall. I applied for that job, got it, and did that for 14 years.

I retired from Lassen but continued to teach part-time for six or seven years until Covid hit.

Nyls Nyman entered collegiate-level education following his playing career and spent many years in coaching and administration (courtesy Nyls Nyman).

Over the years I've worked with the Major League Baseball Players Alumni Association on youth clinics, and developing coaches clinics. Years back, while working at an alumni youth clinic in the Reno-Sparks area, I spoke with the point person. He and I were there early, and I told him that while the youth clinics are nice, we should also be conducting something for coaches. He called me a couple weeks later, asked if he could send an outline of what they had tried to do in the past, and if I could help put something together. I said it would be a dream. I completed an outline for conducting coaches clinics and started helping in their development. It's one of my passions, and whenever someone is looking for someone to do a coaches clinic, I always volunteer.

I've been blessed and fortunate to have a loving family. I now consider myself a full-time grandpa. I have five grandchildren, and it's a joy.

1980s

The 1980s were a time of labor strife, as owners complained of rising salaries. A strike shortened the 1981 season, and major league rosters were cut from 25 to 24 players between 1986 to 1989 to reduce costs. During this time, there was also collusion between owners in an attempt to lower free agent salaries.

After bottoming out in the 1970s, there was a resurgence of minor league affiliated teams in the 1980s. A major shift in pitcher usage also impacted rosters in the 1980s. As relief pitching became more prominent, teams inevitably carried more pitchers.

Two important organizations were formed for players during the decade. The Major League Baseball Players Alumni Association was formed in 1982. In addition to promoting the game of baseball and raising money for charity, the organization has helped former big leaguers maintain a connection to the game and the sense of camaraderie they often miss after their playing days. Additionally, the Baseball Assistance Team (B.A.T.), affiliated with Major League Baseball, was formed in 1986 to confidentially assist former players who have fallen upon hard times, and serve as a bridge to help them become self-sufficient.

The following chapter includes stories from seven players who ended their playing careers in the decade.

Randy McGilberry

Randy McGilberry played five seasons of affiliated baseball, including parts of two seasons in the major leagues. His last year playing in affiliated baseball was 1980. Following his playing career, he entered the drafting industry. He has also been involved in coordinating his own baseball camps and advocacy for corrections officers. At the time of the interview for this book, he was semi-retired and working part-time at his church in Florida.

I grew up loving to draw. I used to buy big poster paper at TG&Y, go out in the backyard, and just draw whatever I was looking at. When I got to high school, my first year I took mechanical drawing, and then I took it my junior and senior years.

When I got to college, I thought I wanted to be a mechanical engineer, but it was hard for a mechanical engineering student to keep his grades up and play a sport. My counselor pulled me to the side and told me, "We're going to have a two-year associate's program here at (Louisiana) Tech I think would be right up your alley." However, I signed pro when I still needed three quarters to graduate, and the rest is history as far as that goes.

I realized my days were numbered as a player on my first day. I went to instructional league right after I signed in 1975. I saw guys come in that were drafted in both the higher and lower rounds. Some of these guys were considered prospects. I watched guys that were gone just two weeks after signing. Their careers were over.

I knew in my first year of pro ball that you're only as good as your last outing or your last impression. I'm a realist, see things for what they are, and I don't try to make more out of it than it is.

I'm one of 22,000 guys that have put on a major league uniform. I'm proud of it because millions have tried. I did something a lot of people dream about but can't achieve. God blessed me with the ability to achieve it and hang in for a couple seasons. However, I also saw baseball for what it really is.

I say this tongue in cheek, but baseball is a business just like everything else. When people look at you, they look at your trade-ability and how much money they can get for you. When I got traded to the Mets, all the Mets and Royals did was trade two pitchers they didn't want. Kevin Kobel took my place with the Royals, and I took his place with the Mets. Both of our careers were basically over that summer.

I already knew my career was coming to an end because I was having a lot of issues with my elbow and forearm tightening up after so many pitches. I remember before the Royals traded me to the Mets, when I was in Omaha, I rolled over one night in bed and told my wife, "Roxie, why don't we just go home. I can get a job. I'll find something to do to support us."

I was only making $21,000 a year. Of course that was seven months a year playing baseball, but I knew a lot of friends at home who were making $30,000 or more working in factories or stuff like that.

I looked at the reality of it and told myself sooner or later, and it's probably sooner, I would have to move on and do something else in life. I figured the longer I put it off, the harder it would get. I watched a lot of guys and their families suffer with them trying to hang on, and I wasn't going to put my wife and son through that. After that season with the Mets, I made the decision to go ahead, be a family man, and quit hanging on.

When I got out of ball I took a drafting job at a local manufacturer. That was my beginning in drafting, and that's primarily how I made a living for 35 years.

I opted to start out as a low-level draftsman for a local fabricator, and I climbed the ladder from there. I saw what was important and I was around good people that wanted others to succeed in the business.

However, if I had not played major league baseball, and I didn't have the name association around Mobile, I don't know if I could have gotten people's attention like I did. Everything I've done has always hinged around that one little thing on my resume, playing major league baseball. My resume is pretty impressive with my design work, project management work, and management experience. However, when they look down and see that, they're like deer in headlights and ask, "You played major league baseball?" They don't want to talk about anything but baseball. Baseball's opened a lot of doors for me, even though I only lasted for a short stay, and it makes a difference to this day that I played in the major leagues with that particular group of Kansas City Royals.

When I got out of playing, I also umpired. You could make good money if you were a good umpire. I was probably making a couple hundred dollars a week umpiring. I would work eight hours as a draftsman, head to the ball field to call a few games, and make somewhere around $80 a night.

Over the years, I just weaseled my way up through various facets of drafting and engineering. I was an engineering manager over casino boats under construction. I've been a designer at chemical plants, a designer in ship building, a safety manager, and a facilities manager. I always stayed close to how I got into the business, which was through design. I made some real good money. I retired from full-time work at Exxon in 2017.

Right before I retired, my son was stabbed as a corrections officer. I started lobbying for corrections officers in the state of Alabama almost immediately. I formed the Alabama Corrections Officers Association and have become a well-known figure at the State House.

My son had PTSD pretty bad. It was compounded because he was in the Army. He had volunteered to go to Kuwait, but they wouldn't take him because he'd injured his shoulders, so they kept him on base in Germany. He often had to get in his dress uniform and escort bodies, and he escorted a couple guys from his unit. He felt because he didn't go to Kuwait and Iraq with his unit, he didn't either take a bullet trying to save one of them or was able to keep them from taking a bullet somehow. My son was that

Randy McGilberry entered the drafting industry after his playing career. Now semi-retired, he is very active with advocacy for correction officers in Alabama (courtesy Randy McGilberry).

kind of man. Eventually, he told them he couldn't do it anymore and got an honorable discharge.

He liked that structured life of the military and got into corrections through a friend. He loved his job and took it very seriously, but he saw so much in that prison. There's so much violence in a prison—death, suicide, inmates beating on other inmates, officers beating on inmates, inmates beating on officers.... It just took its toll on him. I begged him to come home but my son was in a very dark place. The PTSD was pretty bad, and he committed suicide in 2020. As long as I have my expenses covered, I'll continue with the lobbying forever. I gave him my word.

I stay busy.

For over 30 years, I've also had a baseball business. I started that by putting hand printed sheets under windshield wipers, promoting myself as a pitching instructor. I grew it into a 501(c)(3) and do camps. I've had over a thousand students. I try to get communities involved with supporting their youth. About 30 percent of the money I collect goes right back into the communities.

At the end of camps, we have life lesson talks. Everybody wants to play ball but the reality of it is if I've got a hundred kids, one guy out of that bunch might play pro ball. I let these kids know there are doctors, lawyers, teachers, police officers, and a lot of other things you can do to have a lucrative life. I tell them they've got to find what they're interested in and what they're good at.

I'm now on staff at my church. When I retired from Exxon, they offered me the buildings and ground job at the church. I said, "Okay. I'll work 24 hours a week." I often work more than that, but I'm not interested in a 40-hour a week job anymore. I've graduated from that.

Jack Kucek

Jack Kucek played eight seasons of affiliated baseball, including parts of seven seasons in the major leagues. His last year playing in affiliated baseball was 1981. Following baseball, he entered sales. At the time of the interview for this book, he was retired and living in Ohio.

I hurt my arm with the Blue Jays. I knew I couldn't do it anymore and come back.

The transition was quick. I just realized when my baseball career was over, I still had to provide. It was simply called having to pay rent and bills.

It's a little different nowadays. If a guy has been in the big leagues, he should have a little savings. Back in my day, when you ended your playing career, you had to act quicker.

I married my wife the prior year in 1980, and we had a little apartment in Clearwater, Florida. She was working, and I was sitting around doing nothing for a little while. I hadn't sat around in my entire life. I said, "I can't do this."

I started looking around for different jobs. The first job I had after baseball was from answering an ad for cemetery sales. It was in a room with no windows, so I felt like I couldn't get the hell out of there.

After a little experience, I met a guy named Len Gabay, who owned a cemetery. I interviewed with him, and he said, "Jack, I love athletes. You guys are naturals. Stay with me and I'll teach you the business." He did.

Len taught me everything I know about sales. I learned that if you can sell, you can do anything. It doesn't matter what you sell. You can sell jets, or you can sell widgets. If you know how to sell, you'll always have a job.

Len ended up selling the cemetery and then he bought an art gallery. We managed two art galleries and made a lot of money doing it.

Eventually, my folks were getting older, and we decided to move back to Ohio. I met a guy with Bridgford Foods who told me, "I've got this project. You've got the right personality, and I think you'd be perfect for it." I was hired and he had me go into Walmart stores. They had displays on the bottom shelves, and I'd have to talk to their people about getting a rack for pepperoni, beef jerky, and all that.

Following his playing career, Jack Kucek had a long career in sales. His first sales job after baseball was in cemetery services (courtesy Society for American Baseball Research-Rucker Archive).

I'll never forget. The first day I sold about six. The next day I sold 12. The day after that, I only sold three. He called me and asked, "How's it going?" I said, "Man, this is tough." He goes, "How many did you do today." I said I only did three. He asks, "What about yesterday?" I said 12. He asked, "Well, what about the day before?" I said six. He says, "Just keep going and let me know how many you do at the end of the week." I think I ended up selling about 30 that week. I followed up with him, and he told me his guys usually only sold about five a week.

That turned into being a pretty good job and it was one of the best jobs I ever had. It lasted a while, and I loved it. And by the way, their pepperoni is the best you'll ever eat.

Then, a friend of mine was a vice president with Feed the Children. He asked me if I was interested in raising money. I said sure and got hired there. I raised funds on the east coast and went on to raise millions for Feed the Children.

I realized I had to put the same energy into sales as I did into achieving my dream as a baseball player. It was just a matter of replacing baseball with the job I was doing and giving that job the best effort I could.

Baseball will open doors for you, but you've still got to prove yourself. That's the big thing.

Dave Machemer

Dave Machemer played 11 seasons of affiliated baseball, including parts of two seasons in the major leagues. His last year playing in affiliated baseball was 1982. Following his playing days, he spent a short time selling cars before entering a long career as a minor league manager and scout. At the time of the interview for this book, he was retired and coaching high school baseball in Michigan.

In July of '81 I was with Toledo in the Twins organization. I broke my ankle sliding into second in Richmond, Virginia. I was rehabbing and during that time George Brophy, the farm director, came to Toledo.

Cal Ermer was the manager, and he said, "Mac, George Brophy wants to meet with you." I go into Cal's office, and George goes, "Dave, we'd like you to go in a new direction." I go, "What's that?" He says, "We'd like you to manage our Wisconsin Rapids team next year." I say, "Whoa, really? Gee, Mr. Brophy, I appreciate that but in '79, just two years ago, I made the big league team out of spring training with the Tigers. I don't think my playing career is over. I want to continue to play."

Looking back at it now, I probably would have been better off taking that job. The Twins are so loyal to their employees. I probably would've ended up with the Twins the rest of my baseball career and maybe even gotten to the big leagues as a coach. But at the time, I didn't feel my playing career was over.

I rehabbed all winter and went into spring training of '82 with the Twins in good shape. I was called into the office and thought it was the end of the line, but they told me they were going to keep me. However, I was put on the phantom DL even though I wasn't hurt. I still remember the first game I played in '82. It was against the University of Toledo in an exhibition game. I still wasn't on the roster, but I played in the game and got a hit. The guys got the ball and put "first hit as a phantom DL member" or something like that on it. I still have that ball somewhere.

I went on to get activated and was sent to Triple-A that year. There was a time when I was on a little bit of a run. I was playing every day and thinking, "Man, I've got a chance to go back to the big leagues." There were rumors about me going back because I was playing so well. One night the Twins brought in a slew of executives. I was playing third base and just didn't play well that night. I made an error or two and I didn't swing the bat well. I remember waking up the next morning and looking at the transactions. The Twins had acquired Larry Milbourne, who was a utility guy. As soon as I saw that, I knew that would have been my spot.

Years later, during the replacement camp of 1995, I was running the

Expos minor league spring training. Cal Ermer came in as a scout for replacement players. We went out for breakfast, and he said, "I don't know if I should tell you this, but do you remember when there were rumors about you going back up to the big leagues in '82 and the night everybody came in to watch you?" I said, "Yeah. I didn't play well, and they acquired Larry Milbourne." He said, "Well, you were going up. I had your plane ticket in my drawer." I said, "Well, I kind of figured that. I appreciate you telling me although it's killing me right now."

So, after the '82 season, the Twins let me go. Mr. Brophy called at the end of the year and said, "We're going to give you your release." I said, "Mr. Brophy, can I ask you a question? Is that job still available in the minor leagues as a manager?" He goes, "Son, I only offer it once." I went, "Well, in that case Mr. Brophy, I'd like you to put down that I retired. I've never been released in my career. I'd like to flat out retire and have a clean slate." He goes, "I can do that." I don't know what it looked like on the official paperwork, but I let him know I wanted to retire.

That winter I got a phone call from a scout with the Toronto Blue Jays about possibly having a spot for me, but that never came to fruition.

I had two children, born in '80 and '82. My son was just born, and my daughter was two years old. I really felt it was important to spend time at home.

I didn't know what I was going to do. I thought about possibly teaching. I have a teaching degree and wasn't sure if I wanted to do that. But my sister was married to a guy in the car business, and he called me. He was the general manager of an Oldsmobile dealership. He goes, "Whatcha going to do with your life?" I go, "I'm not sure." He goes, "Well, we're opening a new dealership, and we need a salesman. How'd you like to do that?" I said, "Well, I don't have any other offers, so I guess I'll take it."

My father was a mechanic and I've been a car guy my entire life. Selling cars was actually enjoyable for me. However, as more time went on, I knew there was something more that I wanted to do in my life.

I was playing in a beer league around my area and got a call from Bob Sullivan, who I had played amateur ball for before I ever signed. Bob was a legend back here in Grand Rapids, Michigan, and had a famous amateur team called the Grand Rapids Sullivans. He wanted me to come back and play for him. He called and said, "Mac, I want you to play in the state tournament this weekend." I said, "I'm 34 years old. Why don't you go get a college kid?" He said, "A scout said he saw you play the other night," I said, "We're playing against guys who are throwing 75–80 MPH. We're not playing against elite talent." He goes, "Well, I want you to play this weekend. I'll give you $500." I said, "What time should I be there?" I played in the state tournament, and one thing led to another. I went to Wichita,

Kansas, with the Grand Rapids Sullivans, and we won the National Baseball Congress World Series Championship in 1983.

Before one of our games in Wichita, I was up in the stands talking to an old friend of mine, Freddy Beene, who was working with the Milwaukee Brewers. I played against Freddy in the minors. Freddy asked what I was doing, and I said I was selling cars. He said, "You don't belong doing that. You belong in baseball." I was getting the itch after selling cars and I said, "Yeah, I'd probably be interested in doing something." He goes, "Well, if anything ever comes up, I'm going to give you a call."

About a year later I had something like a premonition. I was in real deep thought. I was feeling down and hoping and praying that something would happen. Doggone, the next day I got a call from Freddy Beene out of the blue. The phone rings, and of course, there's no caller ID. I was watching Knots Landing, one of my favorite programs at the time. I want to finish watching Knots Landing but my wife picks up the phone and I take the call.

He goes, "Mac, this is Freddy Beene. Do you remember when I talked with you? Something's come up with the Milwaukee Brewers. We're looking for a manager and I think you'd be a good fit. I've got a phone number for a guy, and I'd like you to call him tomorrow. I think he might give you an interview."

The next day I made the phone call to Bruce Manno, the farm director for the Brewers. We had a conversation, and he said he had received some good recommendations from some people on me. He asked if I'd be interested in flying up to Milwaukee to interview for a job they had open in Beloit, Wisconsin, in the Midwest League. I said sure.

I flew to Milwaukee a couple days after that and was probably in Bruce's office for three hours. We went to lunch, talked some more, and I really pressed Bruce to hire me. He said, "I'll call you in a few weeks and let you know." I go, "No, you don't have to do that. You can sign me right now because I'm the best guy you've got for the job."

I kept pressing him, but he didn't sign me that day. He said he'd call me in a couple weeks. Well, the next day he called me. When I got that phone call and heard his voice, I knew I had the job. That started me on a run from 1985 to 2019 back in pro baseball.

I'm forever grateful to Bruce Manno for giving me that opportunity to get back into baseball. It was something I was born to do. Since I was five years old, baseball has been my whole life.

I started in Beloit. One thing led to another with the Brewers, and I had a 10-year run with them. I continued with a bunch of organizations and it was a blessing. My professional career ended four years ago with the Orioles. I had been a scout my last six years.

The only thing that is bittersweet about it is that I never got a chance to get a big league coaching job, which I thought I was in line for a couple times. I thought my skillset would've worked in the major leagues because of the fact I stole a lot of bases in my career. I thought I'd be a good first base coach. I read pitchers well and had a lot of areas in the game I excelled at. I thought I would have been a good big league coach but I never got the chance to do that. However, you can't cry over spilled milk. I still loved every chance I got to be in the game of baseball.

Now, I'm back in the game of baseball at the high school level, and it's rejuvenated my life again at 72.

I had played a lot of golf—probably 350 to 400 rounds. But I thought, "Man, I need to do something different."

I received a call from a fella that wanted to know if I was interested in getting back in the saddle. He was pursuing the head coaching job at Lakeshore High School, which was actually the high school my kids went to. I'd been involved with the school for many years, had done a lot of work over there, and knew everybody. He was wondering if I was interested in an assistant role. I thought about it and told my wife I'd really be interested, but not really as an assistant. That just wouldn't be me at this point.

Dave Machemer's playing career included time with the Detroit Tigers (courtesy Dave Machemer).

Well, I waited for a call back. I knew the athletic director and eventually called him, asking if the fellow got the job. He said, "No, Dave. He didn't get the job. We're still looking." I said, "Oh, really." He said, "Do you have anyone in mind?" I said, "Yeah, me." He said, "Are you serious? Can you come in tomorrow?" I said, "Not tomorrow, but I can come in the next day."

I went to his office over at the high school and when I walked in, there were six people in the room. I didn't know I was going into an in-depth interview for three hours. It was kind of funny. After the chat we had with everyone, he walked me around the new facilities.

Dave Machemer spent 23 seasons as a minor league manager (courtesy Dave Machemer).

I knew they had a lot of partners who had donated a lot of money to improve their facilities but after I walked through everywhere, I just went, "Wow! This is something else!" There was a new $18 million field house and batting cages. They had new turf, and everything was really nice. I thought, "Man, this would be a nice fit for me."

After he walked me through all the facilities, we walked back to the school. It was snowing and picturesque. We stopped in the parking lot, and he goes, "Well, I'm offering you the job." I'm thinking, "Whoa, that was quick." I told him, "Well, the first thing I need to do is talk to my wife. I want to make sure she's on board with it." That was on a Friday. By Monday I had made the decision it was something I really wanted to do.

I had the urge to get back in baseball and it's been a real thrill for me. We have a great group of kids and I'm excited about the season as we go along.

I have to give credit to my wife who was there by my side every step of the way through my professional career, and afterwards, to make sure I didn't lose it mentally. It's a tough road.

I was blessed my transition went from playing, to working two years, to getting a chance to get back into professional baseball.

I loved to compete. I'm proud to say they called me the "Pete Rose of the Minor Leagues." I considered it a war every night when I went to bat or was on the field.

I miss the camaraderie of the guys I played with too. Every day when you went to the ballpark, you could feel the love in the locker room, from the veteran guy, to the superstar, to the guy that never got out of that particular league. It was a joy to meet all those people, and I'm still friends with many of them. I'll always feel a big highlight of my life was meeting all the people I did in baseball.

Steve Luebber

Steve Luebber played 20 seasons of affiliated baseball, including parts of five seasons in the major leagues. Following his playing career, he spent nearly 40 years as a minor league pitching coach. While his last year as a regular player in affiliated baseball was 1983, he occasionally pitched in games while a coach from 1986 through 1988. At the time of the interview for this book, he was retired and living in Missouri.

I was always one of those guys paying attention to the non-playing parts of baseball, and the business side. I was always paying attention to what's going on with waivers, labor stuff, and why.

Roland Hemond was a longtime GM and a super nice man. One spring training I was fortunate to sit down with him, and he showed me the stuff they had to do to study transactions. So, I understood those things a little bit more than the next guy. I knew some of the uniqueness of the antitrust exemption, why certain things get done and why certain things don't get done.

I knew how the roster rules would catch you differently at certain times, and why you might be pitching really good but wouldn't get called up. They may not have a 40-man roster spot for you, or there might be a guy with no options left, so they can't send him down without losing him. That helps you understand your standing in the world.

The last few years as a player, I was hanging in there because I was still having a lot of success pitching. In 1983 I was a bullpen guy, kind of a player-coach, and doing well. Late that year, I got traded to the Padres and I actually talked to a guy about possibly going to Japan instead. I saw what the Padres had at the Triple-A level, thought I was a better option than a lot of those guys, and figured I may have a chance to get back to the big leagues with the Padres. That's why I stayed.

The following spring they had some roster issues with some of the pitchers they had. Even though I thought I pitched better, I was on a minor league contract, and they had some roster power, so to speak. I didn't get activated at the end of spring, and that's when I entered coaching.

When I was playing, during the offseasons I'd help the Missouri Southern program a little bit to stay in shape. Coming from that, I also started doing some pitching lessons. Additionally, the last few years my pitching career was going on, I was a player-coach in a few spots. The

Padres minor league director knew I was interested in possibly coaching, so that's the way it all fell into place.

Following his playing career, Steve Luebber was a minor league pitching coach for nearly 40 years (courtesy Steve Luebber).

If I had to do it all over again in hindsight, I may have pursued Japan. I'd have probably been a pretty good pitcher in Japan. I was still throwing hard and probably could have made some decent money for two or three years doing that. However, on the other hand, as it turned out, I got in 55 total years doing pitching and coaching.

I think the biggest challenge of the transition was seeing people out there that weren't performing as well as I had been doing. Additionally, while I knew I would be dealing with recent signees out of high school and college, I'd have to do curfew checks and make sure they were taking care of themselves. That was an additional piece to coaching a pitcher I didn't think I was going to have to do.

In 1984 I roved a little bit and then went to Spokane, which was the Padres rookie team at the time. I was fortunate to be with the Padres for seven seasons, but after Ray Kroc passed away, they went through a lot of transitions and changes. No matter how good of a job you did, you might get pushed out, and it wasn't about your performance. I saw that several times.

I was married with a family. I'd finish my season and then sit there and go, "Am I going to get another contract offer?" They may have another person in mind to put in your place. There was one year I was told I was going to come back. I was waiting on the stuff to show up in the mail. Then late in the winter I found out they were going with someone else. I was fortunate that some people got on the phone on my behalf and helped me get the next job.

Most contracts are year to year, but there were a few times I had two-year contracts. They usually went from November 1 to October 31.

Even when you thought you were okay for the next year, you never really knew until things occurred.

You could sense that atmosphere after you'd been through it, and it was not a comfortable feeling. You'd have to sit there and think, "What am I going to do if this happens or that happens? How long can I stay with this before I have to do something else?"

Like I said, I was fortunate that either the people in the organizations helped me out or somebody else took a chance on me. My reputation was good, so that's one reason I was able to stay in the game so long.

Most years I was the pitching coach with a club. I had three years when I was a pitching coordinator with the Rangers in the mid-nineties roving around and spending five or six days with a club and then traveling to the next club.

Early in my coaching career, I pitched in a few games. In 1986, I hadn't played in a few years and was coaching in Beaumont, Texas. Back then you only carried 10 pitchers on your staff. We had somebody get hit by a line drive and he was on the shelf for a little bit. Another guy was a little sore. We were going on a road trip, and our manager asked the minor league director, "Can we activate Luebber and pitch him if we need to?" That's what happened. I got into a few games that year, and the same for the following two years. I did fine. I was still throwing batting practice from the pitching rubber, so I was in shape.

Then, a little bit later, the Senior Professional Baseball Association developed. That had some appeal because it was offseason income. I was able to do that both seasons down in Florida. I was over 40 years old at the time and that was a lot of fun. There were a lot of guys I had played with or against. There were the usual groups of pulled hamstrings and all that, but after a few weeks of play, the caliber of play was actually pretty good.

Right now, I'm helping my nephew's high school baseball team. After being the assistant coach, he got the head job last year at a high school called Webb City, next to Joplin here. When I retired from pro ball after the 2022 season, he asked if I'd help. So, I still have my finger in it a little bit.

Jim Kern

Jim Kern played 18 seasons of affiliated baseball over 19 years, including 13 seasons in the major leagues. His last year playing in affiliated baseball was 1986. Following baseball, he entered a career in hunting and fishing outfitting. At the time of the interview for this book, he was working and living in Texas.

I had a weaning away period. In '83, during the second game of the season with the White Sox, I destroyed my elbow throwing a pitch. However, I played until '86. At the point when I destroyed my elbow, I had eight years and 156 days of major league service time. The maximum pension benefit was 10 years.

The next year, without really ever looking at me, the White Sox released me out of spring training. I was still trying to come back and went to a tryout camp in June that Philadelphia had the University of Texas at Arlington for young players. I just showed up and threw for a scout. I was throwing well enough but certainly wasn't back to the point where I could throw a breaking pitch. I hadn't even tried that with my elbow, but I could throw the ball in the mid-nineties, and I was still rehabbing. I threw the ball well enough that they wanted me to go to Philadelphia and throw before a game. Well, I went to Philadelphia with two days' worth of clothes and that night Tug McGraw strained a muscle in his shoulder and they put him on the disabled list. The next day they offered me a contract. I played with Philadelphia for about 45 days, got absolutely nobody out, and they released me.

Then, Milwaukee signed me and sent me to Double-A in August of '84. I played there about a month, and then they called me up for September and I had a decent September with Milwaukee. I also spent a short time with Milwaukee in 1985 before being released in the middle of June.

All this time, I was trying to incur major league pension days. I knew I was nowhere near where I was in the late seventies. The arm just was not functioning well. I would pitch and then sit in my hotel room with my elbow in a bucket of ice for a half hour on and off to get the swelling down. Then, the next day when I showed up at the ballpark, they didn't know how bad I was feeling. Again, I was just trying to incur major league pension days.

I had been released three times in three years but talked Cleveland into letting me come to spring training in '86. I needed about 70 days for 10 years.

My philosophy was that I would throw all winter and be as good as I was going to get when I went to spring training. The kids hadn't hit all winter, so I was way ahead of them in spring training and looked really good. I would make the team and by about the end of April they would catch up to me, and by June I would be gone.

I go into spring training knowing they are going to take 11 pitchers for the team. Well, there's 27 pitchers in camp and eight spots are already spoken for. Basically, there's 19 pitchers for three spots.

I had to make an impression. I'd been released three times in three years and had to get them looking at me with 19 pitchers. On the first day out, I was throwing the ball in batting practice at 95. I get in the clubhouse and hear all the hitters bitching about me throwing 95, and what an asshole I am because they're trying to get their swings together. But it had just the effect I wanted it to because everyone was bitching and talking about Jim Kern throwing the ball hard too early in camp. It got the coaches looking at me and got me to stand out. I pitched pretty well, but I was basically as good as I was going to get in spring training.

I made the team, but by the middle of May, I was getting my ass kicked. The kids had caught up and surpassed me, and I was getting nobody out.

In June I was really struggling. I walked into the manager Pat Corrales's office, and said to him, "Pat, I'm not begging but I just want you to know I need 10 days for 10 years." Well, 15 days later, I was called into the office. Joe Klein, the general manager, and Pat are sitting there. Pat says, "Do you have your 10 years?" I said, "Damn right. I've got 10 years and five days right now." They said, "Okay, we're going to call Dickie Noles up."

They offered me a minor league coaching job. However, I told Pat, "I've been in the game 19 years. I spent seven years in the minors before getting a shot at the major leagues, and I've been rehabbing in the minor leagues four times in the last five years. If I take a minor league coaching job, my wife will kill me." I thanked him for the opportunity. At that point I had my 10 years and five days, and I was done.

Because I had destroyed my elbow in '83 and played through '86, I had a weaning away period. I knew it was going away. It wasn't something that just happened out of the blue. There was already a three-year transition period there for me. Leaving the game wasn't the biggie. It was finding something else to do.

The hard thing was for 19 years, I had left the house at three in the afternoon to get to the ballpark. The games started at 7:00 or 7:30 and were over at 10. I'd get home, have supper, watch a little television, and go to bed at about one. Then, I'd get up again at 11 or 12 and start the cycle again. I had this cycle for 19 years.

It's really tough when you retire, because it's like somebody reaches inside of you and takes a chunk out. You can't have it anymore. I've been gone from the game 40 years, and still that time between five o'clock until 10 o'clock at night is really a bitch to occupy time. I've talked with other guys that have the same problem. There's something missing from your life and you've got this huge hole that's really hard to fill. It's like having withdrawals.

After I got released in June of '86 I went to the lake in Michigan and spent time with family. I did some relaxing. However, starting in '87 when you don't go to spring training, there's a huge hole missing and you're trying to figure out how to fill it.

I love the outdoors, and I love hunting and fishing. I had leased ranches in Texas to hunt on while I was playing. So, there was a natural progression to starting an outfitting business. I was known as Emu, the world's largest non-flying bird, when I played baseball. That was my alter ego, so for name recognition, we went with the Emu Outfitting Company.

I was lucky. My wife and I got married at 21. She survived all the bullshit years of minor league and major league baseball. It's not as if we got married when I was an all-star. We got married when I was in A-Ball. She was an intellectual and much of the time I played baseball, she went to school. Consequently, she had accumulated both bachelor's and master's degrees in computer science and engineering. When I retired from baseball, she said to me, "I'd like to work." Here I am, just a retired athlete trying to get my feet on the ground for the rest of my life, and I've got a wife with multiple degrees wanting to work. That helped a lot. She went out and worked, and I helped with the kids and such. It really allowed me to get Emu Outfitting up and going.

In Texas, about 98 percent of the land is privately owned. So, if you want to hunt, you basically have to lease hunting rights from a rancher. At that time out in west Texas, you had some big ranches. What I would do was lease a 15–30,000-acre ranch for say $2 an acre for the hunting rights. Then, I would turn around and lease a couple hundred or thousand acres to groups of hunters for $4–6 an acre. I did guided hunts on some of them as well. We had white tail, quail, Rio Grande turkey, and feral hogs in that area.

Then, I started leasing land in the Big Bend area in southwest Texas for desert mule deer. Down there, there were even bigger ranches. Most of those were guided hunts.

After five to eight years of doing that, the ranchers learn you've leased the ranches for $2–3 and acre and then released them for $4–6 an acre. They decide they're not going to release them to you but are going to take the hunters you've already marketed to and lease to them directly, outside of you. So, it got to be counterproductive teaching these ranchers what their land was really worth.

I had been doing hunting and fishing shows, and by doing those shows, I met outfitters from different areas of the world. I found there was more money getting hunters for different operations around the world as a booking agent than there was in running the hunt myself. Consequently, let's say I'd sell a $6,000 summer fishing trip to Alaska, I would make a 20 percent commission for selling the trip for the outfitter, and I didn't have to provide money upfront like I did on a hunting lease. I was still going out and getting hunters and fishermen, but I didn't have to stick my neck out, and I was still making 20 percent for everybody I booked. It was much more lucrative.

Over the years, I started booking hunting and fishing trips in Alaska and the mountain states. By the same token, I held guide licenses in many states and would guide some of these hunters.

You get to the point where you develop relationships with the hunters and fishermen. That helps for marketing too because the guy that spent $6,000 on a fishing trip in Alaska is also the guy that will likely spend $6,000 for a peacock bass fishing trip in Brazil's Amazon or a golden dorado fishing trip in Uruguay or Argentina. I started making deals and meeting outfitters in Brazil, Argentina, and Uruguay, and once they saw how well I could guide and book people, several of them hired me to run their American booking offices. It also morphed into running lodges where we did fishing and hunting trips.

I still do a lot of hunting and guiding, but I do most of my shooting now with a camera instead of a gun. I've been into photography all my life and the photography worked well with marketing on websites, Facebook, and at the fishing and hunting shows. I became rather good at it and have won several awards for my photography. I usually carry $8–10,000 worth of photography equipment wherever I go, whether it's hunting and fishing, or just out and about. It's something I really enjoy.

Jim Kern played in 13 major league seasons (courtesy Doug McWilliams / National Baseball Hall of Fame).

It's been an interesting career post playing. I've also done some commentary for college and major league baseball games, and even had a radio show, Outdoors with Emu.

Unless you're going into coaching, transitioning from playing can be really hard. However, once you're successful at something, it builds confidence. Being around baseball for 19 years, including parts of 13 years in the major leagues, builds confidence that you can go out and do what you want.

However, I think what helped me more than anything else in my life was spending six years in the Marine Corps Reserve from 1969 to 1975. I'll tell you what. If you survive 12 weeks in Parris Island, South Carolina, in the Marine Corps, and then another five and a half years in the reserves, you build confidence. In the Marine Corps, "I can't" is not a phrase they will accept. You'll find a way to make things work.

Following his playing days, Jim Kern entered a career in hunting and fishing outfitting, which included leading numerous peacock bass trips in Brazil (courtesy Jim Kern).

I carried that over into baseball. When I came into a game in a relief situation with the bases loaded and nobody out, I found confidence. I'd tell myself, "I survived several gunnery sergeants in bootcamp. I can survive this." As a result, post baseball, I wasn't afraid of trying things. If you're not willing to fail, you're not going to succeed.

I've been lucky. I played professional baseball and have been doing the outfitting since. It's been a life in which I've always been able to do what I loved. I've never really had a job.

Al Woods

Al Woods played 14 seasons of affiliated baseball, including seven seasons in the major leagues. His last year playing in affiliated baseball was 1986. Following baseball, he entered a long career in law enforcement. At the time of the interview for this book, he was retired and living in California.

I started sensing the politics being played in baseball and it wasn't as fun to me anymore. I got dissatisfied with it. That started the transition right there. I'm not saying I didn't want to play. I still wanted to play.

I could say some of it was my fault. Minnesota wanted me to come back after the '86 season but they had taken me off their 40-man roster. I learned you can't let pride set in and have it make decisions for you.

In 1987 I was still invited to big league camp, and I probably would have made it. I turned them down. At the time I wasn't thinking and was just upset they had taken me off the 40-man roster. Again, I let pride step in the way of my thinking.

Tony Oliva got me into the Mexican League and around the time I came back, Minnesota was looking for some left-handed hitting. I tried to call them, but they turned me down. I could understand because I had turned them down previously.

I thought about going into business and I also thought about going into coaching. I had some offers to do some stuff, but I also had to deal with some other unpredictable things in life that forced me to make changes. My wife passed away in a car accident and I had my daughter to take care of.

I was forced to adjust and fortunate to be able to adjust a little quicker than some people. Some people take a while to adjust, and some people never adjust. When I played, the money wasn't nearly like it is now, but it was still more than most normal jobs. I was fortunate to have known some people that helped open the door for me to different employers.

My first job after baseball was with the Contra Costa County Juvenile Hall System. A friend of the family was an educator in the juvenile hall system for years, and he suggested I apply. He backed me up and that's pretty much how I was able to get that job.

Al Woods spent nearly 30 years in law enforcement following his playing career (courtesy Doug McWilliams / National Baseball Hall of Fame).

Then, after that, I worked at the Oakland airport. We catered for the airlines, and I became a manager there. That was my last job before I started with the San Francisco Sheriff's Department, and I retired from there three years ago.

I never really thought about getting into law enforcement. It was something that just fell in place. At the church I was attending at the time, one of the associate pastors worked in the sheriff's department. He asked if I was interested in working there, and he kept asking me about it. Finally, I took the test, mainly to keep him from bugging me. I kept passing the tests and going through the steps. One thing led to another, and I ended up getting a job there. I took the first test in 1992 and once everything was done, I started in December of 1994.

I worked inside the jails, and in the home detention department for a while, but mainly the jails. I would also work the courts sometimes for overtime. I always relied on treating people the way I would want to be treated, even if they were in custody.

They say hindsight is 20/20. If I could go back, I would have mentally prepared myself differently than I did. I wasn't fully prepared to stop playing and transform. It was a quick adjustment.

Ken Clawson

Ken Clawson played five seasons of affiliated baseball in the Padres and Rangers systems. His last year playing in affiliated baseball was 1987. Following his time in affiliated baseball, he played four seasons professionally in Italy. After his playing career, he worked with multiple baseball schools, including coordinating his own for a short time. He also owned a full design landscaping company. At the time of the interview for this book, he was semi-retired and running a small sports memorabilia business in California.

Before the 1987 season, I was the first pick by the Texas Rangers in the minor league phase of the Rule 5 Draft.

They called me that winter and said, "We don't know if we want to bring you back as a shortstop or as a pitcher." They had wanted to draft me out of high school as a shortstop.

I ended up going to spring training and I had a split contract between Double-A and Triple-A.

I had developed a split finger fastball, so I had a third pitch finally. I was getting everyone out. It was unbelievable. I was very confident.

Spring ends and I go in to look at the list of where you're going to be sent. I started with Triple-A and didn't see my name. I looked at Double-A

Tulsa and I wasn't on that list. I went all the way down to Port Charlotte in the Florida State League, and there's my name.

I went into the office and asked, "What's going on? I've got a Double-A/Triple-A contract. I thought I'd at least be in Double-A." They said, "Well, you had a rough season last year. You're still learning to pitch. If you have a good first half of the season, we'll bring you up."

I had a really good first half. I was 6–1 with four saves and an ERA in the twos. I was really doing well. I had a lot of confidence.

The June draft comes around and they drafted a bunch of pitchers out of the College World Series. I was going, "Okay, that's cool. They'll probably all come here, and they'll move me up." Well, they came to where I was in Port Charlotte, and they stopped pitching me. I only pitched two times the second half. I couldn't figure it out.

My dad used to get my mail. On Christmas Eve he said, "You got a letter from the Texas Rangers. Let's open it up." We were thinking it was my next year's contract. I opened it and all it said was, "You're unconditionally released." I got really bitter. I was angry cause I had just had my best year.

After I got over that, I helped to develop a team here in the Sacramento area of guys that had played minor league ball, and even some guys that played in the major leagues. We used to go down to Land Park to work out and scouts would show up because they knew pros would be down there. We started playing games against Sac City, Sac State, and even Cal Berkeley.

Well, the scout from the Rangers that had watched me in high school, Rick Schroeder, came up to me and said, "Hey, Ken. I have an opportunity for you." I said, "Well, I'm trying to get on somewhere like Double-A here in the states." He goes, "Well, would you consider going to Italy and playing?"

I didn't know much about that, but he told me, "There are only two Americans on a team, and they'd really like you because you're like two in one. You can pitch, play short, and hit well so you'd almost be like having three Americans."

I didn't think much of it. They let me know how much they'd pay me, and my eyes lit up. It was more than I'd ever made, and I didn't think I could even make that in Triple-A. They said they'd also give me a house to live in, a car, and even pay for my daughter's private American school.

I went over there by myself at first because I didn't want to drag my family over there not knowing exactly what I was getting into. After a month of being there, I was very impressed and brought my family over. I ended up spending the next four seasons playing there.

I was able to come back home after the '91 season and buy a house. That meant a lot to me because at that point I had played nine seasons, and I felt I wanted to settle down and have my daughter in a more stable environment. She had been moving every six months to somewhere in the county or another part of the world.

We bought a home in Folsom, and shortly after that my wife and I both got jobs. We were just living a normal life because the professional playing life was crazy. My daughter was enrolled in a new school, and I was so happy to settle down and not have all the pressures to play at a high level.

About six months after that, my wife left. I was bitter about that but there was no time to sulk. I had to put my head down because suddenly I had a home with all the bills, and I was raising a daughter as a single dad. I had to get busy and find a way to make it.

I had been working with kids after starting my own baseball school, doing lessons, camps, clinics, and all that stuff.

Additionally, my parents had some friends who had purchased a franchise called Play It Again Sports, where they'd buy, sell and trade used and new sports equipment. I started running that business for them. It gave me a consistent check every two weeks.

Since it was a big superstore, we did some things that other Play It Again Sports never did or never could do. We had a ski shop where we sold skis, snowboards, and did tune-ups and waxes. We had a full golf repair store inside and sold all kinds of golf clubs. People would bring stuff in all day, we'd buy and sell stuff, and it was awesome.

I had already been working with kids and holding baseball camps. I'd do big camps during the season where there would be 30 kids at a time, and I'd bring out another couple pro guys from the area to help me. I did that through Play It Again Sports. The owners were so kind. They bought hundreds of brand-new shirts that had their logo on the back and on the front was my logo of Ken Clawson School of Baseball.

I always had that entrepreneurial mindset, so to speak. I had the Play It Again job where I had to show up every day to run that business, and with the baseball school it kind of created two incomes that was enough for me to get by with the new home.

I was driving my daughter to school every day and picking her up. Sometimes she'd have to come back to my work and do her homework. I had to cook, clean, and all that. Every night I passed out. I look back and don't know how I did it, but it was something you have to do as a parent just to survive.

Then Folsom implemented an American Legion team, and they asked me to be the manager. They paid me for that. I was doing a lot of stuff. I even started detailing cars in my garage in the middle of the night. I was always trying to create income to make sure I wasn't ever going to lose my home. I knew that was my staple. I worked day and night. It was crazy.

In the mid-nineties I stopped working at Play It Again Sports. I kept doing my baseball lessons, coaching legion, and detailing cars. I knew I needed to find a permanent job, and I was searching for something.

That's when Chris Bosio called me out of the blue. He was still playing with the Mariners at the time and knew I had been working with kids doing all these camps with Play It Again, and that I was doing lessons on the side.

Bosio had just purchased some land in Shingle Springs where he wanted to build a baseball facility. He said, "I want to pay you $3,000 a month because when I get done playing, we're going to do this, and I want you to help run my business." He was just paying me to make sure I was committed to him when he did stop playing. I kept doing baseball lessons and detailing cars, and he was writing me a check every month for $3,000.

He called every month and every once in a while, he'd have me do something. Once he had me design a really nice logo for him. I worked with a lady, and we created a really nice design. Back then you also had to go through a digitization process to put logos on shirts. It wasn't like it is now.

The land he had bought in Shingle Springs was zoned as residential even though it was right off the freeway. He called me and said, "I want you to go to these board meetings. We're trying to get things rezoned from residential to commercial." We finally got it rezoned. The property value really went up because it was commercial, which allowed him to borrow more money instead of having to use his own money to build the building.

Once it opened, I started working there 50 hours a week.

He spent a lot of money on the fantastic building and a great business model, but there just wasn't enough people to support the business in that area.

After a couple years, he had to say, "This is what's going on. We're not making it. You're going to have to go back on your own." I was disappointed. Again, I was still a single dad, and the cash flow stopped.

I went back to baseball lessons, coaching legion, and detailing cars. I was just doing everything I could.

I was sitting at home one day and somebody pulled up right outside my house. They pulled out a lawnmower, blower, and trimmer, and they started mowing my neighbor's lawn.

Well, back when I was nine years old in 1974, my great-grandma gave me a hundred-dollar bill, which was a lot of money back then. I went to Montgomery Wards and bought a lawnmower. My friends laughed at me.

But I started mowing lawns, making cash and buying baseball cards and all kinds of candy. Suddenly, my friends weren't laughing anymore.

So, when I saw those guys working on my neighbor's yard, I thought, "This is something I can do. I can work for myself on my own time. I don't have to show up to punch a clock and be under someone else's guidance."

I turned in a few investments, bought a new truck, commercial mower, trimmer, and blower.

I started knocking on doors in my neighborhood and just sucked up my pride. I was honest with people. I said, "You guys know I live down the street. I'm a single dad and I have just started this business. Is there any chance I could mow your lawn and start taking care of your yard?"

I got a couple of yards and was doing them. Then, just being out, people would stop and ask if I could mow their lawn? I grew that into 10 and then 20 yards. I just kept doing that. People started asking me to fix their sprinklers and plant a few plants here and there.

I'll never forget, one day this guy pulled over and he owned a sandwich shop in Folsom. He said, "I just bought a new house out in Rocklin, and it has a huge dirt backyard. Would you landscape my yard? I'll give you ten grand." I just said, "Yeah, sure!" So, I agreed and was like, "Oh no. Now what do I do?" I had no idea what I was doing. It was a fake it until I make it type of thing.

I called one of my buddies that knew stuff about irrigation and told him what happened. He said, "Let's do it." We were there for three weeks and did a really nice job. Suddenly, that whole new neighborhood where people were moving in started asking us to do their yards.

I got so booked up I had to find people to help me. I never looked back. I did that for years. We were always just kicking butt. We would do a yard in a week and move on. We'd do everything above and below the ground.

I would do design. I learned everything I could about plants, and suddenly, I had a passion for plants, trees, and all kinds of designing. We were working with boulders and started doing walls and concrete, and all kinds of stuff.

It became a full design landscaping company and that's basically when I was able to get ahead in life and not just make it. That was my primary source of income for many years.

Then, I ran into Matt Walbeck. I hadn't seen him in years, but he told me he was just starting the Matt Walbeck Baseball Academy. We went to lunch, and he told me what he wanted to do. Matt offered me a position. I thought, "Let's do this. Let's tear it up. We can really get this thing rolling."

I was working with Matt doing a lot of individual lessons in the evening at his facility and coaching one of his travel teams, which required practicing many days and going on excursions throughout the state and even in other states.

I got kind of fatigued. I was throwing a thousand pitches a day and having to be on the field on my feet, working out at the gym before that, and taking care of my personal yard stuff. It just kind of wore me out.

I stepped away and a couple months after that I had a really bad eye accident. I had a bad detached retina and almost lost an eye. They were able to save it through surgery, but I sustained some pretty bad damage.

I couldn't go on the field anymore because of my vision. I have depth perception problems with things coming at me. I reach for things and miss. I have to be very careful.

I had to retire in 2015, but it wasn't really due to wanting to retire. I had to reinvent myself again.

I feel fortunate to have gotten remarried. Thankfully my wife Lacrisha does very well, and I've been very lucky to have her. Without her, who knows where I'd be. She's the bright spot in my life.

Following his playing career, Ken Clawson worked with multiple baseball schools. He also owned a full design landscaping company (courtesy Ken Clawson).

Now I stay busy working in my yard and with my sports card and memorabilia business.

I've been a big collector since I was five.

I remember in '87 when I was with the Rangers in Port Charlotte there was a gentleman who came into the locker room after our first game, Tony Socci. He was this big, jolly, happy man. He bought pizza for everybody. His sign was out on the outfield wall for Socci's Sports Den, a big card shop in Port Charlotte.

We became good friends, and he was aware of the situation I was in financially. It was kind of weird since it was right in the middle of the season, but he said, "Hey, Ken. When you're at home for a week, you can come in during the day, work at the card shop, and I'll pay you $10 an hour." That was a lot of money for me back then. I'd work five hours, get $50, and I'd leave every day with some money in my pocket.

The shop was right there. I wouldn't have to go back to the condo. I'd go right to the yard. I could eat a meal and have enough money to put gas in the tank. That's how I got through that season.

Fast forward all the way to 2015, from working in that card shop, I saw what you could do. It steered me in a different direction.

I knew you could go to people's homes, look at their collections, and offer them so much. There's a lot of people who have stuff laying around that aren't interested in keeping it. You can pick things out, see if you can sell a few things, and then maybe with that money you could add a few things to your collection.

You have to know everything. You have to know pricing. You have to know how to ship. You've got to be really good at customer service.

I had so much stuff I just started thinking there's got to be a way I can create some sort of cash flow.

I started going on Facebook, friending sports-minded people, and got close to 5,000 people. I started posting things on my page and offering free shipping and no tax, which were always better deals than you could get on eBay. People started knowing that if they didn't grab it, someone else would.

I've been able to add to my collection and make a few bucks, and that's what I do to this day.

1990s

The 1990s were another decade of major league expansion, with the growth from 26 to 30 teams. Minor league affiliates grew exponentially.

The role of relief pitching continued to evolve and impact rosters, as the decade saw the universal adoption of one-inning closers and pitchers used in specialized roles. Rules for the disabled list were modified, impacting the frequency of roster changes. The use of steroids enhanced and prolonged the careers of some players, often negatively impacting the careers of players who weren't using them. There was more labor strife, with the lockout of 1990, and strike of 1994. International talent became more prominent in affiliated baseball. In addition to the continued growth of Latin players, the presence of Asian players on rosters became routine.

In 1992, the Major League Baseball Players Association (MLBPA) and the Commissioner's Office collaborated to begin the Rookie Career Development Program for prospects on the cusp of the major leagues. The program addresses topics such as media relations, finances, nutrition, time management, health, and personal responsibility. Post-playing preparation is also discussed. Several players whose stories follow have referenced that the program was beneficial for both their playing and post-playing careers.

There are 11 stories that follow from players whose careers ended in the 1990s.

Jeff Yurtin

Jeff Yurtin played five seasons of affiliated baseball in the Padres system. His last year playing in affiliated baseball was 1990. Following baseball, he became a successful serial entrepreneur in many industries, initially making his mark in the pool industry. At the time of the interview for this book, he was running multiple companies and living in California.

In 1989 we had a ton of outfielders so I was platooning in left, and would also play first and third. I had a pretty good year although I played the equivalent of about half a season.

The next year they gave me a chance to play every day. I was playing first base and started out the year very well. I was hitting about .400 the first month. In Calgary I got hit by a pitch up and in. The Padres had me go to the hospital to get checked out, and it showed I had torn some ligaments in my thumb. However, I kept playing. I had no power after that, and my average went from around .400 to about .260.

I was lifting, doing leg extensions and leg inflexions at the Las Vegas Athletic Club. I was feeling really fatigued and then had this sharp pain. It was like fire going down the backside in my veins. It was miserable. I made it to the training room, and they said I needed to get to the hospital.

They initially thought it might be a tumor or something impinging on my spine, but it wasn't. They did that test in Vegas and were concerned because they didn't know what it was. They flew me to Scripps in San Diego and ran more tests on me.

I had what's called transverse myelitis, which caused partial paralysis. I spent about 30 days in the hospital and felt like I was getting better every day. However, I did leave in a wheelchair because I had atrophy, and muscles really deteriorate fast when you have something like that.

They set me up doing rehab here in Sacramento. I started to lift, and my leg strength came back, but I had a slight foot drop. I wasn't a fast runner to begin with and just couldn't get back to running the same at all. I would try to force my legs but when you have nerve damage from paralysis, it's just not going to happen.

I never played another professional game.

I tried to rehab. I was still hitting and doing everything I could. The Padres stayed with me for two more years and paid me my regular salary.

I did show up for spring training in 1992. I played but every morning they taped my ankles, then I would put a brace on, then I would put on high top cleats about one size too big. It was ugly. I shouldn't have even been out there and they knew they were going to release me anyway.

One day one of the coaches, Tony Torchia, walked by, tapped me and goes, "It's too bad. You were a pretty good hitter." That's all he said. I thought, "I'm done. I'm getting released here."

The first transition was kind of hard because my father was in ailing health and I had to stay with him for about three years. He needed almost full-time care. He had dementia and at times could go wandering. It got to the point where I had to do pretty much everything. That was the toughest part. I didn't really have time to think about baseball or the past.

As far as that transitioning period, I was learning carpet cleaning through a company called Pressluft. Slowly, I started out on my own. I'd work for Pressluft part-time and would also get my own jobs with apartment complexes, doing the jobs that other people didn't want to do. People didn't want to lug commercial equipment up to the higher floors but that's how I got busy. I got to be full-time with that and probably would have stayed in the carpet business if I hadn't landed in the pool industry.

I got into the pool industry because a guy named Mike Dow, who ran FPI Property Management in Sacramento, wanted me to play on his softball team. He let me know they were having trouble with the guys doing their pools and asked if I could take over. I hadn't done a pool once. I immediately got my commercial pool operator's license and studied water chemistry because I didn't want to have any issues.

When I started in the pool business, I would start at 4:30 in the morning. On commercial pool routes, you would have these 70–80 pound portable vacuum units you'd run to the pools. I knew when I was 50 or 60 years old, I wasn't going to be pulling those off the back of my truck and then lugging them back. It made me think of other opportunities. That was about 1995 and by 1996 I started my website selling pool products.

I saw the margins that were to be made on the internet and figured that was my ticket. I figured I'd sell pool products, and I started operating out of my parents' house, which had three distributors right by me.

I started with 40 products, then grew it to 80 products the next year, and kept it up until I had over 90,000 SKUs. I sold pretty much every part known to mankind in the pool industry and I shipped out nationwide.

The internet was coming about in '96, and I tried to equate things to traveling through different cities in the minor leagues. In my mind, I thought, "It'd be great if I could sell one pool heater in Shreveport, Louisiana, today, or Little Rock, Arkansas, or Pensacola, Florida."

It was fun and just like competing. You're just competing and trying to rank in a different arena in business. Back then it was AltaVista that ran Yahoo and Excite that ran AOL. If you could rank on those two, you did well. I had to figure out how to rank on the search engines on my own. If you typed in pretty much any two-word pool related item, I came up in six or seven of the top ten results because I bought about 400 domain names.

I probably did over $450K in sales in 1996, just running around in my truck. I had one of those big white phones and when I'd get a call, I'd pull over and write down what they wanted, along with their credit card information. Then, I'd go back to an old Tranz 330 terminal, input it, and print a label.

With the worldwide web at its infancy, I had to go through long discussions to talk people into giving me their credit card information and explaining that if the product wasn't as described, they could do a charge back to not be charged for the goods. I was selling the same brand-new pool cleaner that was $799 at Leslie's throughout the nation for $399, half the price. The reason I did half the price was because there was another guy out of Connecticut. If it wasn't me coming up in searches, it was him.

When I got busier in '99, I had a program built that would automate my orders. I had this guy come in and build me software that would automate my orders, have them go into QuickBooks, and then into FedEx or UPS. It saved me a ton of time.

I had a good run from '96 to about 2013. I retired and then got bored. I wanted to do something as opposed to just golfing or waiting for friends to do things. There's only so much you can do, and I wanted to stay busy.

I have some commercial property and a warehouse, and had a lady renting from me. She decided she wasn't going to continue with her business, and at that time I thought I wanted to get back into something.

I got into importing artificial grass about two and a half years ago, and it's been great. The reason I picked artificial grass was because I was getting quotes for my backyard. I thought, "There's no way this stuff costs so much." I looked into it, realized the margins are great, and I could sell to contractors.

I'm also looking into lithium powered forklifts as well. In California, electric forklifts will be mandated in 2026. I've spent a lot of time researching them and am ready to pull the trigger.

I've got those two things now. I'm going to try to build them up within three years, sell them, and then be done. I'll be 61 this year.

Then again, I don't know if I'll ever really stop doing anything. I watch Shark Tank, and my mind starts thinking, "I think I can do that a better way."

I remember my mom saying, "Go to school, get your education, and work for somebody." That's not what I wanted to do. I wanted to do something where I ran everything and was in control of my own destiny. I try different avenues and I'm not afraid to fail.

Baseball prepares you for failure. If you're a hitter, you're failing seven out of ten times, and that's considered good. The failures in hitting make you a little more fearless going into business. You think, "I've already failed a bunch of times in my life. I don't care if I fail again. I'll pick myself up and try something else."

Jim Campanis, Jr.

Jim Campanis, Jr., played six seasons of affiliated baseball in the Mariners and Angels systems. His last year playing in affiliated baseball was 1994. He was a third-generation professional baseball player. His

grandfather, Al Campanis, and father, Jim Campanis, both played in the major leagues. Following his playing career, he entered radio advertising and promotions. At the time of the interview for this book, he was running his own media, marketing, and AI strategies company, and living in California.

I got released by the Padres after spring training in 1995, right before the season was going to start.

When I got released, Bruce Bochy said I should explore other organizations or maybe even play abroad. He even talked to me about looking into Australia, which I did pursue. They offered me a contract, but it was really small money, and I couldn't go halfway around the world for that.

I got a bunch of offers to play indie ball, including for the St. Paul Saints, owned by Bill Murray at the time. I couldn't play indie ball. It was $1,000 a month with no housing and $8 a day in meal money. It wasn't a lot. I owned a home and had a mortgage to pay in Tempe, Arizona.

Also, my arm was killing me, and I thought I was going to need elbow surgery. It was hurting to the point where I couldn't straighten it, and I only had about half the range of motion. The writing was on the wall that I'd need surgery if I kept throwing. The trainers knew that, and they always tell the higher-ups who's hurt and who might need surgery. It's funny, it ended up being bone spurs in my elbow, but I didn't know for several years. I had a lump appear on my elbow, had it looked at, and the doctor asked, "Did you ever have bone spurs? I think that's them." I still have that lump sticking out of my elbow, but at least my elbow works now.

After getting released and exploring my options, I just said, "Screw it. I'll start typing instead of throwing." I decided to go back to school. I was able to exercise the scholarship I got when I signed. However, there was a caveat that the scholarship money was capped at $1,800 a semester.

I decided to go to Arizona State. My house was in the same city. I got accepted pretty quickly and started classes in June for summer school, so we're talking only two months after I got released.

I got a job at a place that sold athletic equipment retail. I'd do my homework, then a customer would come in and I'd have to play salesman. When the customer would leave, I'd go back to my homework. I was doing that and my wife ended up having to get a job. We had a son, so we'd have to find a babysitter. We were a typical young family trying to make it work. It was a bit of a scary moment, but we made it through that first year by working hard. We were scrimping and saving and made the turn.

The dean called me in his office and asked, "You're kind of an unusual student coming back after baseball. What are you going to study?" I said,

"I think I'm going to be an announcer." He looked at me and he's like, "You want to be a baseball announcer after you've played college and pro for 10 years?" I was like, "I don't really know what else I can do." He said, "That's like going back to the minors again. You're going to be on a bus half your life. They'll make you sell ads in the offseason. Why don't you just get into the advertising side of media?" I said, "Someone has that job?" He goes, "Yeah. In fact, we have an internship coming up in a month or two."

When that dean told me about the advertising side, I started changing my curriculum. I had been placed in a couple of courses, and he switched some up. He had me take a public speaking class, and classes that were more related to working in the media industry. I immediately went into that emphasis.

For the internship, I went on a bunch of interviews. There were about 20 media entities in the Arizona area—newspapers, radio stations, and television stations. The general sales managers were there and after we were all done, the dean said, "They all wanted you because you're ready to go to work." I chose the number one radio station in Phoenix, KMLE Country 108.

The sports guy and I hit it off. He'd have me do a segment with him with a sports secret nugget and it was a fun thing. I remember one of the questions I posed to him was, "What's the number one substance used by professional pitchers when they throw spitballs?" He'd say, "We're going to get the answer from a former professional catcher right after the break." Listeners would call in and say, "It's spit." I'd say, "It's snot." Then they'd say, "It's Vaseline." I'd say, "It's snot." No one caught on. Finally, I'd say, "It's snot. Guys would blow snot boogers because mucus is slipperier than spit." I even knew a guy who would put jalapeno juice in his nose. He'd have a runny nose all inning and shoot a big snot rocket into his glove. I didn't like throwing the ball back to him, but it worked.

That was an instance of just having fun and it was similar to being in the clubhouse before a game and goofing off. I found out that often happens in radio. I got lucky finding something I liked to do just as much as baseball, and I was getting paid for it.

When I first got into radio, we couldn't afford the mortgage on our own, so we had a couple of roommates and both of them were musicians. I'd play with them, their friends would come over, and we'd make recordings. I was using some of that for my radio commercials.

Also, from when I was playing, I remembered when Ronald McDonald or some guy in an ape costume from the local radio station would throw out the first pitch. I'd connect the dots. The ape would be from the home station of the team or McDonald's would be a big sponsor of the team. And if someone hit a home run in the seventh inning, everyone would get a hamburger. They were all business arrangements. All these promotions just seemed normal to me.

One of the first things that happened when I went into a radio station meeting as an intern was someone said, "Jim, you're pretty creative. Tell us about your idea for this promotion." I literally just regurgitated some baseball promotion I remembered seeing. They looked at me like, "Oh, that's brilliant." They had me quarterback this thing all the way, and I was just an intern.

Before I knew it, I was basically doing the same things I saw happening as a player when businesses would come in and do what we call activation promotions. Suddenly, I'm doing it for several products. It became fun and had a semblance of creativity. It was fun to learn from. Even when it didn't work, I'd learn we should have done this, or that, or convinced the client to spend more to make it really work better.

That's when I really started to turn the corner in the business. I started getting offers to see managers and be a manager of certain promotions. I knew it was a good fit.

Soon after I started interning, the boss said, "I'm going to talk with your dean because we want to hire you." This was before my internship was even over. It was a huge break.

I started realizing I was performing in front of clients. I was telling stories. I was getting them to believe my product was better than the guy that was just in there, and that my audience was going to buy their product or go to their event. I'd let them know, "I'll make you guys a really good commercial, and here's some music for the background."

Those elements became similar to what I did in baseball. There were a lot of similarities, especially with how we interacted in the clubhouse. It was always a joke fest and there were performances with how people would turn it on and talk in front of the group.

I learned how car dealers operate, how restaurants operate, how manufacturers operate, and how retailers operate. I knew how to connect the dots. I ended up making more money between that following May and December selling radio airtime on KMLE Country 108 than I did my entire pro career, excluding my signing bonus.

I started to see there was a future for me in something outside of baseball. And the more I thought about it, the more I didn't really want to go back to baseball anyway. I was bitter the way it ended. Also, my grandpa had done his infamous Nightline interview, so my name was still kind of famous in a bad way. I just wanted to steer clear of it.

When I first started selling radio airtime, I wouldn't even tell anybody that I used to play baseball. I never talked about baseball to the clients. I didn't want people to think, "Oh, this guy's just a baseball player." I wanted them to think of me as a businessperson who could help their business, not just an ex–baseball player who was doing something because he had nothing else to do. That turned out to be a really good tactic.

Eventually, guys would find out I played. They'd like what I was doing for their business and then ask me about my baseball career. I'd let them know I went to USC, was an all–American, third round pick, caught Randy Johnson, and all the typical stuff.

Sometimes I'd get embarrassed when someone would say, "I heard you played in the pros." Most people think the pros are the majors. I'd have to explain the whole minor league system, Rule 5 draft, and everything to them.

It took me a long time, and basically a healing process, to embrace that past and realize I did all right in my pro career. I didn't get to where I wanted, but millions and millions of young guys would have given anything to do what I was able to do.

By 2000, I had kind of hit the ceiling in Phoenix as one of the top reps in the city with the top station. One of the friends I met in radio moved to San Diego and was working with a head guy at the Dodgers radio network. She set me up with a call with him. I flew out for an interview, he hired me on the spot, and I started two weeks later. I moved out to California by myself while my wife stayed back and did all the necessary stuff for the house in Tempe. We started renting it, and we still rent it to this day.

I worked for that radio network about two years and then started my own company. Some days have been great, and then other times you're wondering where the next dollar is coming from.

When I started Campy Media, I was absolutely killing it. Then, a few years later things started to go backwards. There was the big crash of 2008, and I lost about 90 percent of my business.

Everybody started switching over to digital, and I had no clue how to manage digital. Around 2010 I got a job at a digital ad agency to be their traditional guy. I was actually still making traditional television and radio audio commercials and print stuff. However, at the same time I was learning how digital worked. They started going in a new direction and I lost that gig when they laid everyone off in that department.

I started working in areas I knew I could understand, and started making money with digital deals and learning how the whole social media advertising component works. I was having fun, enjoyed the work, and the creativity that goes into it and out to people.

Sometimes I've felt like the last man standing at these old waves of evolution. I was late to computers. I was playing baseball and didn't really touch a computer until I was 28, then I was late to radio, and then I was late to digital.

I recently started a company specifically for AI. For the first time now, I feel like I'm on the front side. It's trailblazing, which is pretty cool. Since I've also lived and worked for years in Arizona, I started the company there. We're still waiting for some of the tech components to be set up.

One of the components of the AI work is an ad network. Basically, it's an ad network that comes into your car through geofencing. Let's say you're listening to a podcast or music and your gas light turns on. It would come through your speakers and say if you go to the Shell three miles ahead on your right, you can get a free drink as well as five cents off each gallon of gas. There's also a component of generating points you could use in the future for things.

Another component is AI assistance and avatars for healthcare. When you have to set up a doctor's appointment, you open an app, and talk to this avatar lady, and get set up for your appointment. It can see your health records, and it's all in a closed silo. It doesn't use other people's AI. It's created its own version, which makes it quite unique. Again, it's pretty exciting to be on the front side of new technologies and not mopping up the rear.

It's been an evolution and a windy course. I've had successes and failures. Ultimately, it's been great.

I've been fortunate to find a career where I didn't have to be a stuffy guy in an office. When you're at a radio station, you could walk in and see Sting because he's got a concert that night and he's doing an interview. I remember talking to the Hootie and the Blowfish guys and tuning up Darius Rucker's guitar while he was doing an interview. Often at 5:30 when I'd walk up to the front to leave, the receptionist would say something like, "We have two tickets to the Doobie Brothers tonight. Do you want to go?" I'd say, "Why not." All the great perks we got used to in baseball, I saw in radio.

The last four years I've also coached high school, which has been an absolute blessing. I realized I could help these kids. I made every mistake a player could make. However, I figured them out, corrected them, and had some successes. I also have the ability to communicate. I've had six or seven guys that are now in Division I or II, and some other guys playing JUCO. They are constantly hitting me with texts on problems and issues, and sometimes it's a personal thing I help them through. It's funny. Sometimes I still feel like I'm that age. Then, when I walk by a mirror, I'm like, "Who's that old dude?"

Sometimes I miss that 20-something-year-old kid with a 10 plus mullet. I'd have fun with my teammates, hit bombs, go out, chase girls, and I didn't really have a concern in the world. We were living life to the fullest and were semi-famous in little towns. We had a blast. However, that 20-something guy's dead. He's gone.

Once baseball's over, you're an outsider and can't come back in. I felt that when I'd go into the clubhouses to see my friends. They're like, "All right, Campy. We'll see you next time. We have to go catch a flight." I'm like, "Okay. I'll keep watching you." It was weird saying goodbye to them when they were still going off to play baseball, while I was going to work the next day. But that was just part of the healing process.

It helped that I found a wife who understood baseball but was even happier when I stopped playing. She saw that I had talents in other areas too. I've been lucky to have her.

Sometimes, in the past, when I've gotten frustrated, I've blurted out something stupid like, "What if I didn't play baseball at all? What if at 21, I got my degree from USC and just started in business?" My business partner has heard me say that and he's said, "Well, what about all the experiences that you had and all the things you were able to do at such a young age that people would die to do?" That's when I realize that looking back, everything happens for a reason.

Jim Campanis, Jr., was a third-generation professional baseball player. Following baseball, he entered radio advertising and promotions (courtesy Jim Campanis, Jr.).

I've learned about other things and found other things I enjoy through those experiences.

Looking back, the thing I probably would have told myself was, "Forgive yourself for not making it sooner." That's probably the number one thing. I've talked to guys who played over a decade in the big leagues, and they're still pissed off about how their careers ended. I get that we're competitive beasts and that's what makes us get so far. However, at some point, we have to realize there's more to life than hitting a baseball. That was tough to understand at first.

Writing my book, *Born into Baseball*, helped me purge a lot of those feelings because they bothered me for a long time.

Putting my playing days behind me, and not mulling it over, was probably the best thing I could have done. I just decided to have fun in a new world. I've had a blast working on a lot of my projects over the years. Sometimes I just laugh when they pay me, because I'd have done it for free.

Bill Sampen

Bill Sampen played 10 seasons of affiliated baseball, including five seasons in the major leagues. His last year playing in affiliated baseball was 1994. Following his playing career, he worked in sports ministry for many years before developing his own baseball training program and complex, leading him to create a travel ball organization. At the time of the interview for this book, he was working and living in Indiana.

I started realizing it when I was with the Royals.

I had been told by players that once you have kids, it actually makes you a better player because it helps to not be so focused on the failure parts of baseball. You still get to go home to your kids. I totally understand that, but it seemed to be the opposite for me though because it was just so hard to be away from them.

Bruce Kison was with the Pirates organization when I was coming up. I loved the guy. We spent a lot of time around each other, and he knew me. When I got traded to Kansas City, he was the bullpen coach for the Royals. I remember Bruce saying, "Something seems different about you. You don't seem to have the same fire that you did." Honestly, it kind of pissed me off at first, and then I started thinking about it. I'm like, "This is a pretty perceptive guy who saw me in the low minor leagues when I was scraping and trying to be noticed." So, I took it to heart, and then over the course of time, I started to sense it. Even going into games didn't give me the same anxiety and nerves, which shows you care. That scared me a bit and made me think I was getting there.

In 1994 I got sent down from Anaheim to Vancouver, and at that point I pretty much knew. Shortly after they had to make a roster move. I was told, "We're going to release you." I'm like, "Cool." The guy goes, "You're okay with that?" I go, "Yeah. I really am." It just didn't feel the same.

I think the biggest challenge is discovering who you really are. I played for 10 years professionally. Your entire life revolves around training and what you have to do. Even if you're only training three hours a day, every second of the decisions you make are based around that. Everything else is completely secondary.

I didn't think I was just a baseball player. I'd have liked to say, "This isn't who I am. It's just what I do." But no, that's who I was because every second for 10 years I was consumed by it. The biggest challenge was, "What do I do? How do I do it? How do I make a living?"

I didn't play long enough or well enough to not work. I was 32 and felt like an 18-year-old coming out of high school trying to figure life out, but I had two kids and a wife.

I think the mistake I may have made was not looking ahead to that day. Looking back on my career, I had to be seconds from being released on several occasions. I remember in A-Ball I got hurt and was bumped out of the starting rotation. I already had one surgery, and I was 25 years old in A-Ball at the time. The guy that replaced me didn't pitch well. I got back in there, started pitching well, and things took off. At the moment, I never thought about it. In hindsight I wish I would have thought, "This can end at any time. I need to have a plan in place to live." I didn't think that way.

I had a college degree in marketing and economics, so I had an advantage there. I graduated pre-draft as a senior sign. However, I still probably should have been a little more futuristic in my thinking and preparation for life after playing. Again, I was just consumed by playing baseball.

Like most players, I thought professional coaching was an option. That didn't really make sense though because one of the reasons I stopped playing was because of all the travel involved in professional baseball, and I had two kids that were young.

I knew a guy in the ministry who I had met along my path of playing, and I did church ministry stuff for quite a while. I started doing some things in sports programming and it blossomed into where they created a full-time position for me.

I had done some baseball training work pretty much since I stopped playing. In 2009, I opened a training facility. I started it not necessarily trying to make it any huge or full-time thing. However, after a few years, I dove into it head-on. Right now, we have two locations of baseball and softball training facilities, as well as a complex that has four fields. We train kids of all different ages and school levels, as well as travel teams.

All three of my boys played travel ball, so as a parent I was around it for probably 14 or 15 years between the three of them. In about 2015 a couple dads came to me and asked, "Would you ever consider coaching travel ball?" I said I'd consider it. They knew a lot of people and were currently in the travel scene with their kids. They said they could construct a team for me and I'd just coach. We did that and decided to call them the Indiana Expos.

I didn't have any intent of doing another organization. I was just going to coach that group of kids. About the same time there was another team that said, "The organization we're currently in may no longer exist soon, or at least not as it currently does. We have about half a roster. Would you consider adopting us and we'll fill the roster the rest of the way?" I said that was fine. Then, a third group came in with the same scenario.

Instead of me just coaching a team, we had a little mini organization of three teams. From there, I decided to roll with it and see what happens. We held tryouts the next year with probably 400 kids. We ended up with eight teams, and it just grew from there.

We have grown and are pretty much capped out now with 33 teams. It grew very organically. There wasn't any intent to start a power organization. It just came day by day and year by year.

We started the Indiana Expos in 2016 and last year we added another facet, the Indiana Angels with dad coaches. This past fall we became part of Canes Midwest, a large travel ball organization.

I now do more reflecting. We are busy all the time, but I am still kind of stunned I still get to do baseball. I can live by doing baseball. I don't feel I was a good enough player to have deserved that, so I'm pretty thankful. I've got the chance to stay in the game and be around kids all the time. I find it a privilege.

Jeff Schaefer

Jeff Schaefer played 14 seasons of affiliated baseball, including five seasons in the major leagues. His last year playing in affiliated baseball was 1994. Following his playing career, he owned numerous companies before returning to baseball in various capacities to assist amateur players. At the time of the interview for this book, he was working and living in South Carolina.

In 1994 I was with the Orioles in Triple-A and asked them for my release, which they gave me. I signed with Oakland, knowing that if I went to Tacoma for a few weeks, they were going to call me up to the big leagues.

I was in Oakland and could see the strike starting to come our way. I told them, "I'm not playing. You can send me down to where they're playing. I'll take the assignment." Tony La Russa and Sandy Alderson were gracious enough to make that happen. I got out of there before everything hit the fan. I was making good money as a Triple-A player and finished the season out.

I started to realize at that point it was the end. I was 34 years old and trying to compete with 21- and 22-year-old kids. I was trying to sneak in a few more days, a few months, or possibly a year. I wanted to play but the grind to work out was getting tougher and tougher. My body was just not the same as it was years before.

I was married and had kids, and it was just time. The game more or less said goodbye to me because at 34 the phone stopped ringing. We make up the story that we retired, but that's never really the case. When the phone doesn't ring anymore, it's a forced retirement, but I had already started to settle into being a dad, rebooting, and looking ahead to what life was going to be outside of baseball.

I missed a lot. Even though I had a family, for 14 years of my life, my family was mainly the game. You spend more time around the guys in spring training, traveling around, and playing, than you really do with your own family. I had missed quite a bit, so it was catchup.

To be flat out honest, there's damage done in that scenario. You're not as attached to your kids as you should be, or you want to be. There are strains in marriages because of all the travel, especially with as much time as I spent in the minor leagues. There was definitely damage done and that marriage didn't last.

When I got done playing, I was 34 years old. It's not an easy transition at that age in life. When I played, there wasn't a lot of money being made. I never landed anything big in terms of salary from baseball. What I made wasn't going to be life sustaining.

The identity changes from being a major league baseball player to now being an average citizen. There was still some recognition around the area for what I had done but I went from being a major league player to not having those kinds of checks coming in. There's a bit of a shock. I wasn't any part of being destitute, but I was used to living a certain lifestyle and having the luxury of doing pretty much anything I wanted to do. That was an adjustment.

I just kind of regrouped for about eight months. You have to find yourself. I definitely identified myself for all those years as a baseball player but then I had to redefine myself.

I was an educated kid. I had a degree from the University of Maryland. I got drafted after my junior year but went back and finished up while I was in the minor leagues during the offseasons. It took a few years, but I got it in 1985. That was a promise I made to my parents. The agreement was if I signed after my junior year, I had to figure out a way to get my degree.

I didn't go on interviews or anything like that. I started off doing my own thing, creating companies, and being my own boss.

In fact, even before I played in the majors, I had a limousine company in Charlotte, North Carolina. I retired as a minor leaguer after the 1988

Triple-A season with the White Sox. I felt I had done everything I could and deserved to be a September call-up. I was 28 and turning 29 that next May. I figured if I hadn't gotten there by then, I didn't know if it was an option. I basically said, "I'm done." I bought a limousine and had no idea what I was doing. There were no Google maps. You had to get a regular map and figure it out. I got lost more times than I got people to their destinations. My strategy was to carry enough wine in the limo that if I got lost, maybe they'd get drunk and not be mad at me.

In my mind, I was done playing. However, I got a call from Terry Bevington, who had been my Triple-A manager that year, in the offseason. He said he got the first base coaching job in the big leagues, the White Sox were surprised I wasn't coming back, and that they wanted me to come back as a big league roster guy. I told him I had already convinced my wife I wasn't going back and would have to go back to her and say I was going to give it one more shot. I told him I wasn't going back to big league camp only to go to Triple-A. I made the team in 1989 and played much of the next five years in the majors.

After I finally got done with playing, I bought a small company for $20,000. It was a screen printing, embroidery, and graphic design company. I knew nothing about the business. I maintained the employees that were there and had them educate me on what it was. I had to educate myself on how things functioned as a business in terms of taxes, inventories, purchases, negotiations, and all those things. It was a big learning curve for me.

There were perks to being a former ballplayer. When you went in to do a presentation or sales meeting and there was a guy with a picture of a kid in a Little League uniform, it opened doors. It would create a conversation that was lighter than just, "I'm doing this businesswise and need you to buy my product or service." There were definitely benefits to that. However, there were also scenarios where people would look at me like, "You must think you're something special." I'd have to say I was just trying to make a living and take care of my family. However, that wasn't very often. Most people were cordial and would love to sit down and have a conversation. More often than not, you'd find a guy with a passion for the game, dreamed of being a big leaguer, and wanted to hear the stories you had. That definitely assisted with opening doors and building good relationships to help with the transition.

The screen printing took off. It grew on me fast. I literally paid $20,000 for the company and then three years later sold it for a couple million to Speedway Motorsports, which is a large NASCAR company. We started printing for them. At that time, I was being pulled into the corporate world, and I was not built for that. I went from sitting in my office with a t-shirt and shorts on to having to be dressed for board meetings with multimillionaires.

I wasn't accepted. It was like a square peg and a round hole. I just didn't fit. I did a good job for them and did everything I was supposed to do. I made them a lot of money, but I was just uncomfortable. I had a five-year contract, and they were gracious enough to know I did the job they asked me to, so they severanced me out for the last year.

After the screen printing company, I ran a golf apparel company for a short time, and then a denim company. We were making high-end jeans, which was a unique experience with cut and sew rooms in the bowels of North Carolina. We were in the fashion industry, and it just wasn't my world. It was uncomfortable going to shows in Vegas.

I went on another self-search thing, and although I had successes with my companies, none of them really made me happy. It was just mundane. It was the same thing with nine to five, weekends being weekends, and Sunday nights getting anxiety over starting the week by going back to what you really don't enjoying doing.

I started messing around, doing baseball lessons, and having some fun with some kids in a facility in Charlotte. I looked around and said, "I can do this better. I'm going to take a risk here, invest in some equipment and a facility, and see what I can make of it." That was 2007 and here we are in 2024. In that early period, it was a grind, but I've had some successes along the way.

I found peace and a place I wanted to be. Bats, and balls, and gloves, and kids, and fields, and grass, and dirt were all back in my life. I figured this was what I'm going to do moving forward, and I'm going to make things work. If the money turns out to be great, awesome. If it turns out to just sustain me, that's still what I'm going to do because happiness is more important than dollars.

It evolved and here we are all those years later. We've put kids in pro ball. We've got hundreds and hundreds of kids we've moved into college. Not just that, but we've built relationships. We've been around kids that are now doctors, lawyers, businessmen, and in other professions who are extremely successful. I knew what the game did for me. I wanted to be involved in the game and help it do the same for others.

I'm involved with USA Baseball as the regional director for the northeast and southeast. We're basically a scouting division for USA Baseball. We work out players through regional events and select a certain number of kids that go into the USA Baseball National Team Identification Series (NTIS) program. It's basically an identifier for kids to get invited to the 40-man trails for the national team or the player development program.

I also have a company called Advocacy Baseball Consultants with two other guys. We help families navigate through the process of exposure, making sure academics are sound, and understanding the dynamics of scholarships involved in baseball. There are no full-rides like basketball or football. Baseball players come out of school in debt. You must maximize the academic piece to minimize the cost of attending school.

When I got back into the game, I had zero idea how much the game had turned into a business. It had been years since I got out of it. When I played, your local Little League and everything was sponsored. I had guys telling me, "These kids pay us X amount to play in our organization. We travel and do all this stuff." I'm like, "What are you talking about?" I did my research and found, "Geez, this is a big business."

What I've become even more passionate about now is our nonprofit, U Deserve a Chance, because the game that was free for me my entire life is no longer free for everybody. We started the nonprofit to raise money to keep kids involved in the game.

I've always considered myself more than just a jock. Even though being a baseball player was my identity and what I enjoyed, I wanted to test myself. Good or bad, I've always kind of bet on myself. Believe me, I've had the fear of failure, but I think that's motivated me, just like it did when I was playing. I think that was a big piece. The game gave me that. You have to fold tent or figure out how to notch it up and compete. I got creative, hustled, and went after everything I felt I could achieve.

Looking back, if I could have given myself any advice, it wouldn't have been to that 34-year-old at the end of his playing career. It would have been to the guy in his early twenties so focused on the grind of having to be a big leaguer. You lose a lot of perspective on what life is really about. It's such a finite career. It doesn't last long for anybody. I don't care if you play for twenty years, you can't shut the rest of the world off because you have a dream of being something you think is going to bring you a lot more than it really does, because it goes away.

Jeff Schaefer played in five major league seasons (courtesy Jeff Schaefer).

You must be able to separate that time on the field, and make sure you're putting quality time into your family and children, because they're the ones that suffer the most through it because you're not there. Even to this day, with my boys from my second marriage, what I did in the game has carried a heavy weight on them because they were baseball guys. There were unfair expectations and pressures they didn't need.

Following his playing career, Jeff Schaefer owned numerous companies before returning to baseball in various capacities to assist amateur players (courtesy Jeff Schaefer).

If you're a professional player engaged in that lifestyle with a family, your family has to take as much of a priority as the successes you can have in the game.

I do miss the clubhouse, plane rides, and competing against the best in the world when I put that uniform on and walked out on a major league facility. I was always aware of the numbers of who I was amongst. At the time, there were 800 players and 28 teams. When you're the starting shortstop, you are one of 28 in the world. You're like, "Holy cow! I'm a kid from Patchogue, New York, that nobody would have bet on. Here I am standing in Yankee Stadium."

There's an adrenaline rush when you're in there. When they turn the lights on at Yankee Stadium and you're standing there at shortstop, it's like, "Whoa!" You can't find that. I'd like to bottle it up and give it to everybody. But it's like alcohol or another drug, it's a short term high.

I felt like on any given day, I could be the greatest in the world. When I was with Seattle, I could go 3-for-4, drive in the game winning run, and make a good play. Griffey could go 0-for-4, not do anything, and it was like, "Who's the best tonight?" Of course, I wasn't consistent enough because his name has Hall of Famer next to it and mine has limousine driver. But those were the things that pushed me forward.

All the firsts are memorable—your first game, hit, home run, baseball card, and bat with your autograph on it. However, in the end, it's the people and the relationships I've accumulated through baseball that mean the most.

If you come to my house, you'll see baseball stuff everywhere. You're not finding any t-shirt I printed, golf shirt I made, or a pair of jeans from my company anywhere. You're finding bats, balls, and gloves.

Pat Combs

Pat Combs played seven seasons of affiliated baseball, including four seasons in the major leagues. His last year playing in affiliated baseball was 1995. Following his playing career, he has worked in sports ministry, corporate consulting, and finance. At the time of the interview for this book, he was working and living in Texas.

I went through my first injury in '91 and had major elbow surgery. I never thought my career was over at that point, but when I came back, I just didn't quite have the same stuff. As much as I tried, and as hard as I worked, it wasn't coming along as I had hoped. I began thinking about the transition seriously in '93.

Then, I messed up my shoulder and had minor shoulder surgery. In '94 I had a decent season and thought I might be able to get back to the big leagues in '95. When that didn't happen, I looked at it as the time to depart.

Part of it was family. My wife was at home pregnant with our third son. Part of it was not seeing the results on the field I wanted. I started turning towards what's next and how best I could support my family. I wanted to be a full-time dad and husband. Life in baseball is probably one of the worst things you can do to your family. It was a combination of all those things.

I wanted to pursue baseball as long as I could, and I did that. Unfortunately, the injuries took their toll. The injuries were negative because they impacted my playing career. However, they were positive in the sense they really caused me to stop, think, and pray about what's next. I got to the end of my career and thought, "I've done everything I can to be the best in my sport, and in that way, I'm leaving on good terms."

For me there was a lot of prayer and asking God about what's next. I had a great support network. I had a church family. I had my own family. I had a lot of people who I could turn to outside the sport that could help me think through what was next. I've been blessed with a lot of great friends and family who cared about me beyond the sport.

My identity was tied to the game from the time I was a kid all the way through my third or fourth year in pro ball. I got a great part of my self-worth from the game. When I got hurt and that was taken away from me for a time period, I had to determine if my identity was going to continue to be tied to the game or if I was worth something more than that. That was through a lot of prayer and reading about what God thinks of me rather than what I think of myself.

I was blessed and grateful God created me to be a part of the game of baseball for a time. However, there's danger in allowing yourself to be tied to the game in terms of your self-worth and identity. That's a dangerous place to be. I played with a lot of guys in which that was true for them. I saw the destruction of what happened in their lives after the game. I'm so thankful I was aware enough to see it and realize I was created in this life to play the game for a time period, but when it was done, I was okay with it because that's not who I am. Who I am is a child of God and God created me for something much greater than the game of baseball. As much as I love the game, and as much as it did for me, that's not where my self-worth is linked.

That said, there's still a transition you have to go through beyond the identity piece. Organizationally, from the time I was seven to nearly 30, that was my way of life—working at the game and trying to be the best I could be at the game. Suddenly, you're turning to something different.

For about the first year and a half, in the back of my mind, I still felt like I could play the game. I felt at some point my arm would allow me to get back to a hundred percent to where I could compete and play in the big leagues. I still threw and did things trying to prepare myself for if that was a possibility. After I didn't see any movement in that area, I told myself I was going to quit thinking about it and turn to business and other things God wanted me to do.

For me, it was tough, but it wasn't as hard as I've seen it for others because of all the preparation and prayer going into the transition.

When I got back home, I really needed to give myself some time to think and pray about the next steps. I had done some ministry with the Fellowship of Christian Athletes, and they offered me the position of director of development. I did that for a couple years and then worked with a Christian sports camp to raise some money for developing a camp in Texas. That was a lot of fun. Those years allowed me to think through the transition of what I wanted to do in business.

During that time, I also completed my degree. I was drafted as a junior and left Baylor. I always knew I'd go back to school and get that done, it was just a matter of how that would work out with baseball. When I was playing, I couldn't do it in the offseasons because of the semester system at Baylor, so I waited until after my baseball career was over. I completed my degree through the University of Phoenix online.

I had worked in the ministry for a couple years and then worked with the Flippen Group, which was eventually rebranded to Teamalytics. From 2000 to 2005, I was in the consulting field working with leaders and doing work with athletes and various teams around the mental, emotional and behavioral sides. The founder, Flip Flippen, was a psychotherapist by trade and opened a couple businesses for helping leaders become the best they can be through behavioral analytics. I took Flip's processes into sports, and we began doing draft analysis and player development work with some MLB and NFL teams. That grew into working with corporate leaders.

The consulting thing really helped me. I was still in the world of sports, but it developed into working with corporate leaders. I got to meet some great business leaders and folks that I leaned into later when I got into wealth management.

I had a mentor back at the time who was a business leader in Houston. He said I had potential in business and in finance. We would talk about the markets and about investments. He said, "I know that's where your heart is because you talk about it all the time. Why don't you think about pursuing a career in finance?"

I had enjoyed related classes at Baylor, and when I was drafted and got my bonus check, I had another mentor who recommended reading the *Wall Street Journal*. I started doing that and was one of those nerdy guys on the team busses and planes reading the *Wall Street Journal* when everybody else was playing cards and goofing around. Thankfully, I realized early on that even if I had a tremendous baseball career and made a ton of money, I wanted to have the knowledge to know how to invest and grow that money. If I didn't have a career that would allow me to retire after baseball, so to speak, I wanted to be in a position to run my own business someday. I've always been very entrepreneurial.

I interned with a couple wealth management firms to dip my toe into it and see if it was something I wanted to do day to day. I knew I had an interest in it for myself and my family but needed to consider whether I wanted to consider building a business around that. After interning with a couple of firms, I figured out that was the direction I wanted to go.

I went into wealth management with Morgan Stanley and did that for 12 years. When you work for one of the big wirehouses like a Morgan Stanley, they remind you that you don't really own your business, and you work for them. However, in the world of wealth management you have to look at the clients you bring as those you serve, not the interests of the corporate giant you work with.

In 2016, my business partner and I opened up what's called a registered independent advisory. It was our own business, and we brought our clients over from Morgan to our own wealth management firm. I really enjoy working with people, helping them create financial plans, looking at their future, and assisting them with achieving their goals.

My middle son wanted to come into the business and in 2017 he went to work with my partner down in Houston and was trained up. He got his MBA and in 2020 we opened up our own shop, Combs Capital Partners. I've really enjoyed working alongside my son and he really runs the day-to-day now. We talk strategy every morning about portfolios and how the market's going. He's done a great job running things, which has allowed me to do other things.

I've been able to enter my second stint with Teamalytics. It's a blast. I love helping people grow and develop, and helping teams come together. We create strong teams for a complex world and do it all through the auspice of using behavioral analytics and coaching to develop people and teams. That ultimately creates relationships that sometimes turn into wealth management clients. That works really well with what I do.

We got into investing in the crypto ecosystem back in 2017. I became a huge believer after researching the crypto world and we developed a couple of funds. We have two crypto funds that were created for anybody that wanted to invest in the infrastructure side of blockchain technology and tokenization. That's been a lot of fun and we're reaping the rewards of that now.

Also, in the spring I do some broadcasting with ESPN and cover college baseball, mainly the Big 12 and the Baylor home games.

I stay hopping.

Greg Litton

Greg Litton played 12 seasons of affiliated baseball, including six seasons in the major leagues. His last year playing in affiliated baseball was 1995. Following his playing career, he has worked in numerous industries, usually in sales roles. He also spent many years as an inspirational keynote speaker. At the time of the interview for this book, he was working and living in Florida.

In '95 I signed a minor league deal with Seattle with the agreement to go to big league spring training once the strike was over. I wasn't going to cross the picket line. I said I'd come to minor league spring training to get some work in, instead of sitting at home. Well, I get to spring training and I'm doing really well in minor league spring training. They settle the strike but don't invite me to big league camp. At that point, I'm like, "What am I going to do? I know Lou (Piniella) likes me. I guess I'm just going to stay here." I ended up having a great year in Triple-A but didn't get called up at the end of the season.

Jeff Brantley and a bunch of guys were always telling me that I needed to sign with a bigger agent with more pull. I loved my agent to death, and we had been together for years. I ended up calling him and I said, "I love you but before my career is over, I've got to try things with a bigger name agent just to see." I signed with Brantley's agent and after that great year in Triple-A, he couldn't even get me a minor league deal. I figured, "Well, I guess it's just not meant to be. I'm done."

My last few years I had great seasons, but I couldn't get a job. I was never one of those players that was a pain or bad teammate. It just didn't make sense. I figured God was telling me it was time to move on.

I ended up calling my original agent and said, "I just wanted to let you know he couldn't find me a job. Thank you for everything you did. Obviously, I'm done." The next year he calls me in the offseason and goes, "Greg, would you like to play if I could get you a job?" I said, "Yes, you have permission to ask around if you want but don't call me unless you have a job. I don't want to just hear that someone might be interested."

After a year off, he was able to get me invited to spring training with Detroit. It was the weirdest thing. I had a strong arm and could sit in Candlestick Park for 12 innings in the freezing cold, get stuck at shortstop, throw a couple practice balls to first, and throw as hard as I could without any stiffness or anything after the game. Well, after taking that year off, I think my shoulder atrophied because I couldn't throw very hard. I'd never had a sore arm in my life, but every throw was like somebody stabbing me in the shoulder. They flew me to Detroit and thought I had a torn labrum, but the doctor couldn't find anything wrong. The Tigers and I mutually agreed I was done.

There are a lot of reasons why I thought God was telling me I was done. My wife and I were trying to get pregnant, and we had started doing fertility shots. I hadn't seen her in about three weeks, and she flew into Tampa on Good Friday for Easter weekend. That morning, we had kind of decided I was done with baseball. I picked her up from the airport, gave her a big hug, and we walked out to the car in the garage. It was weird because when I gave her a hug I could feel her heart thumping. We got to the car, and she says, "I've got something for you." She handed me a wadded up piece of wrapping paper. I opened it up and it was a pacifier. She had gotten pregnant the week before I left. They say women get pregnant when they give up. When I got that job with the Tigers and went to spring training, she was like, "I'm never going to get pregnant." Well, she got pregnant right then.

That's when my baseball career ended and my family started. So, I didn't miss it. I was starting to be a father and that's the greatest thing I've ever done.

I played for 12 years professionally and was signed out of junior college. I had college tuition in my contract, but I was an engineering major and after 12 years those calculus and physics classes weren't very fresh. I was like, "God, what am I going to do?" It wasn't like I was going to go back into engineering at that point.

When I was playing, the minimum salary for my first year in the major leagues was $68,000. I never made a ton of money, but I saved a ton of what I did make. There wasn't a lot of pressure to make money right away. I had a decent nest egg, but it certainly wasn't enough to completely retire.

I was pretty good at golf and after I was done with baseball, I took about a year to practice and see how good I could get. I learned that game will drive you up a wall. But I gave it about a year before I knew that wasn't going to be a route I wanted to go.

One of my good friends and golfing buddies, who I had met getting my wife's engagement ring, owned a jewelry store in town. He called me one day, we went to lunch, and he told me that his son really didn't have a desire to be in the jewelry business. We talked about it, and I learned a little bit about it from him for a few days. We worked out a deal where I was going to work for him for seven or eight years until his youngest son graduated college. At that point he would retire, sell the business to me, and work with me part-time because he loved the business and didn't want to completely stop working. That was a pretty good plan. However, about the time I was going to take over, he got divorced, which set his retirement back.

I met a guy named Quint Studer at a few functions and we became friends. He owned a healthcare consulting business called the Studer Group, and also the Double-A baseball team here, the Blue Wahoos. He heard me speak at a function and asked if I ever thought about speaking. I was still in the jewelry business, but he had me do a bunch of training with his speech coach. They had contracts with hundreds of healthcare groups all over the country. When I got good enough that they started sending me out on paid jobs, I got out of the jewelry business.

I took a sales job in merchant services and credit card processing because it was only commission and gave me the flexibility to focus on speaking for the Studer Group. I was hoping the speaking would become a full-time career. I would do traditional inspirational topics like setting goals and never giving up. I would walk them through my baseball career and how I wasn't the most talented, biggest, or fastest player. I loved it. Other than playing ball, it's the funnest thing I've ever done. I absolutely love public speaking.

I did professional speaking for many years, anywhere between five to 10 to 12 times a year. However, it never took off to where it became a full-time job. I was always kind of the misfit baseball player in the healthcare consulting business, like, "How does he fit in?" When Studer sold the business, the structure of the company changed, and the speaking deals died down, but I still do a few speaking engagements a year.

I went into the mortgage business and still had residual income coming in from the merchant services business much of that time. Eventually I ended up selling all my customers back to the merchant services company.

The mortgage business was really the only job I haven't enjoyed. As a mortgage broker, you basically make a living kissing up to realtors, which I did not like. A couple years ago, I started to let friends know I wanted to get out of the office and back into outside sales.

About a year and a half ago, I went to work with a good friend who I actually met on a flight for a speaking deal. He owns a restoration company that addresses water damage, mold, fire, biohazard, and anything like that. Most of our work comes from plumbers, property managers, and insurance companies. I work in sales covering the Florida panhandle. I'm on the road, kind of set my own schedule every week, and I love it.

I was never really driven by making money, especially after I got divorced when my daughters were young. Divorce is not the way it's supposed to be, but you have to make the best of it. There were opportunities where I could have made more, but I would have traveled more and wouldn't have been there for my girls. I didn't see them enough as is and didn't want to sacrifice my kids' time for trying to make more money. I wouldn't trade it for the world. My daughters and I are very close, and I'm about to be a grandfather in September.

I'm happy and the only times in my life when I haven't been satisfied or happy are when I tried to put things like baseball or myself ahead of my faith and my relationship with God. Those are the only times I haven't been fulfilled or content. My identity was not as a baseball player, so when I was done, I was done. What you do isn't who you are, and your faith and your family are.

Andy Carter

Andy Carter played 10 seasons of affiliated baseball, including two seasons in the major leagues. His last year playing in affiliated baseball was 1996. Following his playing career, he started his own tree cutting and land clearing business. At the time of the interview for this book, he was working and living in Florida.

I never had a Plan B. I didn't want to get sidetracked. I had one focus and that was to be a big league player and stay there. That didn't work out.

I think the first time I really thought about it was with the Giants in Triple-A in '96. That year the pitching coach told me I should get into coaching. I'm like, "I'm 27. I'm not even thinking about that right now." I figured something's going on if he's asking me if I want to be a coach. I said, "I don't think so."

I understood the business part of it. I got to a certain level at Triple-A where I think I was making about $9,000 a month with the Giants, which at the time was pretty good money. I'm not complaining about that at all. However, once you get near 28 or 29 and you're making that, and there's a kid who's 21 who can do the same thing you're doing for $2,500, there's the business side.

When that coach with the Giants told me I should talk to the front office about coaching, I started thinking about that being a weird conversation. Then, the next year I signed with the Mets and just had a weird feeling. I was going to be the only lefty in Triple-A but when I got there, they had brought in a bunch of lefties. I'm like, "I see how that worked out." I didn't pitch much in spring and got let go pretty early in the first cuts. I wasn't mad. I saw them bring in a bunch of guys that were throwing pretty good and I didn't throw much. That's the way it goes.

After I got released from the Mets, I went and played for Jenkintown in the Pendel League for a few games. It was just a men's league. From there, a guy from Allentown in an independent league called, and I finished up the year there.

I went to Taiwan in 1998 and figured once that was over, I'd try coaching. I returned to Allentown as a player-coach in 1999, but I didn't pitch at all. My arm wasn't feeling good, so I just coached. I liked doing it for that year, but the financial part just wasn't there at all. I was offered a coaching gig but told them I was moving onto the next phase of my life.

I had worked in the offseasons.

I had a friend who was in the tree business and making really good money. He was doing over $300,000 a year. I thought, "That's not bad." He was really busy and didn't have time to teach or show me anything, so

I started working for another guy the last two years I was playing. In fact, when I went to Taiwan, I had already done one year of tree work. I figured once that was over and I gave coaching a try, I'd just go right into working for a tree company.

I started working on the ground but moved to climbing because I figured climbing was a lot easier than dragging brush. I did that for about two years and then went off and started my own business.

The company's name is Carter Tree and Bobcat Services. It's a tree and land clearing business in Florida. I also do forestry mulching which requires a machine to run over all the thicket and stuff. I try to stay as a subcontractor. I have a bunch of equipment, and I'll go work for other companies.

It wasn't easy at first. I had no clue about the business end of it. I was just working and saving up for the equipment I needed. It kept evolving every year.

Bidding on jobs required a big learning curve. As a younger guy, I was lowballing just to get work. Some guys were getting $6–8,000 for trees I was at $3,000 for. There were a couple of guys I grew up with who were in the industry, and they always helped me out. I learned a bunch of stuff from them on the business side of it. When I lowballed something, they'd shake their heads and be like, "Dude, you're way off." I see why I did it, but I would never do something like that again. There's a tremendous amount of risk with doing big tree removals, and there were mistakes made when I was younger.

Andy Carter entered the tree cutting and land clearing business following his playing career. Here he poses in front of a large tree project (courtesy Andy Carter).

I'm getting older now and don't want to do trees much longer, so I'm phasing into farming. I bought some land my brother found. The land was already cleared, and it was a good deal. I've researched different ways to make money on the acreage. Organic blueberries and vegetables seem like they pay for themselves per acre on a smaller farm. It'll be a "you pick 'em" place. I'll let somebody else come, do all the work, and leave some money on the table.

I also have some beef cattle. They're heifers, so we're going to get them artificially inseminated and have a small calf operation.

While I'm still doing the trees, I'll be phasing out over the next five years. I'm definitely getting old enough that I don't feel like climbing trees anymore. I've got a couple of younger kids doing that now. I'll probably pass it on to them, then move on to sitting around and watching people pick blueberries.

For a lot of guys, it's tough when they first get out of baseball. I didn't have an issue when I was done. You're just a person. Life goes on. You're either going to work or you're going to go down the toilet and fade away. I've worked since I was 10 years old. I had five or six lawns I would do weekly for five bucks. I worked in the offseasons. It wasn't a big deal for me to leave baseball and go to work in manual labor. I didn't care. If I was putting food on the table, that was fine.

You just have to work hard. There are days you lose money. It's like having a bad day pitching. You must keep getting up and grinding it out or you're not going to be around. I'd have a couple bad games in a row, but then the next game, I'd usually be fine. I did learn that from baseball. You must keep grinding it out.

Mark Acre

Mark Acre played seven seasons of affiliated baseball, including four seasons in the major leagues. His last year playing in affiliated baseball was 1997. Following his playing career, he entered real estate before eventually pursuing high-level corporate sales jobs. At the time of the interview for this book, he was working and living in Arizona.

I played my last season for Oakland in 1997. They sold my contract and negotiated a buyout with the Yakult Swallows in Japan.

I'll never forget. Billy Beane and I worked together on that. I wanted to go over to Japan to see it first. He says, "I'm going to have Eric Kubota call you." Eric was the Pacific Rim Coordinator. Eric calls me, gets my ticket, and says, "All right, get your passport." I was like, "I don't have one." Billy was pissed. They flew me up to Seattle, I got a passport in less than 24 hours, and I went off to Japan.

My first year there went really well. I had always been a reliever but was starting instead.

In spring training my second year I got hurt and realized it was pretty significant. It wasn't like most of the time in spring training when you have some aches and pains. I was actually hitting BP. I was swinging and felt something in my shoulder. My velocity went down pretty quick, and they were shooting me full of cortisone. My arm was still hurting really bad. I'd get done pitching, and I'd literally have to hold my arm. It was bad.

I was going to throw a bullpen and then start against the Giants. I told my interpreter, Koji Kondo, "I'm going to warm up on flat ground and when I get to the mound if it hurts when I cut loose, I'm going to go over there, take off my shoes, and not pitch again until I get an MRI. I have to see what's wrong." He was really nervous and looking at the executives there in their suits standing by the mound. It looked like something right out of Mr. Baseball. He says, "All right. Go ahead." I say, "All right. I'm going to cut loose."

I threw the pitch, and it took my breath away. It hurt like hell. I walked over to the bench and started taking my shoes off. All the executives came over with Koji. They're like, "What's going on?" I said, "That's it. I'm done."

They flew me to see Dr. James Andrews in Alabama. I had to have surgery, and then they released me. However, they still paid me.

I had a house in Scottsdale but that was rented out because I was gone for 10 months at a time. I decided to rehab my shoulder in San Diego and was put up in a beautiful place. Every day I was doing rehab and going to the beach. This started in May, and it was the first summer I'd had in years. I'd never had a Fourth of July outside of being on a baseball field, and I never even had a spring break. I made some great friends down there while dedicating myself to my rehab. The Padres let me work out at their facility and I would often work out with Trevor Hoffman.

I went back to see Dr. Andrews after three or four months, and I had full range back. My physical therapist was very aggressive with the scar tissue. It broke up, which was great. However, I didn't have a team at the time. I talked to my agent, but they wanted to see me pitch outside a bullpen. They wanted to see me play competitively. It was suggested I go to independent ball, but I didn't want to do that.

I did get an opportunity for White Sox camp in 2000, but I failed the physical. The drive back from Tucson that day was a tough one. It was about an hour and a half and pretty sobering.

The first year, when I was out of baseball and rehabbing in San Diego wasn't too complicated. I thought in the back of my mind I could come back. I remember seeing the Padres play. I was in the stands, watching guys I had played against, and going, "I'm going to come back." However, that wasn't the case.

The realization hit in year two.

I don't care how much money you have. I had more than a million in the bank at the time from Japan and a Lloyd's of London policy I had taken out on my shoulder. But it doesn't matter. I was just so depressed and sad. You lose your identity. It's like a death. I remember my wife literally feeding me in bed. That's as bad as it got. My doctor suggested I take something. I adamantly said no and never did. I wanted the lows to be low and the highs to be high naturally.

I started to read real estate books. I had a couple of great mentors and was really trying to educate myself. I bought a house down the street from me. Then, I bought a 29-unit apartment complex and flipped that. I had some success.

I was working with some real estate guys in Scottsdale, and they brought a deal to me. A stadium for the Cardinals was being built, and there was a nearby apartment complex that was dilapidated. We went in, got some investors, and made a bunch of money in 16 months. Things were rocking and rolling.

I was going to start building custom homes but then ran into a guy that embezzled quite a bit of money from me. It was really wild how he did it. Somehow, he took a signature that was engraved on one of my baseball cards and used it in documents. I had to go to court and testify against him, and he ended up going to jail. I did very well when I did things on my own. However, when I started working with other people was when I got into some issues.

Then, in 2008, the real estate market started to tumble. I was like, "All right, I'm going to jump into the corporate world, get insurance, and have a good stable job for my family."

I went into the corporate world not knowing anything about formal selling, sales techniques, or anything like that. I was talking with friends about medical device sales and went on a couple calls with a guy who was a former baseball player working for a company that did plates and screws. I watched a gal's humerus get put together and all that. Afterwards, he goes, "You passed the test. Let's get your resume together. You have a degree, right?" I said, "No." He goes, "Man, you need your degree. You have to check that box."

I couldn't be in med device sales, so I put my resume on Monster and started working for an IT training company while I started the process of getting my degree.

Ernie Young was my teammate in Oakland, and he was at my house one day. I told him I was thinking about going back to school and he said, "Hey, man. You can get the Roland Hemond Scholarship through Major League Baseball." Hemond was a longtime baseball executive, GM, and a very well-respected man in baseball. I applied for the scholarship, was selected, and went to the University of Phoenix for my degree in business administration. I'd work during workdays and do my schoolwork at night and on the weekends.

It's been a great, interesting ride. I started with an IT training company called New Horizons and have just kept climbing the ladder. I'd meet people, network, and get opportunities. Every step I've made has been a step up, never a step back. All positions have been more money and better roles.

When starting out, I had to change the way I spoke. I couldn't use locker room talk and had to try to be more professional. I had to have business acumen. That was one of the toughest parts, understanding business acumen, forecasting, pipelines, and all the things that had to do with sales cycles.

At first, I was like a robot, mimicking what everybody else did. However, much like with baseball, when you're trying to hit or pitch like somebody, it doesn't necessarily work. You have to be authentic and do things your own way.

I remember one day I was working on a spreadsheet, and this guy was joking around and giving me a hard time. I didn't know how to type very well and would peck type. He goes, "You're pecking. You don't even know how to do an Excel spreadsheet." I turned around and said, "Hey, motherfucker! When you were passing your Excel class, I was getting Derek Jeter out at Yankee Stadium, so shut the fuck up!" Everyone went, "Oh!" That was a big moment for me because I realized I had to be authentic and bring to the table what I had to bring to the table. If it worked, it worked. If it didn't, it didn't. I really thrived after that.

I had to embrace being a former baseball player. Previously, when I'd walk into a room at 6'8" and 250, people would be like, "What the hell did this guy do?" I didn't talk about it and would downplay it. But at that point I told myself, "I'm going to embrace being a baseball player." That was a big turning point for me.

I've had a lot of successes and have been recruited by many companies. Headhunters have called me constantly. When you're in sales, you don't sit somewhere for 20 years. You bounce around to different organizations. I've received signing bonuses, stock, and equity in companies. It's been a really great path for me. People talk about bouncing around, but I think it's fantastic. I've got to work with so many different companies, meet so many different people, and my knowledge base across a lot of industries has become really specialized.

Before getting acclimated to the corporate world, I wanted to walk out and quit a hundred times. I was like, "This isn't for me. I can't do it. I'm uncomfortable." I could talk in front of people all the time. However, when

I had to talk about IT training, Security+ training, implementation, and all that type of stuff, it was challenging, but I made it work.

Obviously, we all love baseball, but it's important to do something outside of your comfort zone. You can't be afraid to take risks. That's what we did on the diamond every day. We took risks with pitches. We took risks with changing positions. You can't always play it safe. People can't be afraid of change. If you get fired, laid off, or something happens where you're leaving a job, embrace it. You never know the reason it happened until it unveils itself later.

Mark Acre spent his entire playing career in affiliated baseball with the Athletics (courtesy Doug McWilliams).

Baseball teaches the ability to adapt. I can adapt to any situation, any role on a team, or any account. I think we as baseball players and athletes have the ability to do that. You could be relieving one year and then starting the next. You could play a different position or hit in a different position in the lineup. You must adapt, have the team in mind, and want to win collectively.

I've always been able to interact well with people. A lot of that came from baseball—signing autographs, doing interviews, and just socializing. I grew up very humbly, so it didn't matter if it was the janitor, the security guard, or someone like Sandy Alderson. I've always been comfortable in conversations across the board, and that translates into business. I've never turned my nose up at anybody. I've always been very respectful.

I don't know what Major League Baseball can do, but I'd emphasize

Mark Acre entered real estate before eventually pursuing high-level corporate sales jobs (courtesy Mark Acre).

the importance of having mentors in place during and after playing that have been through the game. I think it's really important. I remember going to the rookie seminar in Virginia, and Dan Quisenberry was our mentor during the week. He had us in a room and there was no agenda. We just talked about life, where we're at, and post-career. He gave us advice, and I took it to heart. I think mentorship programs like that are really important to help guys make a better transition and avoid some of the tragic events we've seen like the recent suicides. It breaks my heart when guys don't see a way out.

Eric Fox

Eric Fox played 12 seasons of affiliated baseball, including four seasons in the major leagues. His last year playing in affiliated baseball was 1997. Following his playing career, he coached in the minor leagues for many years and spent time in the insurance industry. At the time of the interview for this book, he was semi-retired and living in Arizona.

In 1997 I signed with Baltimore in spring training. I drove up to Rochester, New York, for opening day at the new stadium. We had a parade through the city and to the ballpark. I got hauled off during batting practice and was released because they had a big leaguer getting sent down.

Well, I was about to jump in the car and drive back to California, but Scranton/Wilkes-Barre (in the Phillies organization) was in town and had a couple outfielders hurt. Being a veteran with a presence for the young kids, Scranton told me, "Hey, we might have a job for you for three or four weeks until our guys get healthy." I said, "Okay."

I was supposed to be there no longer than a month, but I lasted the whole season. It was a good experience. At Scranton, Bill Robinson was the hitting coach, and he got me interested in teaching hitting. He let me help with the young kids and I saw how he coached.

I'd play for three or four days and then might sit for a week or 10 days. In the outfield I'd be a step or step and a half behind getting to balls where I would have been.

That year Philly had one of the worst first halves in the history of baseball. They were bad. I saw the writing on the wall, and the realization of not getting back to the big leagues hit me. Once you spend some time in the big leagues, that's where you want to be. I didn't see that realization of getting back at 34 and decided to hang up my cleats as a player.

I wanted to get into coaching right away. I thought I'd be able to get a job in Rookie Ball or A-Ball pretty easily with my experience, but jobs are few and far between.

Eric Wedge and I retired together from Scranton/Wilkes-Barre, and he got the manager position in Columbus for the Cleveland Indians. I ended up getting the hitting coach job late in January the following year. The only reason I got picked up by Cleveland was because the guy they had scheduled to coach in Columbus couldn't make it. Eric knew me and my work ethic, so I got the call when spring training was right around the corner. I got to spring training and was in a classroom for eight hours for three days.

I still had the fire burning in me like I did when I was a player, so I had a hard time during the first half of the season. When one of my outfielders missed a ball, overthrew a cutoff man, or made a mistake, I took it personally. However, it was the manager's job to be the tough guy. Eric took me aside two or three different times that first half.

I had to learn as the assistant coach I was the nice guy and the "go between" with the manager to help smooth things out with players. It took half a season but once I learned that, it became fun. I just kind of kicked back and helped Wedge out, as well as helping the players out.

I made it up the ladder pretty fast from Single-A, Double-A, and Triple-A in three seasons. After a year back down in Double-A as a hitting coach, I switched to managing.

I managed one year in Portland, Maine, in 2002, and I'm glad I did it. However, I considered myself more of a third base coach or hitting coach. I didn't like being the bad guy, yelling at players or umpires. That's just not my personality. I tried managing, got that on my resume, and went back to being a hitting coach and outfield coach after that.

The goal was to get back to the big leagues. That was a dream of mine. To get back, I figured I'd probably become a first base coach first. However, the more I coached third base, that was what I really wanted to do. My ultimate goal was to be a bench coach or third base coach in the big leagues. Unfortunately, it didn't happen.

My last job was with Harrisburg in 2012 and 2013. In 2013 we went to the Eastern League championship and lost to the Yankees. I drove home for three days and then got a phone call letting me know they weren't going to renew my contract. I was thinking, "We just made it to the championship, what's going on?" I was told a story that didn't make sense to me but said I appreciated the opportunity the last two years.

I had also gotten tired of riding the buses and being gone for seven or eight months out of the year. I decided I wouldn't be coaching for a while and got my insurance license.

A friend of mine owns an insurance company called Mustard Seed Financial in Meridian, Idaho, near Boise. He said, "If you want to stay home, get your insurance license and I'll give you some house accounts."

I also had my own little baseball instruction business where I gave lessons. I'd always done that in the offseasons. I had given my insurance friend's kids hitting lessons and helped coach his son's team.

I sold auto, home, and commercial insurance for five years. My love wasn't selling insurance. I'd be in the office six to seven hours, and I'm not one to be in a cubicle. However, I'd do that job and then go give an hour hitting lesson afterwards, which wasn't even work for me. That was my release. I wasn't in pro ball, but I was still involved with baseball.

I'd always loved Arizona since the early eighties when I'd come down from Fresno State to play Arizona State and U of A. Then, I'd be there for spring training. I love the heat, and I love the cactus. In the back of my mind, I always wanted to semi-retire down there.

My wife's job in Boise got outsourced to Taiwan. She was at the 24-year mark and had planned to retire at 25 years anyway. One day she looked at me and said, "Hey, do you want to move to Arizona?" I looked at her, smiled, and said, "That's not a tough sell for me." In 2019 we decided to come down to Arizona.

Eric Fox coached in the minor leagues for many years before spending time in the insurance industry (courtesy Doug McWilliams).

When I came down here with my wife, I took my resume to all 15 teams here in Arizona. I told them, "I live here now. I've coached all over the country and I want to stay here." No one wants to stay in Arizona. They call it the "fire league." Well, I never got a single phone call. Unfortunately, I found they were phasing out guys my age and going with younger guys that do analytics. The game isn't what it was when I was playing and coaching. Analytics are important, but people lean on them too much.

I'm semi-retired now but I keep busy. I

Uber about 20 hours a week and that helps pay for my golf, which can get expensive. I try to Uber two to three hours a day, and sometimes more. I like talking with people, and it keeps me busy.

I also help with the baseball clinics through the Major League Baseball Players Alumni Association around Phoenix. We often get 200 to 300 kids for three hours. They're free camps for the kids and they get a backpack full of school supplies, a free lunch, and an autographed ball from everyone. They help introduce kids to baseball, and some of them have never been on a ball field before. I'm fortunate I get to do that.

As a big league player, I was up and down for four years, and every day was like going to Disneyland. I had heard horror stories of rookies coming up and veterans treating them bad because they thought you were taking their jobs. There was none of that in Oakland.

I'd play for Rickey Henderson in left field, and he'd be one of the first guys to give me high fives. I'd get high fives from Rickey, Jose Canseco, Dave Henderson, Willie Wilson, and it was just a great feeling. There was no negativity. It's funny because Dave Henderson and Willie Wilson took me under their wings when I was a 28-year-old rookie. Now I live four miles from Willie Wilson and play golf with him every Tuesday, which is a treat. The guy has Hall of Fame numbers, and he's one of the most down-to-earth people you'd ever meet.

What I probably miss most are the interactions with fans, especially the people in center field. They'd have a poster up and called themselves the Fox Hounds. They seemed to gravitate towards me because of the type of player I was. It's a bad feeling when the clubhouse guy comes up to you after batting practice and goes, "Hey, coach wants to see you in his office." Those were the dreaded words that you were getting sent down. However, every time that happened, and I was on a yo-yo with Oakland for three years, I would go sit with the fans in center field. I had such a good experience.

Kurt Knudsen

Kurt Knudsen played nine seasons of affiliated baseball, including three seasons in the major leagues. His last year playing in affiliated baseball was 1997. Following his playing career, he entered law enforcement. Since retiring from law enforcement, he has worked in workers' compensation investigation and delivery logistics. At the time of the interview for this book, he was working and living in California.

When I was young, I had two career goals. I wanted to become a major league baseball player, and I wanted to get into law enforcement.

I came from a law enforcement family. My dad was an FBI agent when I was little. He worked for J. Edgar Hoover and would show up to my Little League games in a suit and tie in his undercover car. And during my baseball career, my brother entered the California Highway Patrol. Law enforcement wasn't plan B. I knew baseball wouldn't last and I would get into law enforcement afterwards. That was always the plan. However, when I got hurt in baseball, my playing career just ended a little earlier than I wanted it to.

I got released by Detroit during the spring of '95. I drove across the country and had a tryout with the Giants. I threw a bullpen, and they signed me right after that. I stayed in Phoenix for extended spring training and then was with the Phoenix Firebirds. This was before the Diamondbacks were there.

I was having a pretty good year and went for a run one day when we were in Vancouver. My leg was feeling a little tingly, but I didn't really think anything of it. I just thought it felt a little weird. I got in the game that night and didn't have a good outing.

We came back to Phoenix, and I got into another game. I threw a pitch and my cleat stuck. Usually, my front foot would hop when I followed through. This time, I wasn't able to hop because of the deadness in my leg, and I just collapsed. That was an interesting night. I went to the hospital and found out I had a bulging disc in my back. They injected me with cortisone and 10 minutes later, the doctor came in and said, "Okay, put your legs down and stand up." I couldn't stand up. I was paralyzed from my waist down. He accidentally paralyzed me for 10 hours with the cortisone shot.

My season was over in Phoenix. I came home that offseason and was told the only way they were going to free up the nerve was if I had a microdiscectomy. I had surgery in September or October and was throwing bullpens by January.

I spent '96 rehabbing with Sonoma in independent ball and then signed with the Angels that offseason. I wasn't the same pitcher. I went down to A-Ball and hadn't been in A-Ball in a long time. The writing was on the wall. I could have tried to stick it out, but I didn't know if I had the patience to try and work it out. After the Angels, I had an offer to play in an independent league in New York, but the team didn't even have a home field. I had a wife and child by then and would've had to live out of a suitcase.

I went to an interview with the Sacramento Sheriff's Department, and when I walked out of that interview, I knew my baseball career was done. I went through the academy and then worked in the Sacramento County Jail for a few months.

I had a buddy who was a sergeant with the Folsom Police Department. He was a motor cop and when I was still playing baseball, he'd sit behind the catcher, shoot the radar at me, and tell me how hard I was throwing. He said, "Come to Folsom. We'll work together and it'll be fun." I applied and they picked me up from Sacramento County. The good thing about Folsom is that you go through field training, and since they don't have a jail there, you're right out on the street. I learned a lot from being in the Sacramento County Jail but didn't like hanging out there. The jail was quite interesting.

I was a patrol officer with Folsom and never promoted. I never really wanted to get promoted. I enjoyed being out as one of the boots on the street. As an officer with Folsom, there are additional duties patrol does. I was a motor officer for a few years. I was a training officer. I was the public information officer for two and a half years. I was also on the SWAT team for nine and a half years.

The SWAT team in Folsom is just another job patrol does. I know other departments have a dedicated SWAT team and that's all they do. However, if we got a call when I was on patrol, I would head back to the police department, suit up for SWAT and head out. Sometimes we would carry our equipment in our trunks.

Kurt Knudsen played in three big league seasons (courtesy Kurt Knudsen).

When I came to Folsom and worked nights, we had four or five other cops on those shifts, and we had each other's backs. We were a team. We showed up together, did things, and if you didn't do your job, things could go sideways. That's just like in baseball. I still had the team concept, but the stakes were much higher. I'm backing up somebody for their life. I'm getting into situations where my life can be taken, or other people's lives can be taken. I'm not just out there throwing a ball and having somebody yelling at me because I'm on the opposing team. In a way, they're similar and in a way, they're not. I still had to do the best I possibly could and take care of my responsibilities.

You need the ability to communicate and handle the pressures. When Dave Winfield walks up to the plate and you have a screaming crowd staring you down, you still need to know what to do and remain calm about it. I took that into police work.

When you're on the SWAT team going into a house or entering a dangerous situation, you've got to stay calm. Like with Mickey Tettleton calling pitches, you've got to trust your partners to have your back. When you go into a room, it's "You go left. I go right." Having the experience of being in pressure situations and having to remain calm, I believe helped me a

Following his playing career, Kurt Knudsen fulfilled another lifelong dream by serving as a police officer, including time on his department's motorcycle and in SWAT units (courtesy Kurt Knudsen).

lot. Yeah, they were obviously different situations, but being able to slow things down and think things out helped. I think it benefited me in certain situations because I had to compartmentalize and adapt to my situation as a cop. I still went through the same process I did when I was a professional athlete.

I spent 20 years in law enforcement. There were some changes going on in the police department I didn't really agree with, and it was starting to become almost like baseball. It just wasn't as enjoyable to go to work anymore. I was 50 and we had a great contract for retirement, so I figured it was time for me to go.

I had my retirement but still needed to do something. My brother had his own private investigation firm, and he hired me on as a worker's comp investigator. I would travel up and down northern California for state funds. However, my brother became the lead security officer of a new hotel, so I started working for a delivery service partner for Amazon and moved my way up. After Covid, the company got out of the logistics business. I was head hunted by the company I'm currently with and took my dispatch team and 20 drivers to them. I've been with them for almost three years now.

I think my transition from baseball was a lot easier than a lot of guys because I knew what was to come. Also, I just wasn't the same player I had been, and the fun was gone. If I had been healthy and got cut with nobody wanting me, I think it would've been a more difficult transition. Realizing it just wasn't working anymore helped.

I do miss the camaraderie with all the guys and knowing you are all doing the same grind. I miss getting up, going to the ballpark for batting practice, and the calm before the storm. That was the funnest part. I remember once standing in the outfield of the Oakland Coliseum with the music blaring and shagging balls for Cecil Fielder, Mickey Tettleton, Rob Deer, and all those guys, and just thinking, "Wow. I'm getting paid to do this."

I've been doing baseball clinics with the Major League Baseball Players Alumni Association for a long time, and I'll get a little bit of retirement from baseball once I turn 62. I have 177 days in the big leagues, so it's obviously not a lot of money, but it'll help.

Bob Tewksbury

Bob Tewksbury played 18 seasons of affiliated baseball, including 13 seasons in the major leagues. His last year playing in affiliated baseball was 1998. Following his playing career, he entered mental skills coaching for

athletes and has worked at both professional and amateur levels. At the time of the interview for this book, he was working and living in Maine.

I had set goals for my career to win 100 games and to play 10 years to be fully vested in the pension. I achieved both of those things. Then, it was, "What do I really want to do?" What I really wanted to do was to be home with my family.

My last year, 1998, I still pitched a good number of innings, but I was hurt a lot. The Twins offered me a contract for '99, but I declined it. I retired voluntarily, but it wasn't easy. I probably could have pitched another couple years, but I was tired of the rehab. I had major shoulder surgery 10 years before and got 10 years out of it. It just got harder and harder to stay healthy. Then, being gone from my family at the same time was just something I didn't want to do.

The first year was great, but then it was like, "Now what do I do?" I didn't want to be on the field again as a pitching coach, so I turned down a couple of pitching coach opportunities.

I proposed to the Red Sox to be a pitching consultant. I started with them in 1999. I was a roving guy that was working with Double-A and Triple-A prospects. I would go around and develop relationships with the pitchers. I think one of the hardest times for pitchers, or any big league players, is when you have less than three years of service, you have options, and can be sent down. That was my focus—talking to those players about the challenges of staying in the big leagues. The job was limited and probably 10 days a month. I made my own schedule, and it was very convenient. The Red Sox were great with that. Eventually it grew into mental skills stuff.

I also worked as an analyst with NESN for a few years and even got to be in the studio for the 2004 World Series with Jerry Remy. That was really fun. That was my last year before becoming a full-time employee with the Red Sox as a mental skills coach.

I started in spring training, setting up programs and workshops for pitchers and position players on mental skills, and also having individual meetings with players. Just like you'd have early sessions to work on hitting, I would have early sessions for mental skills. I'd then have a lot of meetings at the hotel after workouts and meet with players that were interested.

Once spring training was over, I'd go to the affiliates like a roving guy. I'd go to Portland for a few days, and then to Pawtucket for a few days. From 2005 to 2013, it was mostly minor league stuff. Then, in '13, I started doing more at the big league level. The program started to expand, and they started to hire other mental skills coaches to do the stuff in the minors.

I left to go to the Major League Players Association for 2014. Before Michael Weiner passed away, he had talked about providing a resource that was not directly affiliated with a team. I basically became an available resource for any players in the union. It was a little overwhelming. Conceptually, it sounds great. However, there's just too many players and too many teams to get to know anybody. No one knew who I was, and no one was talking to me. It was really tough.

I definitely preferred working for a team, especially the minor league guys, because they're more open to it. I'd go to a minor league team and probably talk to half the team. When I went to a big league team, I might talk to three players.

I went back to Boston for 2015 and 2016. When Dave Dombrowski came in, he wanted someone to be more full-time with the big league team. I didn't want to travel with the big league team, so I ended up getting fired.

That's when the Giants called me. The Giants had actually contacted me a couple years before and wanted permission to talk to me about joining them. When Theo Epstein heard they wanted permission, he just said, "I'll give you a raise if you don't talk to them." I said, "Okay, I'll take the raise." I eventually did join the Giants for '17 and '18. When my contract was up, they decided to make a change.

Ken Ravizza, who was Joe Maddon's mental skills guy with the Cubs, had a heart attack and unfortunately passed. Jon Lester, who I had worked with a lot in Boston, was now with the Cubs, and Theo was also now in Chicago. Theo called me and I went to the Cubs for '19 and '20. When Covid came, no one knew what was going to happen, and I was kind of done at that point.

By that time, I was ready to be home, start my own business, and stop traveling anyway. Covid just expedited that a little bit.

I now have my own private practice. It's a mental skills coaching business, and I work with high school, college, and professional athletes on improving their mental game. I do it from home. I have baseball players as clients, but I also have clients from other sports. I work with the University of Maine's women's basketball team. I've also had golfers in the past. However, it's mostly baseball. That's my sweet spot, so to speak.

I just got off the phone with a high draft pick. He's trying to deal with the expectations of being a high draft pick and has lost some confidence. That's part of what I talk about—how to regain that confidence and get back to focusing.

When I work with players, especially teams, I'll ask, "How many people here are playing to their potential?" Nobody raises their hand. Then I'll say, "Okay, there are three areas of performance—physical, fundamental, and mental. Which area is the reason you're not playing up to your potential?" The responses are always mental. We talk about self-talk, imagery, focus and concentration. It's those types of things. It's setting realistic goals, focusing on things you can control, simplifying your approach, and that type of stuff.

I was never on a team that had any mental skills coaching, per se, on staff. I always read Norman Vincent Peale, and was always drawn to the self-help psychology section in bookstores. I certainly knew about Harvey Dorfman, Ken Ravizza, and Charlie Maher, who were kind of the pioneers of this around the eighties. I always had an inkling to it. However, I had no idea what I was going to do after my playing career, other than finish my degree.

When I retired and started working with the Red Sox as a pitching consultant, there was a guy that came to spring training who had his degree from Boston University in sports psychology. This guy wasn't a former baseball player but was working with players. That kind of piqued my interest. I thought if I could combine my professional baseball career with some academics, maybe I could carve out a nice little niche for myself. That's kind of what happened.

I went to New England College, a small school in New Hampshire, to finish up my undergrad stuff. I had a backpack with my kids' Beanie Babies on it. I'd go into class with all these college kids, and I was 38 years old. It was fun to go back to school as an adult. I really enjoyed it. The credits transferred to St. Leo University, so I was able to use those credits to graduate from St. Leo with a bachelor's degree in physical education. Then, I got a master's in sports psychology from Boston University.

An early follower of mental skills development as a player, Bob Tewksbury has worked in mental skills coaching for athletes since his playing days (courtesy Bob Tewksbury).

Everything worked out, but it was difficult. Career transitions can be hard. I actually went to therapy myself just to deal with it. I think part of my interest in entering mental skills coaching was to try to help myself with the transition. I tried to work through it with some therapy. You lose your identity. I'm still known as Bob the baseball player. Harvey Dorfman always used to talk about there being the performer and the person. You have to separate the two.

There was a time when I regretted not playing because physically, it wasn't like I had a career ending injury. I was just really unhappy, and it was probably from being away from my family. If I had reached out and found a way to deal with the feelings I was having at the time about playing and being away, I might have been able to sneak out another year or two. Instead, I went with my feelings and said, "I'm going home."

That's stuff I help athletes out with now. I help with long distance relationships and being away from family. It's a hard life. You must have strong spousal support, which I certainly did. But you have to be strong too. I just felt burnt out. My desire to be home was greater than my desire to play.

However, if I had continued to play, I probably wouldn't be in mental skills coaching now, and I wouldn't have three World Series rings.

Everyone goes through it. Even people that retire from being CEOs, or are presidents, go through difficult transitions. When you've forged your whole identity in your vocation, and you don't have that anymore, it's hard. That's why a lot of people go back to work.

Regardless of what a lot of people think, most players aren't in a position to retire completely and do nothing for 30 years. I certainly wasn't. I had to find something to do that was going to give me some fulfillment, and this has really done that.

When you talk to these young kids, regardless of whether they make it in sports, maybe they'll learn something that they can use in life. It's basically life skills with baseball as the backdrop. That's rewarding.

I'm 64 and still having fun. I don't plan on stopping anytime soon.

2000s

The 2000s saw a boom in off-field statistical analysis. This not only changed the style of play but impacted how teams evaluate players and establish their rosters considerably.

The number of minor league affiliates continued to grow. Triple-A baseball began to be used more frequently to shuffle major league rosters. Baseball adopted tough policies against performance enhancing drug use. International talent continued to grow, especially from Latin American countries.

The following chapter includes stories from 20 players who ended their playing careers in the decade.

Joe Grahe

Joe Grahe played nine seasons of affiliated baseball, including seven seasons in the major leagues. His last year playing in affiliated baseball was 2000. Following his playing career, he worked in sales before pursuing a career in real estate. At the time of the interview for this book, he was working and living in Florida.

I've been doing real estate the last 15 years. I coach high school baseball on the side as an assistant for the same high school I went to, and there's a college summer league here I've coached in. However, it's been mostly real estate since 2009.

I was always kind of interested in real estate. I tried some other jobs I wasn't happy with and ended up doing this. My father was a house builder, and I inherited some of that from him. I was always interested in how things were put together, so it was just kind of a natural progression.

I went to camp with the Phillies in 2000. I was in very good shape and throwing as hard as I ever had in my career. I didn't make the team, which I kind of expected. I could sense things in the clubhouse. That was fine because I wasn't afraid of going down to the minors and coming back. They said, "Be ready." I know how baseball is. I just had to go down there and pitch.

We had a workout in Scranton, the Triple-A team for the Phillies, before the season. It was about 35 degrees. I threw a bullpen, and I felt a little twinge in my elbow when I was throwing. I had it happen before and told myself I was just going to have to deal with it.

I started a few games and did pretty well dealing with it. Then, before a game one night, it suddenly just went out. It felt like somebody had jabbed a knife in my elbow.

I got an MRI and found I had a partial tear to the UCL. They sent me to Clearwater for rehab. I thought it would be one or two months, and I'd still be ready for the second half of the season. It was a very slow progression. It got a little better but never to the level where I could pitch consistently.

I ended up spending the rest of the summer rehabbing. The minor league season was ending, and they let me know it wasn't going to work out.

I expected it and it was fine. But it was frustrating because going into 2000 I had been throwing as well as I had my whole career, and I felt I had the rug yanked out from underneath me. However, that's the reality of it. My story's not unique as far as that goes. Everybody must face it at one point or another.

I was able to get five years of service time, which is nothing to sneeze at. I do take solace in that. Not to belittle the cup of coffee guys, but I'm proud I wasn't a cup of coffee guy. I did have some success.

I think the closing part is what cost me my arm but that's just the way it is. That's why you don't see a whole lot of longevity in closers. A lot of people don't understand it's not necessarily the pitch counts that get you. It's the lack of rest between outings and as a closer, you're usually going out there with a fatigued arm to begin with. I have a lot of respect for the guys that can go out two, three or four days in a row. I tried three days in a row once and my arm felt like a noodle.

My son had just been born before the Phillies released me, so at that point it was time to move on to the next stage of my life.

I had thought about getting into professional coaching at that time, but I saw the sacrifices of the coaches from when I played, especially those in the minor leagues. Looking at the sacrifices they made by being away from family was something I didn't want to put my wife and kids through. I have full respect for the coaches that do, but I wasn't willing to make that sacrifice.

I didn't have a job for about a year. Luckily, I had a little bit of money saved, so I didn't have to worry about it at the time, but it was tough. I was 33. From the time I was 10 to 33 my identity was as a ballplayer. All of a sudden that gets taken away and you're kind of rudderless there for a while.

I think a lot of players, me included, don't want to face the reality of what's next because your mental focus is on it being so tough to accomplish what you need to do as a high-level baseball player on a day-to-day basis. You get completely focused on that, get tunnel vision, and you don't think about what you're going to have to do the second half of your life. It was my fault ultimately but I'm sure I'm not the only one who had that mentality.

I was fortunate to be inducted into the University of Miami Sports Hall of Fame in February of 2001. While I was there, the coach at the time, Jim Morris, told me about a program where if you worked in the athletic department, they would pay for your tuition to finish school. I was a year short.

I didn't think much about it when he mentioned it but on the way home my wife and I were talking. We thought it might be a good idea to go back, finish up school, and get my degree. So that's what I did in 2001 and 2002.

It was an hour and forty-five-minute drive from my house to the school. I had to work 12 to 15 hours a week in the athletic department, so on some Saturdays, if I could get hours, I'd work at the football games. I look back and wonder how in the world I was able to do it. The first semester I had 8 a.m. classes, so I was up at five in the morning to get there on time.

However, I realized how easy college is when you actually go to class and apply yourself. I wish I had done that earlier. I would have been able to graduate a lot sooner. But being a college baseball player, you have a lot more distractions, and you're not as disciplined with your time as you are when you're older in life.

I was able to get my degree after a year, which was cool. I still thank Jim Morris for helping me do that because I never would have known there was a program like that otherwise.

However, I was still trying to figure out what I wanted to do.

I sold cars for a year to get some one-on-one sales and interaction experience. That's a good way to do it, through trial by fire, because people are always on the defensive when they come into car dealers. You have to diffuse that.

The company gave me a lot of training on how to deal with people, slow things down, and whatnot. I'll always say it provided good experience, though it wasn't a good experience. The hours were just too much.

I had a friend that was able to get me on with a company selling copiers and document systems. I did that four years, from 2003 to 2007, and it was a pretty good job. I really enjoyed it. However, they brought in a new CEO and started hacking on the compensation program for sales reps. Then, I went to a local tech sales job, and it didn't work out. I just didn't know what we were selling. It was way above my pay grade.

That's when I finally said, "You know what? I really do like real estate." I was kind of scared to get into real estate because you don't have the health benefits and whatnot that you would have with a regular company. You're basically an independent contractor. That was always my hesitation to do it, but I figured it's something I'd enjoy rather than the other stuff. That's when I jumped in and started doing it.

Baseball's helped. When people ask me about the pressure of certain high-end properties and if I'm qualified to handle things, I can say, "I performed on the biggest stage in my profession 20 something years ago. I can handle this too." I'm not afraid to perform on big stages. I tell people, "I've been booed off the field by 40,000 people. Nothing that's going to happen here is going to bother me."

At the end of the day, I still have the desire to coach. I ultimately would like to coach college because I think I still have a lot to offer as far as taking pitchers to the next level with mechanics, pitching mentality, and those kinds of things. There are a few schools around here. Ideally, I would like to land a college pitching coach job that's local where I could stay in my house and commute.

I love real estate and I'm good at it. However, being able to instruct baseball is still what lights me up and fuels me. I still think I'm young enough to make a difference and if somebody from a college around here offered me a job, I would dump real estate in a heartbeat and move on to that.

I do miss playing the game, but it is mainly the other stuff like the access to things you normally wouldn't have, and especially the camaraderie with the guys. It's been 25 years, and I can honestly say I haven't completely turned the page from the experience. I live five minutes from the Marlins and Cardinals complex. When March rolls around and spring training begins, I still get the blues a little bit, realizing that once upon a time I was out there.

Kip Gross

Kip Gross played 11 seasons of affiliated baseball, including six seasons in the major leagues. His last year playing in affiliated baseball was 2001. Overlapping with his playing career, he owned multiple Curves fitness

clubs for many years. However, he has primarily taught baseball lessons since his playing days. At the time of the interview for this book, he was still giving occasional lessons and living in Arizona.

When I went to Japan, I was sitting in Alan Nero's office. He was my agent, and I'd just signed a decent contract. My wife Jami and I were sitting there, and I said, "Well, we've got to figure out what to do with this money now." Alan said, "I've got some investors I can recommend to you." One of the first he named was Dave Bergman.

Dave was the first baseman for the Tigers when they won the World Series in 1984. The reason he became a financial advisor was because he was one of those guys that got ripped off. He was a very conservative investor and that's why I went with him. Dave asked, "What do you want out of this money, Kip?" I said, "Dave, I don't want to lose it. I don't want to go backwards." So, my money went to Dave Bergman, and he did really well with everything. He was one of the best guys I ever met in my entire life. I would have trusted that man with anything.

In 1999, when I came back to the states, I signed with the Red Sox. I got hit by a line drive that busted my pinky finger. I knew then and there it was going to come to an end soon. My last years of playing I relied on my circle change up with my last two fingers and my pinky. I couldn't throw it very well because my pinky had broken. I still had good stuff. I just couldn't throw what I wanted to throw in all the situations I previously was doing. At that point in time, I knew it was the beginning of the end, although I pitched two years longer.

I had a two-year deal with Boston but declined the second year to sign a minor league deal with Houston instead for 2000.

In 2001 I went to camp with the Dodgers. I knew the manager, Jim Tracy, from when I was with the Reds. I knew him really, really well. I was the last cut in spring training that year. He said, "Kip, go home and take three days off before you have to report to Las Vegas." I was shocked I went that long. I had no chance. That's when steroids were really big. I was watching guys who were throwing 83–86 the prior year who were now throwing 95–96. I couldn't compete against that anymore.

I went to Las Vegas and ended up getting released from there. Afterwards, Tracy told me the main reason was because in the pitcher's meetings I'd take my *USA Today* crossword puzzles with me. The pitching coach thought I was doing the crossword puzzle, but really whatever the pitching coach was telling us about the hitters, I'd write down on the newspaper. When I'd do the crossword puzzles I'd refer back to my notes and see what the hitters were doing. Anyways, I got released from there and went back to California for three or four days.

The Rockies called and said, "We need a starting pitcher in Colorado Springs. Can you be here tomorrow?" I said, "I guess so." I got in my Land Cruiser and drove all the way to Colorado Springs. I pitched the next day.

I had a really good time there. I actually threw a shutout in Colorado Springs that year. It was one of the highlights of my career. In Colorado Springs that just doesn't happen. They actually had champagne in the clubhouse after the game because of it.

It was getting late in the season in August, and they called me into the office. Chris Cron, who was the manager says, "Well, the organization wants to bring up the guys from Double-A and we're going to have to release you." I stood up, thanked him and the pitching coach Jim Wright for everything they did for me, and shook their hands. I let them know I had a blast there. I had an outstanding time, was able to help coach a couple guys, and everything was good. It was a really rewarding experience playing in Colorado Springs.

I still talk to Crony every once in a while. He's told me, "In all the years I've managed and coached, I've never had another player thank me for releasing him."

I had a few teams call me for the next year. I flat out asked, "Have you been watching me? I'm not good." I just couldn't get guys out anymore. I threw that shutout in Colorado Springs, but that was the highlight. If you look at my numbers, they are terrible. The teams just thought I had a good presence in the clubhouse with the younger players. I didn't sign. I just wanted to hang out with my kids.

Around that time, I really wasn't thinking about a post-playing career. I was mainly focused on my family. I had a daughter, and my son was born in 2000, not long before I retired in 2001. My focus wasn't on starting a new career. It was on wanting to be with my kids, doing things with them, and teaching them the game of life.

I never had a problem with retiring because of two things—I had my kids that were young, and I knew I wasn't good anymore. So many people ask, "Do you miss it?" I miss hanging out with the guys in the clubhouse and going to have a drink afterwards. Do I miss being on the field? Hell no. I don't miss it one bit, because I sucked. You just get to the point where you're not good anymore.

A lot of guys can't come to grips with that. There are a lot of ballplayers who go through different illnesses and depression because they can't handle not playing the game anymore. I had zero problems with it. I turned over, and the next thing I knew, my main job was my kids.

I don't remember the exact year, but I was still playing and living in Moreno Valley, California. I had a pretty good friend base of people in the neighborhood. We'd all go out to dinner and one day I was sitting across from a neighbor lady and asked, "How's everything going? How was your day?" She goes, "It was kind of crazy. I went down to Orange County today with a friend of mine who opened a Curves for Women." I said, "I don't know what you're talking about." She said, "It's a fitness place just for women." She started telling me about it, and I got really interested. I thought the concept was fantastic. It was for women only, and like their own little country club with a 30-minute workout.

I went down to Texas where the place was based. I sat down for a couple days, listened to the whole spiel about it, and walked out with a franchise. Within the next three years, I owned three Curves for Women. I was hands-on during the winters when I'd come back from playing. I'd teach a workout with a diet plan. They did really well for quite a few years. I probably should have sold them earlier but ended up owning them for 10 plus years.

However, since I retired as a player, I've mainly just done baseball lessons. I've also coached in high school and a year of independent ball in Victoria, British Columbia. Since I moved to Arizona, I've backed off a whole bunch but when I was still in California, I was giving anywhere from 20 to 40 lessons a week.

Giving lessons wasn't really anything I thought about doing. The whole thing started when a buddy of mine called me one day and asked, "My son would like to get some help. Can you help him out?" I said, "Yeah, bring him over. I'll work with him a little bit." I worked with him, and then did it another time. The next thing I knew, I had another buddy call me and say, "My son wants to learn how to hit. Can you help him hit?" I said, "Bring him on over."

Word of mouth started passing along and I had a lot of guys calling me. I said, "I'm going to start charging for this." I never advertised or anything like that. It was crazy. I started to have to turn kids away after a certain amount of time because I couldn't do it all.

Since I retired from playing baseball, I've been trying to pass along the knowledge of fundamental baseball, which is getting worse and worse even at the high levels today. I think travel ball has a lot to do with it with these so-called coaches. They go out and play game, after game, after game. They never practice so these kids are never taught the game properly. It's become a huge thing in my life to get these kids to understand there's so much more to the game of baseball than just picking up a bat and hitting a baseball thrown by a pitcher.

I've always told my guys that they need to learn the game. Occasionally, I'll have a player ask, "Kip, what do you mean by learn the game?" I'll say, "What you learn about playing the game is how you learn to win a game." I'll say, "You guys have your Xboxes and PlayStations. When you put a game in, do you go straight to level 10?" They say, "No, we can't do that. We have to start lower so we can get to level two and three." I say, "That's exactly what I'm talking about. You guys haven't learned the first few levels and you're trying to play at level 10 already. You can't do that."

I'd much rather have the younger kids. When they get to high school, it gets tough because they have a lot of ingrained bad habits or they haven't been taught properly.

I like teaching one-on-one. I did it a few times with a whole team, but I didn't like it. I like getting personal with a kid, learn his personality, joke around with him, and be able to whack him on the back or arm—whatever it takes.

Baseball is tough to learn. You can't look it up on YouTube and do what they're telling you to do. You don't see yourself in what you're doing. You think you're doing what they're saying to do, but you're really not. You need somebody with eyes that can see what you're doing properly and what you're not doing properly. Until that happens, you're never going to feel what you're supposed to do during practice or a game. You just can't do it. I'm big on feel.

So many of these parents and kids are getting ripped off by these so-called instructors. They don't know it and it's hard to watch. When I'm with a kid, I want to give 100 percent and do right by them. Every night I can go to bed and sleep well. I've always been good to these kids.

I can't tell you how many times where after the lesson ends the parent comes over to pay me and I say, "You're not paying me today." They say, "What?" I tell them, "You're not paying me today because I don't think I got enough out of your son today. That's on my end, not his." People respect you when you do stuff like that because you're ultimately not doing it for the money. Yeah, I want to get paid. However, it's more rewarding when a kid says, "Hey, Kip. I went 2-for-3 in my game this week."

What's even more rewarding is when you get emails or a text from a parent of a player you coached 10–15 years ago that says, "We just want to thank you for everything you did to help him become a better man in life. You helped him develop to where he's at today." That's the cool part about coaching. You just don't realize the impression you're having on kids while you're doing it.

Jason Hardtke

Jason Hardtke played 12 seasons of affiliated baseball, including three seasons in the major leagues. His last year playing in affiliated baseball was 2001. Overlapping with his playing career, he ran his own baseball

academy for many years. He then coached minor league baseball for multiple seasons before entering sales and the mortgage industry. At the time of the interview for this book, he was working and living in California.

I had just turned 30. I'd been playing since I signed out of high school, so I had 12 years of pro ball under my belt. I wasn't that old, but I didn't like the opportunities I was getting going into the next spring training. I did have some offers to go and play, but I turned them down.

I was just kind of done with the life, to be honest. I was tired of packing up and leaving all the time. I was ready to move on.

There were a number of other things that contributed to me deciding not to play as well. I had met my future wife, and we were getting serious. A couple years prior, I had opened a baseball academy and was running the business with my family. I was just ready to move on.

The baseball academy business was doing well, and I was having a good time doing it. However, in the back of my head, I was always interested in eventually getting back into pro ball as a coach. When the business slowed down a little bit around the time of the housing crisis, I thought it seemed like a good time.

I had a great opportunity with the Diamondbacks. The first two years I was hitting coach in the Pioneer League. I was with the Missoula Osprey, which was awesome. Montana's beautiful.

I had my house in San Jose, but we moved to Arizona. The kids were young at the time and in preschool. We lived in Tucson, and with extended spring training and short season rookie ball, we would make the trek up to Missoula for the season, which would start towards the end of June. It worked out well for the kids since it was summer and they were out of school.

From there, I managed our High-A affiliate, the Visalia Rawhide, for two years. During that time with Visalia, we moved back to San Jose. We had renters, but once we were able to get them out, we moved back into our house.

It was a whirlwind for two years.

When I started coaching, it was fine with younger kids. However, when they got older, I was missing a lot. You're not taking time off during the baseball season. You're locked in. Although I was home half the year, during the baseball season, I was just missing a lot. I didn't foresee that getting any better. It was tough missing so many of my kids' activities.

I went into software sales for about a year and wasn't really digging it.

I talked with my buddy Mike Frank, who had played in the big leagues with Cincinnati. We roomed together during the season when we were with Cincinnati's Triple-A team, Indianapolis. Then, we lived together and worked out during the offseason. He was a good buddy of mine and after he retired from playing, he got into mortgage loans on the builder side of things. He said I should give it a whirl.

Mike hooked me up with the company he was with called iMortgage, which has since been bought by loanDepot. I've been a loan officer for 12 years now.

I'm currently with DHI Mortgage. D.R. Horton owns DHI Mortgage, and they are the biggest home builder in the United States. I primarily do new home stuff and am now on my way to a community in Santa Rosa where they're building 125 homes. We'll sit out there and pre-qualify people as the preferred lender, and there are incentives for using us. In a time right now when there isn't a lot of lending going on for homes, the builder business has actually been pretty good.

As an athlete, you have that competitive fire. I think organizations in any industry look at that as positive, and being a loan officer is no different. In sales you're competing. You're setting goals and trying to do your best every day. Obviously, that's going to be a benefit with anything you do, but as a baseball player, and now as a loan officer, it's definitely benefited me.

I loved being a baseball player. I wouldn't trade it for the world by any means. It's helped me with so many things I did then, and do now, but it wasn't everything. Yeah, you have a certain identity as a baseball player, but you move on. I was never under the impression it was something I was going to do my whole life. There was no real remorse. There wasn't a time I was going through withdrawals. It was like, "What's next?" I was moving forward and not really looking back.

I love talking baseball, but I've never been a person that brings it up and says, "Guess what I did?" Like I said, it's always been about moving forward and not looking back. But when I see buddies that I played with, or even current players for that matter, we always have that camaraderie. They want to hear your stories, or tell their stories, and that's the cool fraternity of baseball that you get your whole life. That never goes away, which is kind of cool.

I wouldn't mind getting back into coaching again, or possibly scouting, someday. I'm not young anymore, but I still have the desire, and I still love the game.

Jeff Frye

Jeff Frye played 13 seasons of affiliated baseball, including eight seasons in the major leagues. His last year playing in affiliated baseball was 2002. Following his playing career, he worked as a player agent. In recent

years, he has helped lead baseball camps and been a motivational keynote speaker. At the time of the interview for this book, he was working and living in Maryland.

I don't know the day on the calendar, but I know the game I realized it. I was in Louisville. It was August, near the end of the season. The lineup came out and I was playing second, and hitting second.

Well, earlier in the year when there were injuries to the outfield, I told the manager I could play the outfield if he needed me to. So, he stuck me in left field sometimes, and I did pretty well.

We had a player, Ruben Mateo, who was now with the Reds, and he was on the disabled list. We got word he was coming and was going to be activated. The lineup comes down and a new lineup goes up. Suddenly, I go from hitting second and playing second to hitting seventh and playing left field. I'm one of the leading hitters on the team and I'm like, "This is kind of weird." I'm standing there in the outfield and thinking, "How am I going to get back to the big leagues hitting seventh and playing left field for Louisville?"

After the game I was kind of bummed out and I called my best friend, Mike Hamilton, who was the video coordinator for the Rockies. I had a heart to heart with Mike. I said, "My back's killing me, dude. I've been hurt all season and get my back adjusted sometimes two or three times a game just to be able to get through the entire game. I think I'm done." He goes, "Quit. You have nothing to prove. You've had a great career."

I went home, talked to my wife, and showed up at the field the next day. It was a Sunday day game, and I was the oldest guy on the team, so a lot of the time the manager, Dave Miley, would give me Sundays off. He did and I wasn't in the lineup. I knocked on his door and said, "Hey, can I talk to you for a second?" He goes, "Sure." I said, "Skip, thank you for everything but I'm going to the house." He goes, "No, you're not. You've just got the day off. You're good." I said, "No, honestly, I'm going to the house today."

I went in, started packing up my locker, and all my teammates came over, trying to talk me out of it. I said, "I love you guys, but I've got to do what I've got to do." That was it.

I was driving back to Texas and Mike Berger, who was my teammate coming up with the Rangers, and a longtime friend, called me. He was a scout working with the Astros, and Jimmy Williams, my former manager with the Red Sox, was managing the Astros. Mike says, "Hey, we're going to need a utility guy if we make the playoffs. Do you have any interest in going to Triple-A for us and playing some shortstop?" I knew I couldn't, but I wanted to try. I could barely play shortstop when I was healthy because I just didn't have the arm strength. Well, I went to New Orleans for two and a half weeks and didn't play well at all. They ended up making a trade instead of calling me up and that was it. I never tried to play again after that.

I'd been playing baseball for 15 years. I was gone for seven and a half months a year, and even longer when I went to winter ball. I had little boys and wanted to stay home.

Thad Levine of the Rockies called me almost as soon as I retired and asked if I would consider being a scout. I said, "I don't know. How many days a week am I going to have to be at the ball field?" He said, "Probably six days a week." I said, "No chance. I don't want to be away that much."

I had another longtime friend call and tell me that if I ever wanted to get back on the field in uniform to let him know and he would get me a coaching job. I didn't want to do that either because I didn't want to jump on buses in the minor leagues.

Then, I had a friend approach me about becoming a sports agent and starting our own sports agency. He had been an agent with Scott Boras for a number of years. I figured he knew what he was doing so we started our own agency. That was probably around six months after I retired. Until then, I had no idea I was going to jump into something like that.

As luck would have it, I had barely been an agent for a month when I got a phone call from Darren Oliver. He was my teammate with the Rangers, and I had also played against him. He called me Fryedaddy and goes, "Hey, Fryedaddy. I need you to help get me a job." He was represented by Scott Boras but fired him and asked to see what I could do.

I didn't know what to do but called my friend Mike Hamilton with the Rockies for Dan O'Dowd's number. I called O'Dowd and said, "Hey, Dan, I'm calling to see if you have any interest in Darren Oliver." He goes, "What? I thought he was represented by Scott Boras." I said, "He was, but he just fired him and hired me." He goes, "That's interesting. Scott called about six weeks ago but at the time we had no interest in Oliver. Some things fell through, and I think we would have some interest now." So, within 24 hours I got him an invitation to big league camp with the Rockies, and he played for 10 more years in the major leagues after that. Other than Oliver, I think we had one client at the time, and Oliver wasn't even really a client yet.

I had a lot of contacts in the game, and so did my original partner. We started using our contacts, going to games, and trying to recruit guys. We started accumulating clients and grew by word of mouth.

Scouts knew I was an honest and trustworthy guy. They'd call me up and tell me about players here and there. We started gaining more and more players. I think at the peak we had nine or 10 big leaguers and 30 or 40 minor leaguers.

However, I learned over the years that it's a very cutthroat business. There's not a lot of integrity and loyalty, and that's just the opposite of what I believe in.

I had represented my last major league client since he was 16 years old and we went all the way through the minors together. He had a decent big league year, and that offseason I got fired in a minute and 14 second phone call.

This kid's dad stayed at my house the prior season with his youth hitting instructor. I took him all over and it was almost like we were family. Then, I get a minute long phone call from the kid saying he needs a different agent. I was like, "I just don't know if I can do this anymore. I don't want to lose sleep over other people not being loyal." I'm loyal to a fault, and I couldn't take it.

I've started to get into speaking.

I talked at a high school and a couple of other places, sharing the story of my call-up, and all the stuff that happened prior. People started telling me, "You have an incredible story. You should start telling it more." I'm like, "All right. I might do that."

Well, I then went to an event and saw a guy speak. I thought he was pretty good, but he didn't knock my socks off or anything. I asked my friend there, "How much does that guy get paid for doing that?" He said five grand. I said, "I could do that." He said he thought I should, and I decided to start down that path. I began growing my presence on social media and letting people know I wanted to do it, and in recent years, I've started to do some keynote speaking stuff.

I've also worked on hitting and fielding camps. I'm working on a deal with an organization to start doing baseball clinics all around the country that will talk about character development and leadership with kids.

I started to notice how many guys are out there just bamboozling people with their drills. Unfortunately, a lot of parents don't know any better. They see these guys with a lot of social media followers and figure they must know what they're talking about. They're not teaching the basic fundamentals and the proper techniques I developed as a kid. They think they have a cheat code to being a great hitter and try to teach every kid to hit like Aaron Judge. Obviously, they're not 6'7" and 280 pounds. We've never seen anybody with his size and athleticism. They can't do what he can do.

The Shegone Nation started as a joke. I just made a funny video where my son videoed me in the backyard and I imitated one of the baseball drills I saw. I said, "The lightbulb went on." It was just a joke. However, all these guys came after me, calling me names, and threatening me. I'm like, "What's going on here?" That got me fired up.

These guys also have cool names like the "hitting doctor" or "pitching doctor." I was like, "How do they get these names?" They didn't earn those names. I figured I had to come up with a name for myself and came up with the "Certified Hitting Guru" just as a joke. I have over 50,000 followers on Instagram under that tagline. It's funny.

I think probably the biggest challenge with the transition from playing was being home all the time. I welcomed that because I got to be around the house with my boys and do a lot of stuff with them. But I got bored a lot of the time at first.

The sports agency thing let me still be competitive. I always want to be on the side of the player and not the organization. I could never picture myself being a coach and knowing one of my guys is getting released but

Jeff Frye became a player agent after his playing career. In recent years, he has helped lead youth baseball camps and been a motivational keynote speaker (courtesy Jeff Frye).

not being able to tell him at the time. Being an agent allowed me to be on the player's side, work for the players, fight for them, and still be involved in the game. I also kind of made my own schedule. It was a good scenario for me.

I do miss my teammates, the time we got to spend together, and the bonds we developed. I miss practicing and the games. You've got to enjoy it while you're there because it can be gone overnight. It doesn't last forever.

Mike Trombley

Mike Trombley played 14 seasons of affiliated baseball, including 11 seasons in the major leagues. His last year playing in affiliated baseball was 2002. Following his playing career, he became a financial advisor and took over his father's investment and retirement planning firm. At the time of the interview for this book, he was working and living in Massachusetts.

I always knew I was going to enter business with my father as a financial advisor. Baseball just kind of derailed that for a while.

My father started the business in 1965, and I was born in 1967, so he had been a financial advisor my whole life. He loved baseball, but he also loved talking about financial planning. We would sit down and talk about it, so I was always very well in tune to that.

I was never a huge first round prospect with a bunch of scholarship offers. I never thought, "I'm going to play professional baseball and then figure it out later." Baseball almost happened by accident. When I signed with the Twins as a 14th round pick in 1989, my parents figured, "You might as well try it." I always knew I had something to fall back on, so I think that kind of relaxed me a little bit. I knew if baseball didn't happen, my life wouldn't be over.

I'm not downplaying baseball. Of course I wanted to be a major league baseball player. I'm a competitive guy and when you're in that world, you want to do well. I wanted to be in the big leagues and stay for as long as possible. However, knowing what was next after playing, and not having a lot of expectations placed on me as a baseball player, made things kind of gravy for me.

I was lucky to get a lot of breaks throughout my baseball career, but it spiraled down quickly.

In midseason of 2001, I was traded by the Orioles to the Dodgers. Honestly, I was a fish out of water in L.A. I didn't pitch well and lost my confidence. Then, 9/11 happened.

My wife was pregnant with our third child. She was due 9/11 but was late. When 9/11 happened, I figured I wouldn't be able to get home to see the baby born. Well, the season was suspended for a week, and I got the chance to fly home on the 16th.

It was one of the first flights out of LAX after 9/11. Many of the people had loved ones that were missing, and the whole plane was crying. I remember sitting there thinking, "I'm going to see my baby born and all these people just lost loved ones and family members." The light bulb went off a little bit for me.

My youngest daughter was born on September 17, and then I got back on a plane on the 18th to fly back to L.A. I remember thinking, "What am I doing here? I don't see my kids anymore. 9/11 just happened. My baby was just born and my wife's home alone with the kids. I'm going to be selfish again to go play baseball?" I wasn't even having fun because I wasn't pitching very well.

I didn't have a good end to the season, and the Dodgers released me out of spring training in 2002.

I went back to the Twins, and they probably figured, "When Trombley comes back here, it'll be the same as before." Well, I wasn't there mentally, and I didn't pitch well. That was really devastating for me. I was going through all these thoughts about 9/11, my kids, and all this stuff. Then, I went back to Minnesota and felt like I really let them down.

The Twins wanted to send me down. I said, "No, just release me. I need a break mentally." My thought was that I would take the rest of 2002 off and come back in 2003. However, at the beginning of 2003, I just made the decision I was done.

I was almost relieved. I felt like, "Here's another chapter." I got to see my kids more. I could get back to a bit more of a normal life, coach my kids, and start working. Again, I knew what was coming. I had been around financial planning my whole life. I wasn't settling. I was excited about doing something else.

The plan was for my wife and I to take over the business when the time was right. My wife and I had gone to Duke together. She ran track and I played baseball. After Duke, she got her master's at NYU and was working for Pricewaterhouse as a CPA in the financial world, but she quit her job to be a baseball wife when I was still in Triple-A. I had gone to Duke to become a financial advisor but left early when I signed with the Twins. I remember my mom made me promise her I'd finish right away. In fact, after a good first year with the Twins in the minor leagues, they wanted me to go to winter ball. I told them no because I had promised my mom. I finished the next fall in 1990. So, I already had my degree.

When I got done playing, the first couple of years were about just spending time with my family, getting off the rollercoaster, and relaxing a little bit. I was getting licensed, and we were living in Fort Myers, Florida.

My father and I talked about opening an office in Florida. However, my mom got sick with cancer in 2007. My dad said, "I need you guys up here because I'm going to retire." Rather than my father working longer and us having two offices, the plan changed to going up to Massachusetts where the business was based.

I worked with my father about two years before he retired and my wife and I took over. My father did that on purpose because clients were used to seeing him and talking to him. They needed to become familiar with me too. Of course, many knew me because I grew up around them. However, they knew me as the kid that went to Duke and became a baseball player. They didn't know me as their financial advisor. At first, I thought that might be a detriment like, "Do they really want to invest with a baseball player?" It was a much easier process than I thought it would be, and after two years, it was all ours.

Both my wife and I are advisors, run the business, and it's been terrific. It's been a great balance because some people connect with me more and others connect with her more. We've been married 33 years and maybe she'd tell a different story, but we see each other every day, work together, and get along well. She hasn't kicked me out yet.

We're whole financial planners. It's not just, "Mike, I have $50,000, what stock should I buy?" We don't really do that. We work on financial plans that include social security, pensions, 401k's, family challenges, or whatever it may be. It's full financial planning.

I must mention I've always been very careful not to push any financial planning on any of my former teammates. I've spoken with and helped some, but I've never pushed it to get paid. I've given a lot of free advice, and my wife's also given a lot of free advice to some of the wives. I hear so many stories about people thinking the money's going to last forever. In the baseball world, everybody has a friend or guy who wants you to invest in this or that. I never wanted to be that guy but sometimes I wish I had offered more advice.

My father always said, "I started the business from nothing, and you guys have taken it to the next level." Our plan is to have our son join us in a couple years and transition the same way. I joke that my son is a better version of me. I think he'll do a terrific job. He's much more tech savvy and he'll take it to the next level. We're always evolving. We're in our 60th year now and I'd like to see someone to take it to a hundred years.

I'm proud of both my careers. My baseball career feels like a lifetime ago and I don't want to downplay it. I miss the camaraderie with the guys and the competition. However, I really enjoy being a financial advisor, especially growing up around a lot of my father's clients that are now my clients. We have their kids as clients, and now we're often even into their grandkids. It's been a wonderful transition for us.

Marty Cordova

Marty Cordova played 15 seasons of affiliated baseball, including nine seasons in the major leagues. His last year playing in affiliated baseball was 2003. Following his playing career, he entered real estate before co-founding a media company. At the time of the interview for this book, he was working to open a wellness center and living in Nevada.

I had signed with the Orioles through 2004. I played part of 2003, got hurt, and had to have surgery. I was recovering from Tommy John and thought I could come back at least as a DH, but the Orioles were not doing well at the time, and it was easier for them to keep me on the injured list and have insurance pay part of my salary. I'm not sure how much they insured players for, but they weren't going to let me back on the field.

In 2005, I went to spring training with Tampa. I was really working out hard and my lower back was just killing me. When I got there, I knew there was no way I was going to make it through spring training. Just standing there in the outfield and shagging, all that would just kill me. I was trying so hard to get in shape it got to where I was having trouble walking. My back was really that bad.

Lou Piniella was the manager. I told him, "My back is so bad. I'm pushing myself to do exercises, but I can barely stand up. It's crazy. There's no way I can do spring training." He said, "We'll work with you."

I loved to work out and to do really strenuous cardio. I loved being in great shape. It just got to the point where it was no fun to train that hard with it being so taxing on my body. Tampa was really bad that year and I was like, "Do I really want to be on a team where I'm struggling physically when we're also losing all the time?"

Once I decided I wasn't going to play anymore, I immediately had surgery. The first surgery didn't work, so a year later I had another one. That worked for probably the next 10 years. I was pretty good without having any back pain, but I started getting it again when I'd work out. You don't really know how bad back pain is until you have it. I've gone so far as to going to Cellular Performance Institute in Mexico to have stem cells injected into my back. I had another surgery in October and I'm trying to avoid another.

Everyone who's played a decent amount of time will have a lot of injuries from playing, from back, to neck, to knees. I've been pretty lucky except for my back. My lower back has been a nightmare.

With everything you have to do to be an athlete to be in shape, from lifting weights, to dieting, to two-a-day workouts, and all those things, I told myself I was just going to retire and take it easy. I was like, "I have a place in Laguna. I'm just going to go to the beach and it's going to be awesome." I was 35 at the time and realized everybody I knew was working. It was boring. You can only go to the beach by yourself so much. It wasn't exciting to me at all. I realized I had to do something else.

That's when I started getting a little more involved. Even when I was playing, I was a passive investor in real estate here in Vegas. A friend of mine had built my house, so we started building custom homes together. However, the market crashed in 2008, and I moved on from that.

In 2009 I started a media company with two other guys called Bent Pixels. The company manages YouTube channels. We had podcasters like Joe Rogan and Bill Burr, to eSports teams, to gamers, and quite a few others. We went out and sold their content to advertisers so they could advertise on videos. We also did rights management. For example, if other people were uploading Joe Rogan's podcast, we had a team of guys and software we developed that would find those videos and claim them. Then, we would either take them down or capture the revenue.

That kept me busy for a long time. I was doing that until about five years ago when I was kind of getting burned out. I didn't really want to be in that business anymore. It wasn't doing anything to make me want to come to work every day. One of my partners had big aspirations for the company and I didn't want to go in the same direction. I just wanted to move on. I was bought out except for still owning something like 7 percent in the business.

After that, I just spent the next few years focusing on my mental and physical health. I had been traveling, having fun, overindulging, and drinking. It got to be how I dealt with stress. Eventually, you're just somebody that's drinking too much and not enjoying life. That's when, five years ago, I decided to fully change my life. I stopped drinking completely and stopped doing anything that was bad for my body.

I wanted to figure out a way I could do something I was passionate about, and that was helping other people in need of help. I knew that was something I needed to do to find peace and happiness. I couldn't find that through material things, so I set out on a quest.

I started cold plunging, meditating, journaling, and many other healthy things mentally and spiritually. I was trying to figure out if I wanted to open up a rehab, or what it would look like.

About two years ago, I got an idea going with my friend Jackie, who I've known for about 20 years. She has a business where she does lymphatic flush. When you have surgeries, doctors will send you to do a lymphatic flush to recirculate your lymphatic system and remove waste and toxins from the body. In talking with her, I realized it was something that I wanted to do, but I envisioned something bigger with a wellness center.

I have a friend, Brent, who owns roughly a hundred McDonalds. I also know Maxx Crosby, who wanted to do something in this space, help people, and give back to the community. I got with Maxx, Brent, and Jackie, who had another couple people who wanted to invest on her side.

We started a business and right now we're in the middle of constructing this wellness center. It's going to be around 2,800 square feet here in Vegas.

That's what I'm working on now, and it's been taking a lot of my time to go through the plans. It's a lot more than people may think. It's worse than building your own custom home with all the permits and regulations.

We'll have a community room with four cold plunges and an infrared sauna that can hold six to eight people. Then, there's going to be two private rooms that have their own cold plunges and saunas for people who are super meditative or just want to do it privately. We'll have a float tank, a hyperbaric chamber, and a red light bed. We're also going to have two lymphatic flush rooms. Eventually, we're going to have IV services. We're even potentially partnering with a friend of mine that's a doctor doing exosome treatments, where they take your blood, send it off, break out the exosomes, and then put it back into your system.

We want to provide a high-end finished look where people can go with a communal aspect. You'll get to meet people that are into the same things you are. We're going to have weekend activities and maybe DJ type stuff where people can get together who just don't want to go to clubs anymore. They can meet people that are healthy and like-minded.

Baseball helped a lot by providing me with the proper work ethic to go into the business world. I was always the first one to the park and the last one to leave. Baseball was my job, and it took priority over everything, probably to a fault. It took priority over family, friends, and relationships. Looking back, I probably needed more balance. But going into the business world, I've just never been the type of person that quits. When I started the media company, there were just two other guys and me running the business. I was doing everything. I had to do whatever was needed for however many hours it took.

As far as being a professional athlete, fortunately for me, I didn't love being a baseball player. I loved being around the guys, and I loved playing the sport. However, I didn't like being identified as an athlete. Some guys have a hard time stepping away from the limelight, and they do things after to seek more attention. I didn't really care about the attention, so that part of the transition was easy for me. I never wanted to be famous.

The challenge for me was figuring out what I was going to do with my time. As a baseball player, you're used to doing something on a routine. Your day is so regimented. You come home from the field, maybe hang for a little bit, then go to bed. Then, you wake up, eat, and you're back to the field at one o'clock for the next 12 hours. You're busy, and you're traveling.

I thought I could just retire and that having fun the rest of my life was going to be easy, but it's not. You find at some point it's an empty feeling and you need something you're really passionate about in your life. You realize you're going to live a long time and that you have a lot of time ahead of you. You need to find what you're going to do and your new goals.

I wasn't really passionate about the media business. It was cool to start a company, grow it, and sell my interest. That was awesome, but I didn't really like going to work every day.

Now, my biggest focus is to do things that are positive for people, and providing this wellness center will do that. If it makes money, great. Who doesn't want to make money? I do owe that to my partners. However, I'm not doing this for money. I'm not doing it for anything other than just trying to help other people and provide services I'm passionate about.

Jalal Leach

Jalal Leach played 14 seasons of affiliated baseball, including one season in the major leagues. His last year playing in affiliated baseball was 2003. Following his playing career, he formed a baseball school with his brother and has worked as a scout. At the time of the interview for this book, he was running his own baseball business focused on hitting instruction and living in California.

In 2003 I started in Mexico with Saltillo. However, the manager in Tacoma with the Mariners organization, Dan Rohn, was my winter ball manager in Venezuela the year before. They had some injuries and needed a Triple-A outfielder. He called to see if I could get out of my contract. Somehow, I got out of the contract and went to Tacoma.

I injured my elbow and was playing hurt. I knew at my age I had to take care of the injury on my own. I had been in the game a long time and knew everything was written down, categorized, and monitored. I didn't do any treatment in the training room. I knew I'd likely be the first one they'd get rid of, so I was just taking care of it on my own to survive.

I was with Tacoma about half the season before eventually getting released. I went up to play independent ball with Winnipeg in the Northern League before finishing up in Fargo-Moorhead, also in the Northern League.

Because of my relationship with Dusty Baker, he got me a spring training contract with the Cubs in 2004. I got into a few big league spring training games before being sent to the minor league camp, but I could see the writing on the wall. They released me and I tried to get on with another team, but no one wanted a 34-year-old washed up guy.

I ended up sitting at home for about a month before I got on with the Monclova team in Mexico. I told them I'd done no baseball in about a month with two little children at home, and that I'd need five to seven days to get my legs under me. Well, as soon as I got off the plane and went to the ballpark, I was asked to play because the team had been struggling. I just rolled my eyes and said yes. After that first game I didn't recover before they tried to trade me. I told the general manager not to trade me but just release me. I knew I was getting to the end and went home.

Mike Easler, who was with Yucatan at the time, called and asked, "Do you want to come down here to Southern Mexico? I need a lefthanded hitting outfielder." I told him, "I think I'm at the end." He goes, "Come on. Give it one last shot." I went down and played for him but knew as that was evolving it was time to move on.

I had started to lose the passion for being out there, and physically I couldn't keep up anymore. I just had to play it out of my system.

I enjoyed the ride and have no regrets. Sure, I wanted to play in the big leagues longer and make more money. However, at the end of the day, my dream was to play in the big leagues, and I did that.

When I got to the end, I had to figure out what I wanted to do.

While I was finishing up in the Mexican League, my brother, who had played in the minor leagues with the Padres for a few years, was doing baseball lessons with a kid. He would email me, and I'd send him some drills to help the kid with hitting. They worked and the kid's dad spread the word. Well, when I hung them up, I basically jumped right into lessons with my brother.

We didn't know what we were doing at first. We didn't have a business plan or insurance, and we just came up with a small flat rate fee. We were doing Sunday hitting clinics out at a high school and at the peak we'd have about 40 kids out there. The majority of the kids were from that high school, so the high school coach was okay with it.

We did that through the fall and when the weather changed, we started looking for a place to go inside. I searched the area, found an indoor place, talked with the owner, and negotiated what it would cost to rent a cage. We kept growing and growing.

It got to the point where we needed to find our own place. I found a place over in Natomas on the backside of my parents' church. I'd been in enough batting cages I knew what it needed to look like. I knew how the tunnels, walkway, sitting area, cash register, and everything needed to go. I looked at the space and drew it all out of my head.

My brother was a cop at the time and was coming in after his cop job. We were doing lessons, and it became an avalanche.

We were teaching kids, and they were getting better and better. The parents eventually pressured us into creating travel teams and I think we had up to 10 travel teams at one point. Then, they wanted us to find college opportunities and we started helping them with that. There was a lot of excitement, and it was a whirlwind developing the kids. Although I don't like taking credit, I think at last count there were 14 of the kids that we coached who have played in the major leagues.

In 2009, the pro scouting director of the Yankees, Billy Eppler, called me and offered me a job as a pro scout.

As a journeyman player, having to bounce from organization to organization, I guess I was scouting when I played. People were telling me I had been evaluating players the whole time.

I remember a story with my old teammate and roommate Kevin Jordan. He was in the big leagues, and I was in Double-A with the Expos. I called him and told him about a guy on my team named Vladimir Guerrero. He asked, "Is he Russian?" I said, "I don't know what he is, but this guy can do everything on the ballfield but slide." He laughed. I told him, "Be on the lookout because he will be a force within the next year or so." When Guerrero came up to the big leagues, Kevin told some of his big league teammates, "My boy played with this guy and said he's going to be something." The rest is history, and he ended up having a Hall of Fame career.

I guess I was always scouting not knowing it. I used those instincts throughout my playing career and took them into scouting. I just had to learn the 20–80 scouting scale and the scouting lingo so I could write reports and evaluations, and the front office and other scouts could understand what I was saying.

I scouted 15 years with the Yankees, then the Giants, then the Marlins, and then the Giants again before I was let go last year. I did pro scouting and also worked in the Pacific Rim.

With pro scouting you're basically scouting the other team's organization. We scouted from Single-A all the way up. You wanted to know their organizations from top to bottom just in case you had any dealings with them—trades, free agency, release of players, and any other purposes.

Now, data and analytics have evolved to where they're not scouting the upper levels as much. They think they have a lot to cover that. However, I still believe there's something to be said about sitting in a ballpark and watching players. You have the weather elements, the energy of the crowd, and the way players interact with teammates. You might catch if a player is playing hurt or if he has a clutchness about him if you go watch him play. I think the teams that realize that will have an advantage over teams that don't because we're humans.

When I was scouting in the Pacific Rim, I was watching the KBO in Korea and the NPB in Japan. Basically, when those players are posting to come across, you want to have as much data and information on them as possible. If you feel they could be a fit for your organization, you want to be able to make a pitch at them. I was over there to see how their skills would translate to the major leagues and if we felt they would, and they had what we were looking for, we'd pursue them.

They play a different style of baseball in the KBO and NPB. You have to figure out how it's going to translate. For Korea at the time, their average

Following his playing career, Jalal Leach has worked as a scout and runs his own baseball instruction business (courtesy Jalal Leach).

fastball was about 88 miles per hour, while we were probably at 93–95. For the hitters, you had to figure out if the guy was going to be able to adjust to catch up with the velocity. Japan is getting closer and closer to the big league level. They've been winning the WBC as of late and you're seeing more guys come over.

Since I was not rehired by the Giants after 2024, I went back into the youth training space. I had always dabbled with lessons on the side and worked them around my scouting schedule.

My business is called Leachy Elite Training, and I do it mobile. I focus mainly on hitting, but I do know pretty much all the positions. I have kids from seven all the way to college level. I'm just a one-man operation right now. I keep all the stuff in my car and all I need is a cage and an L-screen. I've got everything else. Most of what I do is individual, but I do groups as well. I'm also in the process of trying to do stuff online because people want to work with me who aren't in the immediate area.

Once I get a player's mechanics dialed in, I focus on the approach. I talk a lot about approach and the mindset of a hitter because I know how it feels to stand in that batter's box. It can be lonely. You can feel the pressure, the tension, and all those variables. I talk about how hard hitting is and not to be hard on yourself when you get in there because it's not easy.

This week they're having all these Easter tournaments. I get out in the mornings to watch these guys play and I can see the differences between the cage swing approach and the swing they take in actual games. So far, with the kids I've been working with, the swings I've seen have been really good, if not better, than in the cage. That tells me it's not just the mechanics we've been working on but that they've also heard me when I talk about approach.

It's been awesome working with the kids. I didn't know a year ago that I'd be back in this space. I thought I would still be scouting. I can't look into the future but I'm having a blast training kids, watching them do their thing, and develop. I'm staying present and enjoying what I'm doing now.

Jeff Reboulet

Jeff Reboulet played 18 seasons of affiliated baseball, including 12 seasons in the major leagues. His last year playing in affiliated baseball was 2003. Overlapping with his playing career, he has worked as a financial advisor since his last season as a player. He also established his own baseball academy. At the time of the interview for this book, he was working and living in Ohio.

As a player I had the reputation of having a pretty good grasp of basic finances. A lot of guys would see me researching stocks and ask questions.

Those were always interesting conversations. I remember Kirby Puckett talking about being worried about a certain guy but saying, "Reb, I'm not worried about you at all. You've got it figured out."

However, I always thought I was going to be an agent. Towards the end of my career, my agent knew I liked finance and that I had younger kids that were getting ready to start school soon. He basically said, "You don't want to be an agent. That's 24/7. You'll be gone all the time like when you're playing." I didn't want to be a 24/7 agent traveling all the time. I wanted to work from home and be with my family.

After my 2002 season and going into 2003 I was having those discussions. I was almost 39, so I obviously knew I was near the end of my playing career. My agent said he could get me a spot with a New York firm and get somebody to mentor me in the financial industry. I already had some financial guys helping me, and after he met those guys, he recommended I work with them.

I had a meeting with my financial guys in early January of 2003. They said they'd love to have me and would sponsor me if I wanted to try to get my licenses. I started the process and got my Series 7 in a month and a half. By the time spring training rolled around, I was Series 7 licensed.

I went to spring training with the Orioles and got released on the last day of spring. I ended up with the Pirates and went to Triple-A because I hadn't played in a few weeks. After a couple weeks, Pokey Reese blew out his thumb, they called me up, and I was starting every day.

With my Series 7 license, I was meeting with players on both my team and other teams. I'd have breakfast meetings, then play a game, and then go out and meet with guys at night over beers to talk about finances. It got pretty exhausting. There were full days for a few months there. As soon as the season ended, I pretty much knew I was done playing. I had a couple opportunities to come back but playing wasn't on the top of my mind. You have to be fully invested to continue playing at that high of a level.

Once the 2003 season was over, I went and got my Series 66 license, which is for insurance and other things. At that point I was fully licensed.

The transition wasn't as hard for me as it is for a lot of guys. The hard part for a lot of guys is finding value in what they're doing. They go from people screaming at them for their autographs to sitting at home and doing nothing. It often takes a couple of years to figure out exactly what's next. I was lucky. I thought I was going to do something, and it turned into something else pretty quickly that wasn't far off from what I originally planned to do. I found a lot of value in helping people.

I missed the camaraderie with the players in the clubhouse, but I was still getting a lot of that in the financial world. I was going to spring training, sitting in the manager's office, and talking with players I'd played with or against. I had access. I could go anywhere I wanted to. A lot of people knew who I was. I would set things up with clients, hang out during batting practice, and because I wasn't a bad dude, people would say, "Come on in." Now it is a little different. Baseball had a lot more baseball people in it years ago. I don't know as many people as I once did.

I'd say about 90 percent of my clients are baseball guys. Some are retired. Some are current managers, players, coaches, trainers, and recent draft picks. We focus on the relationship side of things, so we have a smaller clientele. It has to be a good fit for both us and them. Everybody sells financial products but at the end of the day it's really about planning, communicating, staying active with clients, and talking with them through the next steps for what they want in life. We're not just there during their playing careers. They're a client for life with us.

When you're in the big leagues and have money, you see how many people are trying to get access to you as a player. That's always intrigued me and has been a major thing for me because I see where people make mistakes. I've made my own mistakes. People are always trying to get you to invest in a restaurant or something like that. There's a lot of private equity stuff that comes up. Every year there's something new. We talk with our clients about whether something is investing or speculation. We're not into speculation.

Shortly after I retired from playing, Major League Baseball and the Major League Baseball Players Association asked me to work with their Rookie Career Development Program. They take former players that have been in the big leagues and have them mentor top prospects, either guys that have recently entered the big leagues or guys they think will be in the big leagues within the next year or so.

Traditionally, each organization would send three guys for the four day in-person program. They'd learn about what to expect in the major leagues, from how to deal with the media, to finances, to situations that come up in the clubhouse. They even cover post-career. There's a lot of really good information. Since Covid, we've been doing it through Zoom, so we can have more players. It's been an honor to be involved.

I have a series of things that I like to bring up, and one of them is networking. When you're in major leagues, you're in the greatest network in the world. I always felt like I was a good dude and had a good reputation. I built it up from playing for 18 years. I felt I could have done anything I wanted to do because I knew a lot of people I had good connections with. I was the lead player rep in 1994 with the Twins during the strike year and I think that led to being a Rookie Career Development guy. People see what you're doing, and that creates opportunities for you going forward.

I've been involved with Major League Baseball and the Major League

Baseball Players Association through other things as well. I've done the Hank Aaron Invitational in Vero Beach, the MLB Combine, and the USA 18U trials.

I enjoy giving back to the game. I think giving back is important. I started my own nonprofit, REB Sports Academy, many years back for youth baseball, and we've started a little bit with softball. We have programs, hold clinics and classes, and put teams together. It's a growing endeavor. We're trying to make Dayton, Ohio, baseball better and ensure everybody has access to quality coaching.

Matt Walbeck

Matt Walbeck played 17 seasons of affiliated baseball, including 11 seasons in the major leagues. His last year playing in affiliated baseball was 2003. Following his playing career, he became a minor league manager before starting his own baseball academy. At the time of the interview for this book, he was employed by the California Department of Parks and Recreation and living in California.

I was going to be a major league manager. That was my goal. I learned so much from so many great baseball minds. I had the ability to lead, motivate, teach, manage, be well organized, communicate, and all that sort of stuff. Being a catcher also helps lend itself into managing or coaching. And because I had so much passion and love for the game, it just seemed like that was what I was meant to do.

I think it started right away. When I was playing and learning from my coaches and managers, I was enamored by how much there was to the game and how much fun it would be to someday coach. I was always learning that along the way while I was playing. In the back of my mind, I'd think someday when I'm coaching or managing, I'm going to do that, or I'm definitely not going to do that.

I always had the ability to coach, help instruct, and see things. I have an eye for certain things. As a kid, I watched games, read box scores, and would just be glued to it. It just became a language to me. Certainly, I knew my playing career was going to come to an end, and at that point I'd transfer all the knowledge I'd learned into being a coach or manager, help players improve, and enjoy the game.

After the 2003 season with the Tigers, (Alan) Trammell and (Dave) Dombroski talked to me on the last day of the season and said, "Hey, we appreciate what you've done, but we're not going to have a spot for you next year as a player. We'd like to offer you a managing position in either short season A-Ball or full season A-Ball."

Mind you, that Tigers team in 2003 finished 43–119. It made me realize if I can't play for one of the worst teams of all time, it's probably a good time to make a career path change. That's how it all started to transpire.

I started as manager of the West Michigan Whitecaps in the Midwest League.

The decision was pretty easy, and the transition was pretty straight forward. Thankfully, I was going from one of the catchers of the Detroit Tigers to a manager for the Detroit Tigers organization. I knew the Tiger way. They knew I was a rookie manager and there were things I had to learn.

I talked with, and asked as many questions as I possibly could, to the Tigers coaches in the clubhouse. As a former player, it was interesting to sit in on meetings and hear what actually goes on in those meetings. I was just a sponge. I wanted to succeed. I read John Wooden's books and other books on sports psychology.

I reached out to Marv Foley, one of my former managers. I had a system I learned from Marv that I really believe helped my teams win. It was an offensive strategy with a developed plan for various categories. For example, if you're leading off an inning, you would get a point if you saw eight pitches, lined out, or reached first base. If you did any of those things, I would pay you 50 cents. If you didn't do any of those, you would pay me 25 cents. If there was a runner on second with nobody out and the situation called for that runner to be moved over, and I didn't give you the bunt sign, you had to find a way to get that guy over. Strategies like that. It kept everybody realizing there's a game within a game, and instead of going up there and just trying to hit the ball over the fence, there was a plan.

I started developing and building teams to get everybody to feel like they're part of a group that's bigger than just themselves. I realized how treating your 25th guy on the roster is just as important, if not more so, than your number one draft pick, because you want everybody pulling together.

I suppose the biggest challenge was that my muscle memory, brain, and everything was so competitive. I had to realize I wasn't going to be able to share everything with the players and be as close. You sort of become an outsider in the clubhouse. Even though you're the manager, you have your own office. There has to be a line.

I was fortunate to have a really good pitching coach with West Michigan in A.J. Sanger. He was fantastic and had been coaching for a few years, so he was able to mentor me also.

I was surrounded by great baseball people—Toby Harrah, Bill Freehan, Al Kaline, Mick Kelleher, Jon Matlack, Larry Parrish, Britt Burns....

The list goes on and on of all the guys that played baseball that you could learn from their experience. It was a passion for me, and I really dug it.

2004 was fun. We won the league championship. In A-Ball they play a first half and second half. We squeaked in the second half and ended up winning the whole thing.

I had a lot of great players and coaches, and success because of that. The Tigers front office allowed me to do my thing and gave me the freedom to kind of do what I wanted.

In November of 2007, I got a call from Glenn Ezell. He was our field coordinator and my boss. He said the Texas Rangers reached out to the Tigers front office and asked if they could interview me for their third base coach position, spring training coordinator, and catching instructor. Basically, it was three roles for one person. He asked if I was interested, and I said absolutely. Looking back at it in 20/20 hindsight, I probably should have given deference to the Tigers and said, "Whatever you think is best." I probably shouldn't have been in such a hurry to promote.

I had nine years and about 35 days of major league service. I played in 11 seasons, but some of those included the minors. Getting back to the big leagues would've made me fully vested.

I accepted the interview opportunity. The Rangers flew me to Arlington, and I did great in the interview.

I was thrown into spring training coordinator, catching instructor, and third base coach on a team where I didn't really know anybody—coaches or players. It was quite an eye-opening experience, and things just didn't work out. I was told they were not going to renew my contract the next year. As far as I knew, everything was amicable.

Then, I interviewed with the Pirates to manage their Double-A team. At first everything seemed great. Slowly I realized it was not the baseball I grew up learning and playing. It became difficult for me to do stuff I wasn't true to. What was really the nail in the coffin was after the 2010 season, when we won the Eastern League Championship, and I was named Manager of the Year, they fired me just to prove a point. I supposedly had to do everything my way, which probably was the case. But then again, you have to be true to yourself.

It wasn't until right before Christmas when the Braves flew me out to Atlanta and interviewed me for their Single-A job in Rome, Georgia. I was hired there for the 2011 season, and I sensed immediately something was wrong. People were like, "This guy has to do things his own way." I had a reputation for being kind of a renegade or maverick.

I was warned early in the season. Supposedly, I was making them hustle too much and working them too hard. They said, "You can quit, and we'll continue to pay you, or you can change." I said, "Well, I'm not going to quit. I'll try to change." I tried to adjust but when that happened everything just fell apart.

The next thing I know is they're calling me, saying they're in my office and they need to talk. I drive to my office, they're sitting there, and they say, "We're going to let you go." I was kind of relieved, but I was certainly disappointed.

I think when I started to close out my managing career, the game really had started to swing in the facet of where it was more about developing tools and skills, not teaching them how to play to win. It became apparent I didn't fit that mold. It happened much faster than I could have ever imagined.

I started doing private lessons and that's when I began my baseball academy with the help of my business partner Glen Gross.

We started out very small renting single cages and using online scheduling software. Then, as business grew, we ended up renting our own space. As that continued to grow, we expanded. Shortly thereafter, Covid hit, and it threw things into a tailspin.

During that time, Glen and I created a web-based app that was subscription based with over 400 videos and a filtering system. Basically, someone would subscribe and have access to the content that was on there. Little League coaches could prescribe drills for their players to watch, and then the coach could actually see if the players watched the video. Most of the drills were designed to be done in small, confined spaces so kids could practice in their garage or backyard.

I got to the point with the state that baseball's in now with all the different training methodologies that teach less of the feel for the game and more about just pure strength, spin rate, and all that sort of stuff, I just wasn't inspired to do it anymore. With social media, everybody's got the new best drill. I realized that what I like to teach is just not applicable in today's game. It seemed to me a lot of the people teaching and making decisions, even in the front office in Major League Baseball, didn't have much experience on the field.

Once I got to that point, not knowing what I was going to do was the biggest challenge for me. What am I good at? What do I want to do? Taking baseball out of the equation, I had no idea.

I made a spreadsheet of all my contacts I thought could have some sort of advice or opportunity on something I could maybe be inspired to go after.

It was difficult to find anything at my age and with my experience. I don't have a college degree. I signed a professional contract when I was 17, so it was difficult at 53–54 to find something I could be successful at outside of baseball.

It's tricky. I feel the reason I made it to the major leagues was because I never had a backup plan. I never thought, "Well, if this doesn't work, I'm going to do this." I knew it was going to be so hard to get there that I couldn't even have one inkling of jumping off the ship and trying to do something else.

A lot of successful people can do that. A lot of guys go to college and get a degree. They are so wise and smart to realize, "Well, I'm going to play this many years and then I'm going to start this career doing financial advice, selling insurance, becoming a cop, or whatever." For me, because I was undersized and such a long shot, I felt I had to sell out and give it all I had to get there.

For the most part, I don't have any regrets. I don't really wish I would've done anything differently. But again, it was a challenge not knowing what I wanted to do after baseball.

I had a sales job for a little while where I was only making commissions. I was driving all through northern California selling fire equipment to firefighters. It was a great experience, and I learned a ton. I worked there for I think four months. I was under the impression it could be something that would take off and I could develop fire stations that would call me and ask for turnouts and other tools, helmets, cleaning supplies, and stuff like that. It was tough because I found many fire stations had been working with the other companies for a long time. Honestly, I didn't really know anything about the industry. I was a fish out of water. But again, I learned a lot. I learned how to cold call, knock on doors, and introduce myself.

I'm friends with the gentleman who is the executive vice president of 4LEAF, Inc., an engineering consulting firm. A position came up in Sea Cliff and Aptos for managing a debris removal project. They needed someone to monitor the trucks that come in and take the debris. He said they didn't have anybody on their staff to do it and asked if I was interested. I said I was definitely interested. I had a phone call with him on a Wednesday, and I was on the job site the following Monday.

I had to follow the trucks to the dump, take pictures, and verify all the material that was being disposed of. It was a crash course on how to write reports, and I fit right in. I had some really good mentors.

I would commute back and forth. I would stay down there, come home to Fair Oaks Friday evenings, and drive back on Sundays. I did that for a few months before I was relocated to Folsom Lake where I managed another debris removal project.

As that project started to wrap up, I was talking with my current supervisor about a consulting role in more of an administrative position with FEMA projects throughout the entire state. I went through the process of taking the exam and other processes that need to take place to become employed by the state. I then went through the interview process and was hired.

I'm now with the California Department of Parks and Recreation in their facilities management division, and part of managing FEMA projects for disasters that have occurred in our state parks statewide. I'm learning from some really experienced people that have been with parks for a long time.

I'm very happy with this full-time position. My goals are to continue to learn and help my supervisor and our team provide good services to the parks of California.

This is my first full-time job where it's not a one-year contract or I'm running my own business. The work-life balance is unbelievable. It's literally 8:30 a.m. to 5 p.m. Monday through Friday.

Sometimes it is somewhat challenging to grind it out for eight and a half hours with a 30-minute lunch break. It's just a different feeling. But if you've played in the major leagues, you can adjust and figure out a way to do it. It just takes practice.

I think a lot of us players attach ourselves to having been a former major league player and have a tendency to hold ourselves in a little bit of a higher regard because of that at certain times. I've learned that most people really don't care. Some people do, but at the end of the day, they're going to be your friend for who you are as opposed to having played in the major leagues. At the same time, I think we have to tell ourselves that what we did was extraordinary. Very few people have ever played a day in the major leagues so there should be some sense of accomplishment and pride for having achieved that dream.

Matt Walbeck played in 11 major league seasons (courtesy Matt Walbeck).

I'm still involved with the Major League Baseball Players Alumni Association. They have what's called Legends for Youth Clinics. Former major leaguers will be contacted, and we'll get together to put little clinics on for Little Leagues throughout northern California. This happens throughout the entire country and even in different places throughout the world. They're free clinics that promote the game and help teach kids fundamentals.

As a minor league manager, Matt Walbeck celebrates winning the 2010 Eastern League Championship with the Altoona Curve (courtesy Matt Walbeck).

I think a lot of us, when we're out of the game, miss the adrenaline. We miss the moments of bliss when you're in the zone and able to tune out 45,000 screaming fans and not hear anything. We miss the camaraderie of our teammates. We miss the battle. We miss the grind. I haven't been able to find a way to replace that.

I played men's league baseball for a few years and the thing I liked most was the camaraderie. The grind wasn't the same. You show up and play catch, and the next thing you know it's time to play ball. Whereas, when you're in the big leagues, you show up at noon for a seven o'clock game. You have a routine, and that routine becomes part of you. It's like a comfort blanket. You want to get into that zone. We chase that feeling of being in the zone where you're in the moment constantly.

I've taken up guitar heavily and practice a lot. I play live and perform with bands. That gives me those jitters and a nervous belly, which believe it or not, I like. I like the nerves and performing.

Before that, I got into flyfishing a lot and really would get into the moment doing that.

You have to find an outlet. Some guys get into gambling, drugs, and alcohol because it becomes numbing. You must find something that's healthier where you can still get those moments of being in the present. I think that helps with the post-playing career.

You have all the energy, and it may even be like PTSD for certain people. There's so much high stress and then suddenly you have a big hit or something and you get this rush of adrenaline. After a while, your body gets used to it.

I can remember even when I was out of the game and had stopped coaching, when spring training would start to come around, I'd find myself walking around the house doing dry swings and giving signs like I'm a third base coach, not even thinking about it. It's like my body was ready to go to spring training. There were dreams at night about being in the clubhouse, not finding your uniform, and stuff like that.

Psychologically, there's a lot us players must fight through to get into that next stage of life.

Scott Forster

Scott Forster played nine seasons of affiliated baseball, including one season in the major leagues. His last year playing in affiliated baseball was 2004. Since his playing career, he has worked in pharmaceutical and medical device sales. At the time of the interview for this book, he was working and living in Pennsylvania.

I had a couple surgeries on my shoulder. My head was saying, "Keep going." My body and arm were damaged goods so to speak, but I kept telling myself, "I can get myself back."

I played on a couple independent teams. I was reaching out to all the coaches, managers, and organizational people I knew just to get an opportunity. I exhausted everybody that I knew. Then, I went to people that I did not know.

It started creeping into my mind. It had been on a lot of people's minds, but nobody was going to say that to me. They knew I wasn't ready and needed to get it out of my system.

I was calling and emailing every single major league GM I could find contact information for. I wound up speaking to Brian Cashman of the Yankees. He got me a private workout with Rob Thomson, who is now the manager of the Phillies. I did the workout and Cashman called me about a week later. He had broken down every stat for every pitch I had thrown—percentage of fastballs for strikes, percentage of sliders for strikes, and all that. This was even before analytics became a big thing. He dropped those stats on me and didn't sign me.

I remember I was at my buddy's place in Florida and went out to his pool. I was in a pool chair, and my dad called me. He asked, "How'd it go?" I said I didn't get it. He's like, "Well, Scott. I think it's time to come home." I literally broke down in tears because I knew he was right. I went inside, packed up my stuff, and within two hours got in my car and started driving from Florida to Philly.

I had graduated college before I signed and was glad I did. There are so many kids that get drafted out of high school, play for five or six years, and have nothing to fall back on. Then, they're late to the party so to speak and struggle. A lot of my friends really struggled. They took the money dangling in front of their faces to get drafted and pursue every kid's dream. I'm glad I had finished college because it helped my resume, and I didn't have to go back to school to finish up. I was lucky there.

When I was first playing, during my first couple offseasons, my uncle put me on the payroll of his insurance company. I got my insurance license and learned the family business. However, it just wasn't for me.

During other offseasons, for seven or eight years, I would work at an indoor facility. I gave private lessons, group lessons, clinics, coaching teams, you name it. I worked with lots of kids and got a base clientele of about 250 kids. I got to know a lot of parents and what they did.

I was really close to one couple, and they were both in pharmaceuticals. They said, "When you finish playing, you should get into pharmaceuticals. You have a personality that would be a great fit for it." I was still playing at the time but kept that in the back of my head. When I finished playing, I reached out to them. They made a couple calls and got me an interview.

I wound up not getting the job but the guy I was interviewing with referred me to another company and I got hired there. I spent almost five years with that company and then switched over to medical devices. I did that with a few more companies and did well.

An opportunity presented itself about five and a half years ago. I sat down and interviewed with a guy, one of my cousin's best friends, in a pair of shorts and flip-flops. He said, "It's August. I'm wearing a pair of shorts and flip-flops. You can do the same." We went to a casual Italian restaurant and sat in the bar section. He had already seen my resume. We just sat down, talked, and had a few beers. He was a huge Yankees fan and knew I played. We wound up talking about my baseball career more than we talked about my resume. He asked, "Do you want the job?" I said, "Sure." That was it. He hired me and it'll be six years there in August. I've done extremely well with the company, so it was a great move for me.

I was in pharmaceutical sales for five years, and for the last 12 years I have been in medical devices.

I was fortunate to get a job in pharmaceuticals about six months after I stopped playing. I had a story to tell, and it was fresh in my mind. I went from the field to trying to get doctors to write prescriptions for the drug I was selling. It was a new competition for me.

I felt like, "You made it to the top in one career, now let's make it to the top in another." That's how I approached it. I missed the camaraderie, the locker room, the games, and everything that comes with a baseball career. However, I just channeled that energy into trying to be the best at my next journey in life.

I felt the work ethic I picked up in baseball, and especially surviving in the minor leagues, helped translate into my corporate career. Being able to climb the ladder knowing I'd have a limited opportunity with each team only carrying 12 or 13 pitchers prepared me.

I dealt with having to adapt to managers, to coaches, and to players from all over the world. To be on a team with them, talk with them, adapting to changes and being a professional about them, and learning personalities, helped. I was able to adapt to a doctor's personality, a nurse's personality, or a CEO's personality. I feel like instead of dealing with players, pitching coaches, and managers, I'm just dealing with doctors and pharmacists. Baseball definitely prepared me.

Getting to the majors was my ultimate goal when I played baseball. With the job I have now, I won salesman of the year last year and I'm on pace to do it again this year. I don't need accolades and recognition, but it is satisfying for me. I was recognized as the best player in the company for what I do. It's like me getting to the major leagues again in a way.

Micah Franklin

Micah Franklin played 12 seasons of affiliated baseball, including one season in the major leagues. His last year playing in affiliated baseball was 2004. Following his playing career, he worked for five years in the financing of black cars and limousines before returning to baseball. He has worked as a minor league coach and scout. At the time of the interview for this book, he was running his own hitting instruction business and living in Arizona.

I played for 15 years. I lived in Japan, Korea, Mexico, the Dominican Republic, and Venezuela with my wife and daughters. It's really different than most people's careers. I signed and left a few days after graduating high school. I was not in the regular world until I was 32 years old.

It came about organically. I was ready to be done with the grind and the mental wear and tear on your mind from playing baseball. I think it happened within that last year. I wasn't told I was done. I was still performing high in Triple-A, and a team overseas wanted me. However, I was just physically and mentally done.

I was in Tucson in Triple-A. At the end of 2004, I told the team I was retiring that last week of the season. They were going on the last road trip, and I didn't join the team. I retired and drove a car three and a half days to New York.

I had wanted to be a firefighter. My brother was a firefighter, and I thought that was so cool. But when you play for 15 years and have nine surgeries, being a firefighter is kind of out of the question. I still think it's absolutely awesome and one of the best jobs out there for people that are athletic, like to do things as a group, and look out for each other. Coaching and scouting were other things I thought of doing when I was done but it didn't turn out that way at first. I went into the business world.

I had a family business my grandparents started. My grandfather was a taxi driver for years and he started a brokerage in New York. My uncle turned that into an amazing business. He had an idea for me to start a company with him, and we started a financing company for black cars—limousines, taxis, and things like that. This was obviously before Uber and Lyft.

I had bought a house in Long Island. After I retired and drove there, my brother and cousin helped me do a quick renovation, and my wife and daughters came the next week. Shortly after, the business was up, and I had customers.

I was the owner operator of the management of the loans. We did the financing for drivers who needed to get a car, and I did that for five years.

The business was doing unbelievably well. We were killing it. My uncle was amazing and a great businessperson who taught me a lot. However, I missed baseball. I told my uncle I wanted to get back into it, and he already knew.

I spent about a year sending letters and making phone calls to teams. I got a lot of rejection letters.

Then, Tommy Allison, the scouting director for the Diamondbacks, had an opening in 2009. He took me under his wing and taught me a lot. It was an awesome time. Peter Woodfork was there, and Jerry Dipoto was in the front office. There were a lot of good people I had the opportunity to learn from.

I started scouting and learned the lingo. That was a great process, and I really enjoyed it. I got to sit in on five amateur drafts and be part of a couple of them. It was cool to see how that all works.

I even coached the Diamondbacks Elite Scout team, which was amazing. In the summers for two years, we had a select team. Mike Fetters and I selected all the players. The Diamondbacks paid for everything. The kids didn't have to pay for one thing. We practiced every day at Salt River Fields. It was awesome. From that team, we had 23 players make it to professional baseball and seven made it to the major leagues. That gave me a coaching kick.

Then, I went up to Seattle for three years and was a major league scout. I absolutely loved that. It was intense. You have to do reports on every major and minor league player that you see and are responsible for. When they call, you had better be ready with an answer. It's do this trade or don't do this trade. Millions of dollars are at stake. It was a lot of fun.

I missed coaching and wanted to try it, so I went back to the Diamondbacks. I was a hitting coach with their organization for five years. Then, De Jon Watson brought me to the Nationals. However, after two seasons, Washington needed to cut money.

Things evolved into me planning to do hitting lessons. I was getting tired of pro ball and listening to people who never played the game telling you all the drills that a hitter needs when they have no idea what a hitter needs mentally and physically. It wears you out.

I was planning on doing lessons full-time, but the Oakland Ballers called me about their manager job. I should have realized it was too good to be true. It didn't work out and I have no one but myself to blame for that one.

I am enjoying my new venture, called 7to22. I am working with amateur and professional hitters doing private hitting coaching, and I absolutely love it. I do some groups, but mainly one-on-one amateur. Kids come in for an hour session, I work with them, and then another kid comes in. I usually do about six or seven lessons a day. I rent out a cage and I'm usually booked 2–4 weeks out.

I came up with the name 7to22 when I was with the Nationals working with Darren Baker. The name 7to22 is a play on bat path metrics that create line drives through the middle of the field. They were saying he was hitting too many ground balls that wouldn't be hits in the majors. We looked through the computer system and his metrics were unbelievable when he hit the ball between seven and 22. I started looking at a lot of people and found the best hitters hit the ball between seven and 22. I named it 7to22 and it's a great starting point for people to start asking questions.

I didn't know how bad amateur coaching was for all these kids. I brought in stuff we do with the pros—how to hit the ball and move correctly. I make it simpler than all these fancy people are trying to make it. I work with kids and help them understand that a lot of these complicated things out on social media, while not necessarily wrong, are not what professional hitters are focusing on and doing. There's an organic result of moving the correct way. There's a lot of people trying to make kids move in slow motion. In turn, when they go fast, everyone's dragging and spinning off the ball, not staying on it and hitting line drives through the middle of the field.

When I started, I had about 3–4,000 followers on Instagram, but I was big on the pro side. Pro players would follow me because that's who I worked with. I didn't work with amateurs then. However, I put an ad on social media for parents, began to put myself out on social media more for younger amateur kids, and the algorithms grabbed things. In a few months, I went from 3–4,000 to just short of 21,000 followers on Instagram. I show my videos and I'm one of the few people that show the whole routine because I want kids to learn it correctly.

I learned early on that you're playing the odds game in baseball. If you do things correctly, realize what you're good at, and do it as many times as you can, the odds are in your favor. It's not always going to work out, but the odds are in your favor if you do it enough. In Vegas, there's a reason the house wins, right? They're going to lose sometimes but the casinos have the odds in their favor. For the most part, those fancy buildings and casinos are built on people losing because they're not playing the odds. So, if you go on your strengths, you're going to be successful.

Everybody wants to be Barry Bonds or those amazing hitters that can do everything. Most players are not that way. Those are very few and far between. I find out what a hitter's strengths are and work with them. I let them know, "This is your strength. If you continue to do this as much as you can, the odds are that you're going to have good numbers at the end of the year, and you're going to be successful. If you

Micah Franklin as a minor league hitting coach with the Arizona Diamondbacks.

keep trying to do something you can't do, you're not going to be successful because the odds are not in your favor." It's as simple as that.

You also have to talk to them about the struggles they may go through during the year—how they're feeling at the moment and how their body's reacting. You must understand that versus always looking at a hitter when they're at their 100 percent strength and ability to perform. When you understand what players are going through, it definitely helps with coaching.

There are all kinds of things you go through when you're done playing. It doesn't matter what you tell yourself, you're still going to have to go through it to understand it, and it can take a long time. There's depression. Thankfully, I have an amazing wife and daughters that helped me through it.

I don't care who you are. If you were an elite player, you have visions of being better than you ever were. I made it to the majors but wanted to be better. Those who were better, wanted to be Hall of Famers. Guys in the Hall of Fame wanted to be a top Hall of Famer. You must handle that even though you didn't necessarily fail, you did fail to get to where you really wanted to be. The goal posts always move, and you must understand that. It takes time to accept.

Jason Jimenez

Jason Jimenez played eight seasons of affiliated baseball, including one season in the major leagues. His last year playing in affiliated baseball was 2004. Following his playing career, he entered law enforcement. At the time of the interview for this book, he was working and living in California.

I think my story's a little different because I was a late bloomer. Professional baseball was kind of plan B honestly. Plan A was always to be a police officer.

My grandfather on my mom's side was a police chief for over 20 years. He was my role model and someone I wanted to be like. I used to ride in his cop car and hang out with him in his chief's office. I always wanted to be a police officer.

I wasn't very good at baseball as a young kid. We all have dreams of playing, but the reality is I didn't think I was good enough. I continued to develop through high school, then junior college, and then I started to get some attention at San Jose State. I was blessed to get drafted in the 28th round by the Tampa Bay Devil Rays. You always hope you get to the big leagues but as a 28th round draft pick, the odds are not very good.

When I got drafted, baseball obviously became my priority. Law enforcement then became my plan B. I knew as a professional baseball player the day would come, and I knew what was next. I didn't know how long the journey was going to be but I'm super grateful for the eight years I got to play professionally, and the opportunity to pitch in the big leagues for both Tampa Bay and Detroit. That's something I'll always cherish.

In 2004, I didn't think my career was coming to an end. I got hurt and was eventually diagnosed with a partial tear. I saw Dr. James Andrews and he basically said if I wanted to keep pitching, I needed to have Tommy John surgery. At the time, I wanted to keep playing, so I elected to have the surgery.

Unfortunately, I was a free agent. I was responsible for my own rehab and didn't have a team with a plan of how I was going to come back. I had to figure that out on my own. That was a challenge. Looking at how rehab from Tommy John is today, you see guys coming back much quicker and much stronger than before.

I remember waiting to get the surgery and sitting in a hotel room in Reading, Pennsylvania, praying and basically telling God, "I'll do whatever you want, whether it's continue playing or law enforcement. Lead me to which way you want me to go."

That's when I started to consider I might be at the end, and how to proceed in law enforcement if that was the case. I started to do a lot of research for what that looked like, read books about law enforcement, and talked with friends back home that were already sheriff's deputies or police officers. I gathered all that information and data, trying to prepare, so when that time came, I knew the steps needed to begin the journey down that road.

I ended up having the surgery at nearly 30 years old, and at that time my wife and I had two young kids. I was a free agent, and I didn't know what was next.

I had a connection with the school district here in town and they had a police department. To get my feet wet, so to speak, I became a school service officer to see what that was like. The first year or so there I was still trying to figure out what the next step was, whether I was going to go back to baseball, or go explore more opportunities in law enforcement.

As time went by and I continued to rehab, I could tell I didn't have the drive I needed to be successful playing at the professional level. For the kind of player I was, I had to be at the park early every day, well before everyone else, to get extra work in to make sure I could perform at that level. Having done it for eight years as a professional, I knew the drive and work ethic I was going to need, and probably more, coming back from surgery. No offense or disrespect to independent ball, but I made the decision that when the day came, I was never going to scratch and claw to try and hang on. I felt it was time. Ultimately, I sat down with my wife, we had a discussion, and I told her I thought I was done.

Those years as a school service officer were valuable for me. I was able to provide for my family, and it provided good training and experience for the transition into becoming an actual police officer.

I went into the police academy, and I was fortunate to get hired by the police department here in the town I grew up in. It's a medium sized department. We're over 300 employees, and I've been here 18 years now. I don't regret a minute.

At first, I really wanted to work my whole career as a patrol officer. I loved working the streets, and I worked graveyard for lots of reasons. For the first couple years, it was just because I had no seniority. However, it allowed me the opportunity to be present for my kids' activities, events, or whatever they may have going on in their lives. It was important to me to be present for them, and I could sacrifice a few hours of sleep to make sure I was there for my kids and wife when I needed to be.

Graveyard also allowed me the opportunity to coach as I began my journey as a high school pitching coach. Once I stopped playing, I didn't really watch, read, or talk about baseball. I was done. However, then, around two or three years later, I started to get the itch about the game again. That's when I started coaching high school baseball, and that helped fill the void for me.

A friend of mine was a coach at Elk Grove High, my alma mater, and they had just lost their pitching coach on the varsity team. They were already a pretty successful program, and I just wanted to be a freshman coach. Well, when I mentioned it to my friend, he said, "Well, we just lost our pitching coach, and there's no way you're going to be a freshman coach. You're going to be on varsity." I ended up meeting with the varsity coach, Jeff Carlson, who's a legendary coach now, having won a tremendous number of games, and having had quite a few players get to the big leagues, including his own son, Dylan. There have been six or seven players that I've coached that have reached the big leagues. I'm grateful for my time with Jeff and all the coaches I've had the privilege to coach with. It's been an awesome experience.

Recently, I was telling this story about when I first started coaching. I used to cringe when the kids called me coach. I felt like that was just like someone calling you old. As time has gone by, I know it's a term of endearment and respect from the players. Sometimes I'm in the grocery store or somewhere else and hear "coach" from a grown man with a family wanting to show me what he's become. Two years ago, I was in Nashville for a weekend trip, and I ran into a former player who's in law enforcement there as a police officer for Metro Police in Nashville. I get a lot of pride in seeing these guys as contributing members of society doing great things. Some are doing it in baseball, and some are doing it in other areas, whether it's military, teaching, or whatever. For me, that's a thrill and I think the most rewarding part of it. I love high school coaching. I think this is year 16 or 17 coaching at my alma mater, and I've been fortunate.

As for my work with the police department, after about seven or eight years on patrol, I was fortunate to be selected to be a gang and narcotics detective, which I did for three years. I got to work with my best friend from high school, and we had a lot of fun. We both share the same desire to be proactive and make a difference in our communities.

Eventually, a friend and mentor of mine here in the department pushed me to test and try to promote to become a sergeant much earlier than I had originally wanted to. I'm glad he did because being a sergeant has been a fun position. I say that because in the end, as a sergeant, you probably have the most important job in the department. You have the ability to help mold officers that are going to be out in the streets interacting with our community day in and day out. Those interactions are extremely important.

Every interaction has an impact, good or bad. But in the end, we want our folks to be able to treat people with respect and fairness. I grew up here. I live here. I want them to understand that my family, or their families, could be out there. You want people treating those people the same way you'd want our families and friends to be treated. It's been an extremely important position for me, and I enjoy it.

As a sergeant, I ended up being asked to be our public information officer. That's a position, honestly, I never in a million years would've told you I wanted to do as a cop. I loved chasing bad guys. I didn't have a communications or journalism background, or any of that. I really had to learn this job from ground zero. However, it's been one of the most rewarding positions because I had to learn and develop. To this day, I'm still trying to learn new stuff and get better at it.

I was asked to create a media and community relations team. I now supervise a team of seven people. Not only do we do media relations stuff, we're also responsible for the department's community events and outreach. We are pretty active and involved within our community, and over the last three years, we've done over a hundred events each year. I'm so grateful for the chiefs I've worked for while in this position. They understand and realize the value and importance of being entrenched in the community and being one with the community. I haven't been told no anytime we've come up with ideas to continue that mission.

We see the value and importance of having a community that's

As a sergeant with his hometown police department, Jason Jimenez leads the media and community relations unit (courtesy Jason Jimenez).

overwhelmingly supportive of our folks. But at the same time, we also know that's fragile, and we have to be mindful of that every day.

I've been wearing the badge for 18 years now. I think athletes tend to excel in this profession for several reasons through what they learned by playing sports. You have teamwork and communication, but because of baseball I got to travel and get to know people from all over the United States and world. You're exposed to diversity, different cultures, ethnicities, and people with different backgrounds. Some people communicate the same way while others don't. You can learn through baseball how to deal with all of that. Ultimately, I've felt like that was a huge piece for me, and has helped me be successful.

This job is all about knowing how to talk to people and how to deal with people. Officers that tend to have trouble are robotic, and don't know how to relate to or talk to people. For me, starting this profession at 30, and having that life experience of playing baseball all over, and having teammates from all over, has been extremely beneficial to me as a law enforcement officer.

You also learn how to deal with adversity. You have failures in sports. You're not going to be successful all the time. You may not get promoted or something may not go your way, but you keep your head down and keep working, and it'll pay off. Sports teach a lot of life lessons you end up using in this profession.

I've been blessed to have fulfilled my two lifelong dreams—to play in the major leagues and to serve my community as a police officer. At the same time, I've been fortunate to be a high school coach and have an impact on young kids' lives. It's been rewarding to find those wins in life outside of playing the game.

Scott Sanders

Scott Sanders played 13 seasons of affiliated baseball, including seven seasons in the major leagues. His last year playing in affiliated baseball was 2004. Following his playing career, he opened his own baseball academy. He has also worked in sales. At the time of the interview for this book, he was working and living in Louisiana.

In 2001 I went to Japan. After that year, I felt my arm was shot. I felt like a shell of myself and figured I was done. I didn't want to embarrass myself trying to come back. Instead of throwing 93–94, I was throwing 88–90. I decided to transition away from playing.

A buddy of mine who was going to be an agent asked me about coming on and working for him. I told my agent, and he was like, "Well, why don't you come work for me Scott?" He was out of Encino, California, so I moved back to California. For about a year, I worked for him. I was recruiting players, evaluating players, and all that stuff.

When spring training of 2003 started nearing, he asked me to show some of the young players how I had trained and got ready for spring training. I started going out some days and working out with the guys. The next thing you know, my arm was feeling pretty good. I told him my arm was feeling good, and he asked if I wanted to make another run at it. I figured I'd try it out.

I started getting in shape and went to Dodger Stadium to work out for the Dodgers. I then flew out to Arizona right before spring training and worked out for a few teams. Nobody bit.

I was getting in better shape, and my arm kept getting stronger and stronger. When April came around, my agent set up a tryout and 19 teams showed up. I was back to throwing 92–93.

The Marlins signed me. I flew down for a week of spring training before ending up in Alburquerque, and I stayed there the rest of that season. That was the year the Marlins won the World Series and there were numerous times I was right on the cusp of getting called up. It just didn't work out.

In 2004, during spring training, I tweaked a ligament in my wrist. I pitched pretty much that whole season but had to get a bunch of cortisone shots. I mainly did it because my kids loved it. They were young enough to come to the games and sit in the dugout. I sucked it up and after that season, I retired again.

Everything happens in life for a reason. I was in Albuquerque for about a year and three quarters, and my kids still talk about it. It was a really fun time for me and my two older boys. They came to the park with me every day and even went on some road trips with me. It was a blessing.

After that 2004 season, I retired again and moved back to Thibodaux, Louisiana. I had a couple offers to be a pitching coach in the Marlins and Padres organizations. I decided not to pursue them. My kids and family had been giving up their lives all those years to chase me around, and it was time for me to slow down and make it about them.

It was a very easy transition for me. I got done with that 2004 season in early September and as soon as I got back home, I started a Dixie Youth baseball team with a buddy in the same neighborhood. Dixie Youth is basically the equivalent of Little League throughout the south. We literally started practices about three or four weeks later. I took a bunch of kids who didn't really know a lot about baseball and had only played machine pitch baseball and put my heart and soul into teaching those kids baseball. That's what I did that first fall and it was a lot of fun.

Coaching ended up being a big passion of mine because of the kids on that team. They didn't know how to run bases. They didn't know how to pitch. Some knew how to hit, some didn't. Some could barely throw or catch. It was a great story. The next summer we went to St. Louis for the major division World Series and came out fourth. I was pretty proud of that crew.

The transition from playing wasn't hard because of my kids and because I was still involved in the game on a different side. I really thrived off teaching the game and giving back to the game that gave so much to me. I was blessed.

It wasn't like I missed the game of baseball. Did I miss the big paychecks? Obviously. I missed the roar of the crowds, and the adrenaline rush I would get on that mound. Still, to this day, there's nothing I can do in life that can replicate the adrenaline rush I had from 50,000 people either cheering for me or booing me, and trying to strike a guy out. I missed that part of it. However, coaching brought a different kind of adrenaline rush. It was calling pitches and coaching third base—putting on hit and runs, steals, squeeze plays, and anything I could do to make our team better and win. The rush wasn't the same, but the thrill of success was the same. Now I was just living through the success of the kids instead of myself.

I was doing lessons on top of that coaching, and about a year and a half later, I opened a baseball academy. I had planned to open it earlier, but Katrina hit and that backed everything up. I opened the Sanders Baseball and Softball Academy in 2006. That was the main thing I transitioned to and really enjoyed.

While I focused on mechanics, I also worked on the mental and confidence side. It's amazing. When you give kids confidence and mental strength, mechanics don't always have to be perfect. Believe it or not, it's really about confidence. It's not about being cocky, conceited, or arrogant, but confident that even on bad days you can get guys out or hit the baseball.

I enjoyed the baseball academy, but I really only did it at night. The kids were in school, so during the day I basically sat around and did nothing.

I was doing lessons with a kid from the little town over, and his dad owned an oil field company. One day he emailed me, asked if I wanted to grab lunch, and let me know about a proposition he wanted to run by me. He was looking to buy into a company that had a machine that would kill staph infections. He thought I'd be great on the sports side with selling it to high schools, colleges, and pro teams. I said I'd be interested but one thing led to another, the money didn't work out, and he didn't do it. Well, everything happens for a reason.

About a month later, he asked, "Can we have lunch again? I've got something else to run by you." I said, "Sure." We go have lunch again, and he asks, "What do you know about the oil field?" I said, "Absolutely nothing but that my dad worked for Texaco in personnel." He said, "Well, I want you to come sell for me." I never had a sales job in my life. He said, "You're tall, nice looking, and you have a National League championship ring. Go out there, sell yourself, and the rest will take care of itself. You don't have to know a lot about the oil field." I said, "Let's do it."

I started with him about a week later and had a lot of success. I didn't really know a lot about the oil field, but I went out and made contacts. I carried myself well and had a good time. I met guys that were obviously intrigued that I played professional baseball. I'd take them to lunch, hunt, fish, and different things. I helped turn his business around which was a blessing for everybody.

I'd work my oil field job during the day and then at night I'd go to my academy and do lessons. While the kids were in school, I'd get on the road, work my territory, and go straight to my academy around four o'clock. Then, I'd do lessons until about nine at night. I was loving life because I was getting out to see people during the day and then teaching kids at night.

I worked at the oil field job for about seven or eight years. Then, the son, who I had done lessons with, was getting out of college and coming into the business. Together, we helped train him and introduced him to my contacts.

About two years later, I sold the academy to a local business owner who wanted to keep the facility as a baseball academy, which I was really excited about.

Nowadays I am a regional director for Jani King Gulf Coast, which is a big commercial cleaning company. It's weird. I got my current job through baseball also. At the time I was retired for the second time. I wasn't really looking for a job. I was just enjoying my kids' sports and living life.

Every weekend I would go watch my kids play, and my mom and dad would often come and watch too. This particular weekend I was in Florida watching my son Scotty. That day the Jani-King CEO and a franchise owner were there handing out koozies. Well, my dad had taught the franchise owner in college, and they stayed in contact. I had also coached against the franchise owner's kids. He asked my dad, "What's Scott up to?" My dad said, "Scott's actually looking for a job." Again, I wasn't looking for a job. My dad just thought it might be a good opportunity.

The franchise owner called me, and we spoke a little bit about Jani-King. Then, the next day someone from the company called me. It took about five or six months before I slowed down and got the baseball season out of the way, but eventually I joined Jani-King and started out doing sales. I had a lot of success, and they made me a regional director. I've been a regional director for almost seven years.

It's funny how baseball is the way I ended up at Jani-King because they were at a game handing out koozies. It's a small world and it's just another blessing baseball has given me.

For the first few years at Jani-King, I'd still do lessons at one of my good buddy's houses. He has a big garage behind his house, and I put a pitching lane in there. On Tuesdays, Wednesdays, and Thursdays, I'd work at Jani-King until five o'clock and then do lessons until around eight thirty. However, since I moved to Baton Rouge about four years ago I haven't done any lessons because I've been a lot busier. When I get done with the workday, I'm a lot more tired. I head home, hit the sofa, and watch baseball most nights.

I don't regret not pursuing professional coaching with the Padres or Marlins because of the success of my kids and of the kids that I've coached, not just through baseball but through life. I still occasionally get texts from guys that are now 28–29 years old that say, "Coach, thanks so much. You don't know how much you molded my life, and I'll never forget everything you've done for me." I get chills throughout my whole body thinking about it. I've been able to touch so many lives, and they have touched my life as well.

Following his playing career, Scott Sanders ran his own baseball academy and worked in sales (courtesy Scott Sanders).

The game of baseball taught me a lot that helped in my non-baseball jobs.

Baseball taught me confidence and control. When I walk in a room, rarely do I ever feel intimidated. I pitched in front of 55,000 people, screaming down my neck. If I'm not intimidated by that, when there's 10 people in the room, I feel I can control the room, just like I could control the game.

In the oil field job, even though I hardly knew anything about the oil field industry, I was able to go in and sell myself with confidence. I just made sure the guy who was going to rent equipment from me got to like me. If he got to like me then he'd say, "What do you have? I want to rent something from you."

Now, with Jani-King, I run a team here. I have 10 people in my office. I have a hundred franchises, and those franchise owners have 2,000 workers. I have thousands of people who count on me every day to come to work and have success. Being a player on teams, I run my office like a team, my franchise owners like a team, and make sure those franchise owners run their employees like a team.

A team is only as good as the weakest link. We're going to have good days and we're going to have bad days. We're going to make mistakes, but it's how we handle them.

The team aspect is what's helped me be very successful. You can't treat everybody on the team the same. Some people are sensitive and some aren't. You have to pat some people on the back when they're down and kick some people in the butt when they're down. You have to get to know each person in your team and figure out the buttons you must press for them to go out and have a successful day.

Baseball has really helped me, and set me up for success, in all the different things I've done along the way.

Dave McCarty

Dave McCarty played 15 seasons of affiliated baseball, including 11 seasons in the major leagues. His last year playing in affiliated baseball was 2005. Following his playing career, he worked in commercial real estate. He passed away April 19, 2024, shortly after the interview for this book.

I was lucky to have my economics degree from Stanford, so getting a job was not going to be a problem for me. It was just figuring out what I wanted to do and where I wanted to do it.

I grew up in Houston and took some courses at Houston Community College the summer after my senior year in high school. I went into Stanford a quarter ahead and over the course of the next three years took heavy loads in the fall quarters when we didn't have games. I had done that plan so if I signed, great. If I didn't, I could double major or maybe start working on a master's degree. After I signed, I went back for the fall quarter of what was my senior year and was able to finish and graduate early. That was after the 1991 season. I went to High-A and Double-A that year, and then went back to the Bay Area to finish up school.

I think a lot of guys finish up the game and then say, "Oh crap! What's next?" Unfortunately, the vast majority of them don't have their college degrees, and a lot of them are very far away from having their college degrees, so it somewhat limits their opportunities.

I think one of the hardest things about the transition is that you eat, sleep, and live baseball for so many years. For guys who are in the big leagues, or even the minor leagues, when it comes to an end, that's what they've done since they were kids. The hard part is not just transitioning from one job to another. It's not just what you do, it's who you are. You've always been "Dave the baseball player," until suddenly, you're not. Then, you must ask yourself, "Okay, well who am I now?" Unfortunately, most guys don't really put much thought into that while they're playing.

At the time I retired, there weren't a lot of resources for guys when they retired. In recent years, The Major League Baseball Players Alumni Association has been holding conferences for players who have recently retired, or near the end of their careers, and are looking to figure out what's next. They'll have speakers in different fields, whether it be broadcasting, real estate, insurance, money management, and all sorts of different things. They can go to breakout sessions where there are typically three different folks from three different fields. They share what to expect, what's realistic, and what it takes to succeed in a particular career so they can make a decision with eyes wide open rather than kind of going into it blind without having given it any thought.

I was lucky to have the foresight to start thinking about it when I was still playing but part of that was because of my role in the major leagues.

In 1999, I knew I was a bench guy in the big leagues. I knew I was not going to make the kind of money to just retire. And quite frankly, I wanted to do something when I was done playing. I started reaching out through some of the connections I have with Stanford baseball—some of the guys older than me who were in different fields.

One of the best things players can do is when they're in the big leagues, when everyone's door is open to them, is to take advantage of that to meet with people, build their network, and get a feel for what they want to do when they're done. I did that and considered a bunch of different things. I was considering money management, sports agency, staying in the game in coaching or the front office, broadcasting, and commercial real estate. I had narrowed it down to those based on the conversations and meetings I had when I was still playing.

In 2005 I made the (Red Sox) out of spring but had to sign a 45-day contract. If you have enough major league service time and make the team on day one, the team is responsible for your salary the entire year. However, there's a loophole. They can get you to sign a 45-day contract whereby if they get rid of you within the first 45 days, then they are not responsible for your contract that entire year.

The Red Sox really wanted a left-handed hitting backup first baseman. They ended up signing John Olerud, and shortly thereafter, they designated me for assignment. When that happened, they had a deal in place to trade me to another team. It was a team that was not very good, and I played on enough bad teams in my career, that I preferred to just go out on a high note.

Additionally, 2005 was the first year my kids were old enough that when I went to spring training, they said, "Dad, we don't want you to go." That was tough. Our son, our oldest child, has special needs. We had a house in the Bay Area near my wife's family so she could have additional support when I was gone. Unlike a lot of other families, they couldn't just come to where I was full-time because there were all the therapy and medical appointments my wife had to be available for. When I was gone, I was gone. That was really hard. That, coupled with making the choice to go to a team that wasn't very good at the time or just retiring on top, led to my decision to retire.

When I retired, the Red Sox offered to create a hybrid position for me that was part-time on the field and part-time in the front office so I could figure out which route I preferred. I ultimately decided I wasn't going to do that.

As much as I love the game, what people may not realize is that the lifestyle is horrendous. You're gone eight to nine months out of the year, so you only get to see your family in bits and pieces here and there. It would've been great to be in Boston or here in the Bay Area. However, you have to think long-term and consider all the eventualities. What if a GM position or managerial position opens up someplace? There were some cities where I wasn't going to move my family, which would then lead me back not seeing them again.

Additionally, people don't realize you work a lot of hours in coaching and the front office. You are at the field all day and night. I just decided that I really wanted to be able to spend more time with my family after missing the kids' first five to seven years of life. I didn't want to miss any more of their childhood.

I ultimately decided to get in touch with Tom Werner of the Red Sox about if there was any shot I could do some part-time broadcasting. He made the connections there and NESN hired me to do four weeks a year of pre-game and post-game analysis. I did that for four years. They would fly me back there for a week at a time and put me up in a hotel near the NESN studios. I would go into the studio or to the field, depending on if the Red Sox were at home or on the road.

During some of that time with NESN, I would work on commercial real estate in the morning before I had to go into the studio.

Around the time I retired from playing, I went to my wife's high school reunion. The managing partner for Lee & Associates (a commercial real estate brokerage firm) went to high school with my wife and I had known him for as long as my wife and I had been married. We were sitting there talking and he asked me what was next. I told him commercial real estate was one of the things I was considering. He said, "Well, we're going to be opening a new Oakland office and I'm going to be heading it. If you want to join us, there's a spot for you." I thought about it and said, "Okay. Done."

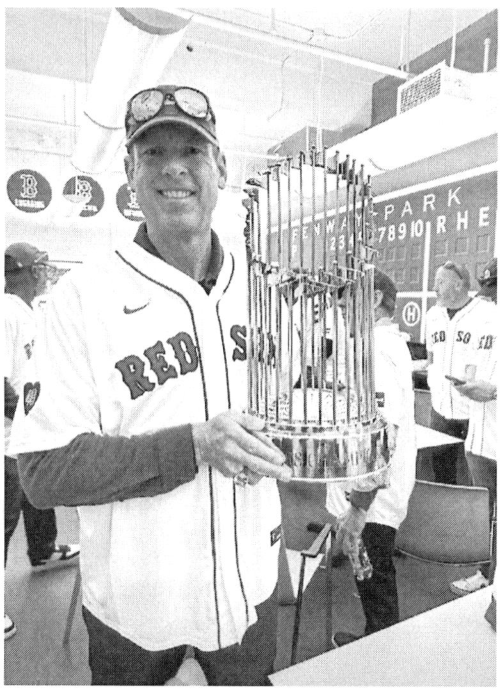

Dave McCarty entered commercial real estate following his baseball career. He attended the 20-year 2004 Boston Red Sox reunion less than two weeks before passing away (courtesy Dave McCarty).

I've been in commercial real estate for 18 years now. We specialize in leasing and sales of office and investment properties in the San Francisco Bay Area. It's kind of weird when you get to the point where you've been doing the second gig longer than baseball.

I think the skills you learn as a ballplayer translate very well to commercial real estate. It's the ability to kick yourself in the butt, motivate yourself, and work as part of a team. Once you get in the business world, you realize there are a lot of people who don't have those skills. You must communicate well and work with people that are not always your best friends. You have to do that in baseball too.

In commercial real estate, there's nobody to motivate you and kick you in the butt. You have to do that yourself. Going into January 1, your salary for that year is $0. It's all commission. You can work your butt off and make nothing. That being said, you can work your butt off and there's no limit to what you can make. You reap the rewards of your hard work and the seeds you've planted year after year after year, doing the things you need to do to be successful. Ballplayers, and athletes in general, don't have a problem with that. Baseball's the same way. You work your butt off and when you're in the minor leagues you're making nothing relatively speaking. Then, if you get to the big leagues, you can make really good money. Careers in sales or real estate are the same way.

Athletes tend to not have a problem with that because they know they can motivate themselves. We like the competitive nature. When you're working on a deal and the negotiations are going back and forth, it gets the juices flowing again. It's a way to replace what you don't have with baseball anymore.

Most former players don't miss playing the game as much as we miss the camaraderie. Nobody ever tells you that the bill comes due on the abuse your body takes over the years. You get to your forties and fifties, and suddenly, your back's hurting, or your knee, or elbow, or multiple things. You see people who have had regular jobs their whole career and haven't destroyed their bodies. They're a lot more mobile and you think, "Wow, must be nice."

I miss the camaraderie most and the special bond with teammates, especially with the Red Sox and the 2004 team. Having gone through what we did to battle and win the World Series, it really creates a special bond. We had our 10-year reunion, and I hadn't seen some of those guys in literally 10 years. It could have been the day after we won when we got back in the same room together, joking around and just having a good time. The relationships don't skip a beat. We have our 20-year reunion coming up on the ninth of the month, the home opener for the Sox this year. I'm really looking forward to seeing those guys again. It's definitely the camaraderie that you miss.

David Lee

David Lee played 11 seasons of affiliated baseball, including five seasons in the major leagues. His last year playing in affiliated baseball was 2006. Following his playing career, he worked briefly in sales before

starting his own baseball instruction business. At the time of the interview for this book, he was working and living in Pennsylvania.

It all worked out in the end. I knew I'd land on my feet, and something would work out, but it was just getting started that was the challenge.

In 2006 the Astros picked me up and I was in Triple-A. I was doing well at the time, but the manager told me, "Dave, you're never going to get called up. You're 33." When he told me that, I knew my time was going to be limited and I had to get in the right situation and place. I bounced around two more places that year and ended up with the Red Sox in Pawtucket. I couldn't have pitched any better in the last month, but they didn't call me up.

That offseason my agent told me no one wanted to sign me. I didn't believe him. I called up every major league team myself and didn't get any interest. In 2007, I kept throwing and playing on a semi-pro team. Unfortunately, I still thought I could play.

I was naïve. I was going to play forever. That last year, the writing was on the wall.

The transition was tough. I didn't really do anything for a couple years. I don't know if it was just that I couldn't believe it or what. I still thought I could play and no one else did. There was a shock factor of having to accept I was not playing anymore.

It's not as easy as people may think it is. It's the reality of not playing baseball when you've done it since you were a kid, until you're about 35.

The biggest thing for me was just figuring out what I wanted to do. I wanted to stay in the game and was thinking about being a coach or a scout, but I realized if I did that I would be traveling, and away from my family. I wanted to be around them and not miss anything. That was the most important thing to me.

I never lived above my means and was never someone flashy who had a bunch of stuff. That made the financial part of the transition easy. I had made some money and had things squared away for my retirement, which was good. There are some guys who are fortunate that don't have to work or do anything the rest of their lives, but I wasn't one of them.

I just needed to find something I liked to do, and I was good at. That was the hardest thing. I never really had a job in my life. I didn't consider baseball a job. It was more fun than anything.

It's tough not doing anything and just sitting around. I can understand if you've worked your whole life and retired but I was going nuts. I was obviously doing yard work and stuff around the house but that wasn't enough.

I had a buddy who did medical device sales, and he was doing really well. I decided to do that and was doing well for about a year. Then, a big merger came in. They bought out our company, and the next thing I knew, they eliminated my position.

Then, I had another friend in commercial insurance. He goes, "Dave, you'd be good at this. You know a bunch of business owners and are friends with them." I did that for about two and a half years but then there was another merger and a lot more eyes and pressure on me.

I did those two things, and it was an eye opener. I was doing well, and there is a lot of money to be made in those fields, but I think all things happen for a reason. They just weren't my calling.

I had been doing baseball lessons on the side and just decided to go into

After a short time in sales positions, David Lee started his own baseball instruction business (courtesy David Lee).

business for myself full-time. I think my calling is working with kids and making a difference. I've helped send a lot of kids to college.

I train kids all the way from seven to college-age. I try to help them on and off the field and teach them life lessons too. I let them know about recruiting and try to tell them, "Use your athletic ability to go to school so you can have a 40-to-50-year career after going to school." It gives me a good feeling to be able to help these kids out.

I'm realistic when I'm training these kids. I let them know their chances of turning pro are slim. However, at the same time, I let them know almost everybody told me I couldn't make it, so why not them. Ultimately, I try to encourage them to use their athletic ability to get into college and burden some of the costs.

Before the 1996 draft, I went from a projected first round pick to a 23rd round pick because I hurt my arm. I got drafted and went to short season A-Ball in Portland, Oregon.

Clint Hurdle was the minor league hitting coordinator for the Rockies at the time. I played for a lot of great coaches and managers, but Clint was always my favorite. You always knew where you were with Clint. He was a hundred percent brutally honest. He communicated well, and he cared about everybody.

In '96 he came in for a mini camp in Portland and I remember him saying, "You know what guys? I know you guys were just drafted or signed. I wish all of you could play for 20 years, make all kinds of money, and go to the Hall of Fame. But sometime in your career someone's going to tap you on the shoulder and say you can't play. It might be tomorrow, it might be next week, or it might be in 20 years. However, it will happen." He wasn't lying. Sometime reality will hit hard, and you must deal with it.

I do miss the guys in the clubhouse. I miss playing and competing. There's no better feeling than when the game's on the line and you do something to help the team win. But there's also the feeling when you don't do that. I've been cheered by 50,000, but I've also been booed by 50,000.

I did everything I could and worked hard at it. Looking back, I'm very fortunate to have played. I got to play in every major league stadium from 1999 to 2004. I was fortunate to play in five big league seasons. I wish I could have played 20 seasons, but that just wasn't in the cards. I gave it everything I had and played with a lot of guys that never made it. I'm in the books and no one can take me out.

Josh Stewart

Josh Stewart played eight seasons of affiliated baseball, including two seasons in the major leagues. His last year playing in affiliated baseball

was 2006. Since his playing career, he has worked in software training and support, primarily within the health care industry. At the time of the interview for this book, he was working and living in Kentucky.

In '99 I got drafted. I was excited as a left-handed pitcher going to the White Sox, as I should have been. That's how everybody is when they get drafted. Then, in 2000, when the new draft came, I saw they drafted more left-handed pitchers. Then, in 2001, they drafted more pitchers. You start to realize there's a baseball circle of life.

I kept advancing and doing well. In 2003 and 2004 I had a couple of injuries, but those were also the years I spent time in Chicago. I went to Japan and then the Marlins. Once I got hurt with the Marlins and had elbow surgery in 2006, it became very transparent that my days were winding down. From 2003, when I got put on the 40-man and got called up, it went from to getting all this attention—calls from my agent, companies sending me gloves, and all those things—to nobody calling.

I was looking for another team to sign a minor league deal with. In December of 2006, I turned 28. It's very young in years, but it's kind of older when you're trying to continue a professional baseball career unless you've already established yourself somewhere.

It was tough because it was all I knew, and everything I knew to be. I realized I wasn't the decent prospect I was only a few years prior, and it was tough to deal with mentally and emotionally. It happened organically. It wasn't like a door closed one day. I got hurt, bounced around a little bit, and then the next thing I knew, I was a 28-year-old minor league free agent nobody wanted.

There was a limbo time before the next season in 2007. I was still working out, throwing, and running as if I was still a professional baseball player. Guys sign all the time, and I didn't want to miss out on that. My mind was still set on baseball. I would work odd jobs while still pursuing baseball and waiting on that call to come, which never did.

My kid's mom and I were married at the time, and she had gotten a full-time job. She was the breadwinner, and I was trying to figure my life out, so to speak. It was difficult because you don't want to start on a new permanent path when you're still wanting to play baseball and hoping to get that call. But you also don't want to keep chasing a dream and avoiding reality.

In 2007 I had an opportunity to play independent ball, but that was my only offer. Some guys go play independent ball, stick with it, and get their chance. More power to them. I'm glad they do, and I wish them all the success in the world. In my mind that made me figure, "The writing's on the wall. It's time to come home."

I know this will probably sound generic, but at that point you must realize what you want out of life. I had a few coaches and mentors in professional baseball say, "Keep playing, keep fighting, and make them take that jersey off you." That's one piece of advice. If baseball would've been the only thing I ever wanted out of life, then I probably would've followed that advice. However, there's the reality of it. Independent leagues don't pay anything. We had a mortgage and a one-year-old at home. I didn't want to be a thousand miles away playing baseball and basically losing money.

Finding something to transition to was difficult. I needed to find a profession for the rest of my life.

At first it was an identity challenge. Coming home after the seasons of 1999 through 2005, everybody would be like, "Hi Josh, how's baseball?" When I lost that the following year, it was like, "Hi Josh. What are you going to do now?" It was definitely the identity. Everything slowed down. I was used to traveling and always being on the go. Then, the world just completely slowed down. I was so used to having that passion for what I was doing. Then, I was sleeping in my own bed every night and wondering what I was going to do.

There was definitely a financial part of it too. I didn't do anything to get rich in baseball, but I was making a living. I went from making a living to making zero in a one year span. In accounting or another profession, if you lose your job, you can go to another firm and actually work your way up as you age. In athletics, you don't age gracefully.

I was in my late twenties and thought about the baseball route in coaching, scouting, or doing lessons. I have a lot of friends who went those routes. However, I was a little burned out on the baseball lifestyle. I had a kid, and I missed a lot of time with him his first year. I wanted something that would not take me away from home all the time.

There was a local place hiring for software training and support. I took a job and started going back to school. I was working and trying to start a normal life. I had left the University of Memphis after my junior year to pursue baseball. I finished my bachelor's degree at Murray State, near here in Paducah, Kentucky. More recently, I went to Bethel University and got my master's degree in healthcare administration.

I found another passion. I loved going to school, and I love the business world.

It took a little while and a couple companies with similar roles, but then I landed at Baptist Health about 11 years ago, and it feels like home. Baptist Health is a hospital system in Kentucky and Indiana. I'm based out of Paducah, pretty far west in Kentucky. I work in the training and supporting of electronic medical records. I'm the statewide director of training and support, which is a pretty far cry from baseball, but I love it. I work with some wonderful people and am part of a wonderful health care system.

I think from an intangible standpoint, baseball has helped in my current job and industry by helping me get out of my shell a little bit. I grew up very shy. I was a wallflower. Baseball helped me become more internally confident. When you're pitching in front of 40,000 people, that helps. It also helped with meeting people from different backgrounds. From having teammates all over the country and world, and including my stint in Japan, it gave me life experiences to help broaden my cultural horizon, so to speak. It helped me understand people more, and where they're coming from.

There was a time in my life where I was bitter at baseball. I went through some depression about not being able to play anymore and not being able to figure out what I wanted to do. I'd see my teammates from previous years on television and think, "Why am I sitting here on the couch?"

This might sound silly, but for probably five years when mid–February would come around, I'd be like, "Okay, it's time to go to Arizona for spring training." My body and mind were still there because it was what I was used to. But no, I was working eight to five. That adjustment was tough. Now, I don't know how I could live that life. I've become used to working eight to five and having dinner at a kitchen table.

Maybe it was because I was trying to transition into different things in life, but there were a few years I just didn't want to watch or even talk about baseball. I live in a relatively small town. It would be like, "There's Josh. He used to play baseball." There was a time when I didn't like having that baseball part added to my name. It was like, "Why can't I just be Josh?"

I eventually reached the perspective that it was a kid's game I got to play, and just one part of the life I get to live.

I do miss the preparation as a professional baseball player. I know that sounds stupid or nerdy, but I always loved to practice, throw bullpens, and get ready. I knew I wasn't one of those guys that threw a hundred miles an hour or had all the exceptional skills some guys had. I was very average for a professional baseball player, so I had to take it upon myself to work harder than everybody or at least try to. I do miss the gym, running, and exercising, and trying to prepare to be the best I could be out there.

I miss the camaraderie with the guys, but there was a weird fine line. You have the camaraderie with the same guys you're competing with for roster spots. You root for them, but you're also shooting for the same job and call-up. I do miss the guys though.

Since his playing career, Josh Stewart has worked in software training and support, primarily within the health care industry. In recent years, he has become involved with Major League Baseball Players Alumni Association activities (courtesy Josh Stewart).

Life was simpler back then. I was traveling everywhere and living out of a suitcase. I don't really miss that part. However, I do miss walking into a stadium and taking it all in, being able to play a kid's game for a living for a while.

I love my life now. I recently got remarried. I have a wonderful wife, a wonderful family, and a wonderful job with a wonderful work team. Over the past few years, I've become more involved with the Major League Baseball Players Alumni Association and helping them do kids' clinics.

It's very difficult to go from something you're so passionate about to a normal life, so to speak. However, I don't think people should get so caught up in the moment that they make rash decisions. A lot of people don't know what they want to do in their middle ages, so if you're starting after baseball at nearly 30 years old in a brand new career, it's okay.

I'm very blessed to have been able to play baseball and very blessed to have found my current career.

Tom Wilson

Tom Wilson played 16 seasons of affiliated baseball, including four seasons in the major leagues. His last year playing in affiliated baseball was 2006. Since his playing career, he has worked as a scout, apart from a few

years as a minor league coach. At the time of the interview for this book, he was working and living in Arizona.

In 2005 I had a really good year at Triple-A but didn't get a chance to go back to the big leagues. I was kind of frustrated.

I was sitting at home around the start of spring training and got a call from Gary Tuck and Joe Girardi, who were with the Marlins at the time. I was talking with Tuckie and he asked, "What's going on? Where are you at? Who are you in camp with?" I said, "I'm at home, man. I don't have a job." They asked if I wanted to play. I said, "Yeah, for who?" They said, "For us." I said, "Sure. I'd love to."

Joe got on the phone with the people down there, I got a contract, and within the next day or two I went down to Jupiter for spring training. I spent that year in Triple-A with Albuquerque and we had a really great group of guys that year—dudes I had played with or against over the years. Quite a few of the guys had over a thousand hits in the minor leagues and had grinded it out for a while.

That season I missed a couple of months with a concussion after I got hit by a bat. I played well the last month and a half or so but again didn't get a chance to go back to the big leagues. Joe and Gary had battled for me, but it didn't work out. The last day of the season I was just like, "I'm done. I'm over it." I didn't like playing well and not being rewarded for it, especially after having some big league experience.

I was fortunate to originally come up through the Yankee system. I had some great mentors with them, especially Gary Denbo and Mark Newman. They really took care of me when I was a young kid in the Yankee system, and I learned a lot from them. I had a good reputation as a player in the 10 years I spent there and thought at some point when I was done playing, I would be working for them.

After the 2006 season I got home and knew I was done. I honestly don't remember if Mark called me or I called him, but we had a very simple conversation about coaching. I said, "I'm done." He goes, "Are you sure? I've told you previously you have to be done. You can't make a commitment and then go back and play." I said, "No, I'm done." He asks, "What do you want to do? Do you want to manage or be a hitting guy?" The managing job was in rookie ball, and I really didn't want to do that. He said, "I need a Double-A hitting coach." I said, "I'm in. Let's go." That was my interview. I talked to him for about 20 minutes, and then I talked to Gary. It wasn't much of an interview. I had known those guys since I was a 20-year-old kid.

I was the Double-A hitting coach in 2007 and 2008. After those two years, I felt like I needed a little bit of a change, and to get out of the uniform a little bit.

In the winter of 2008, Billy Eppler, the director of scouting, called me on a kid the Yankees had a chance to acquire. As a hitting coach, you keep notes on every pitcher you see for your hitters to reference as they come up. Billy knew I saw him, and I broke down what kind of pitches he had, how he pitched, yada, yada, yada. He goes, "Have you ever thought about scouting?" I said, "I haven't. Why?" He goes, "That was a pretty simple and efficient breakdown. You didn't even scout the guy and haven't seen him in months."

I talked to Billy and Brian Cashman about getting into scouting and then went into pro scouting. My first year of scouting was 2009 and I did that all the way through 2015.

In the winter of 2015, Gary Denbo was now vice president of player development. He asked if I'd come back and be the hitting guy in Triple-A Scranton for a season. I went back for a year, and it was another great experience. In 2016 we had Aaron Judge, Tyler Austin, Gary Sanchez, and just a really good team. I loved working with the kids and seeing them get better. It was a lot of fun.

I remember we were in Rochester, New York, and both Aaron Judge and Tyler Austin went to the big leagues at the same time. We had talked in the hotel lobby the night before and the next day they had an afternoon game. They both played and hit home runs in back-to-back at bats in their first at bats. I remember sitting in my hotel room, watching the game, and thinking, "That was awesome!" I don't have kids of my own. So, not having kids, it was like being a parent seeing guys you spent a lot of time with, and helped in some way, have success in the major leagues.

It was more rewarding than I ever could have imagined to coach kids and see them get to New York and have great careers, knowing you influenced them in whatever way possible. I loved coaching but disliked being away from home.

Going into that year, Cashman said if I took that job for 2016, I could go back into scouting after the season if I wanted to. At the end of the season, he was in Scranton watching us play and asked, "What do you want to do?" I told him I wanted to go back into scouting. So, from 2017 until now I've been back in pro scouting for the Yankees.

With scouting you get to have a little bit more of a life and be home a little bit during the season. Whereas with coaching you're basically gone for eight months, which is pretty rough. With scouting we have to travel, but within a certain extent, get to pick where we see the teams at.

I think being a former catcher helps with both scouting and coaching. As a scout, I'm basically looking at the same view evaluating pitching and defense that's happening on the field in front of me. On the coaching side, as a catcher, you're responsible for what happens on the field every night. You're basically an extension of your manager. Then, you also must manage the personalities of your pitchers, which is a part of coaching too.

This is my 35th year in professional baseball. I still enjoy the game. I enjoying seeing young kids play and the challenge of sorting them out and saying, "This is how I think this swing is going to play out over the course of a few years and what this kid at 18 years old might be at 21." It's pretty fun.

I've been lucky. I can never state enough how lucky I was to have great mentors in Gary Denbo and Mark Newman.

It's pretty special being part of the Yankees. My first year with them was 1990, and I came up through the system with some really good players. The Yankees have always been a class act with doing things the right way, and the expectations they instill in their players. It's the most storied franchise in all of sports. I've been very fortunate.

Jim Rushford

Jim Rushford played seven seasons of affiliated baseball, including one season in the major leagues. His last year playing in affiliated baseball was 2007. Following his playing career, he worked as a heavy equipment operator at a copper mine before entering medical billing coding. At the time of the interview for this book, he was working and living in Arizona.

I was not signed going into the 2008 season. I went up to Tucson the last year the White Sox were there for spring training. I talked to Buddy Bell and basically talked my way into a minor league spring training invite. I performed well, but the numbers were against me.

I think they may have been considering me as a future coaching prospect. However, I was afraid if I approached them about it, I'd kill my chances of playing another year. To me it was worth taking the gamble to see if I could get one more year in Triple-A. However, I didn't make the team.

Then, I got signed by Oaxaca in the Mexican League. That only lasted a week before I went home. I met the team on the road in Duranga and played a series there. We then went to Nuevo Laredo for a series. The coach came to my hotel room and said they were going to release me. I was doing fine, however they were only allowed four import players. The other three were doing really well and I was just getting started. They had an opportunity to get someone who they thought was going to be a big bat and play third base for the team. They thought it would be easier to replace me and grab that guy.

I realized the writing was on the wall. I was offered a contract to play independent ball. However, at about that same time I had gone to the local copper mine, which was only a couple miles from my house. I told them I had just finished a long baseball career, had a family to support, and that I needed a job. They hired me and it was a good paying job with great benefits. I had done everything I was able to in baseball. Although I would have liked to have played another season, I wasn't going to give up a good long-term, solid, steady job at the mine to play a few more months of baseball. I would have been in the same situation again.

I didn't make a ton of money playing baseball. My net worth was negative at the time with a mortgage, car payment, wife, and three kids. I needed to put my family first and make sure they were taken care of.

The only other career I had thought of possibly pursuing after playing was coaching. However, I didn't do that because I wanted to be home with my family. My three kids were at the age when they were either in school, or about to be, by then. I couldn't just pick up my family and move or be away over half the year.

I took the copper mine job, and they trained me how to drive a 200-ton haul truck. They're as big as a two-story house and have 12-foot-tall wheels. The mine taught me how to drive them in about six weeks. All I had to do was show up with a pair of steel toe boots and a hard hat.

I had been working for the mine about eight months. Then, the housing bubble popped, and it trickled into the financial crash on Wall Street. A couple days before Christmas in 2008, I was laid off.

Nobody was hiring, and there were no prospects of landing any type of job. I got on unemployment, which was not very good in Arizona. I had to make the decision to stop paying my mortgage but was able to keep up with my other bills.

After a few months, I saw there was going to be an independent baseball team in Tucson for the 2009 season. I had only been out of baseball for a year and could go back and play, which I thought was great. There were no other job prospects, and it was better than unemployment. I went and played for the Tucson Toros that summer and had a fantastic time. It was like my last hurrah, and it helped me get over how my playing career ended quite a bit. I thought of it as a bonus year I never thought I would get. I did really well, and we made it to the championship series.

Following that season, the economy started showing signs of life again and the copper mine started bringing people back. About a month before I was evicted from my house, which was being foreclosed on, I got my job back. It was a real stroke of luck because I didn't know what I was going to do. I had no income because the baseball season had ended. When

I got my job back, that enabled me to rent a house in my neighborhood, and things went back to normal.

For 2010 I worked out a deal with the copper mine and Toros that allowed me to play in just the home games. I did that for a while, but it was just too much. I would work 12-hour shifts going back and forth between nights and days, and then try to play baseball games. Also, I didn't really feel like I was part of the team because I wasn't going on road trips. Additionally, I felt bad because I knew I was taking somebody else's spot every time I'd come in. I didn't make it through the entire season.

For my very last game, we were down by one run late in the game. I hit a double in the gap to tie it up. We went into extra innings, and I came up with the winning run on third. With the infield pulled in, I hit a chopper over the infield for a walk-off single that scored the winning run. The team piled on me, then packed up and went on a 21-day road trip. That's when I called it quits.

I stayed at the copper mine for 14 years.

It was a tough job, a little dangerous, and the hours were difficult. It was a good job for a long time though. Eventually, they started making cuts, mostly to benefits. I was kind of going backwards.

There was always the threat of strikes. We averted a lot of them along the way but finally in 2019 we went on strike. I started substitute teaching and coaching baseball at the local high school. By that time, my son was on the high school team, so that was a lot of fun for me although it was a little stressful with the money. Unfortunately, about eight games into the 2020 season Covid hit, and the season got cancelled.

The strike ended after about a year, and I went back to the copper mine. I worked there a little over another year, but once I had the opportunity to move into something else, I took it.

I had an in for the healthcare company my wife worked for and decided to make the switch. For a little over two years, I've been working in medical bill coding. It's a really good job where I can work from home and have flexible hours. I just have to do my eight hours a day, which has enabled me to continue some coaching and see my kids' games and events. It's improved my quality of life a lot.

As far as the intangibles, my experience in baseball has helped in my other jobs. In baseball you learn grit and tenacity. You learn teamwork, and how to overcome challenges when your back is against the wall.

Baseball's kind of a microcosm of life. When things are going bad for you on the baseball field, that's when you learn what you're really made of. Are you going to cave in and quit, or are you going to find a way? When you go through that enough times, it becomes part of your inner self and your personality. You take that into the working world. You learn how to survive the cut and how to work your way up. There are many things about the game that apply to aspects of real life. If you've been a professional baseball player, you bring a lot to the table at any job due to those experiences.

However, as far as tangible skills, I think the thing that hurt me was becoming institutionalized by the game. I only knew baseball. I didn't know how to work on a computer, and didn't have any sales or business skills. I came away without many marketable skills. There are a lot more resources now. They've realized this is a problem for guys.

A lot of guys go into sales careers. That's always something you can step right into. However, I'm not really a salesman. That's not my personality. Some guys come out with money and can make investments in businesses like opening a baseball facility. I wasn't in that position. I wish my younger self had learned a blue-collar skill like welding, plumbing, or electrical. Those are things you can do in the offseason and then step into afterwards to make good money. I was lucky with that copper mine job. All I had to do was show up and they taught me.

The advantages I had were that I had finished college before my professional playing career started, and I had some experience knowing what life was like without baseball. I had a couple gaps towards the beginning where I gave up on playing. I was doing independent ball, then I'd quit for a year, and then I'd go back out again. Most guys don't have those experiences without baseball. All they know is that they're a baseball player, and their self-image is built around that. Suddenly, it's gone and all those things that made you feel good about yourself are no longer there anymore. It's a tough adjustment. Since I had some experience where baseball was not a part of my life, I was able to think back to those times and use those memories to assist with the transition into the next stage.

You must find a new passion and dive into it. That helps. However, when you do that, you also must realize nothing's going to be as great as having been a professional baseball player. You have to find something that makes you excited for the next day. I got really into politics and economics, and read dozens and dozens of books. I found it fascinating. It kept me busy. Also, I continued with some of my old hobbies like weightlifting, running, and playing the guitar a little bit. Those had been things I had picked up when I was younger and got back into.

I have three kids and got to do a lot of things with them.

My son, Milo, is now a professional baseball player, and I get to do the whole thing over again with him. Everything I did wrong, I try to fix for him. I am a nervous wreck watching Milo's games. When I played, I knew I had some control. When I watch him, I'm helpless. I don't know how to

Jim Rushford on deck during his major league debut with the Milwaukee Brewers in Chicago (courtesy Jim Rushford).

watch. I have to practice watching. I'm getting better at it, but I still haven't quite settled in.

I'll always have peace of mind because I did get that cup of coffee in the major leagues, and specifically hitting the one home run. Nobody can erase that from the record books. I would've loved to have been a superstar and made millions with everyone cheering for me. That wasn't in the cards, but I can feel good about everything I did, especially due to the fact I had such a difficult journey.

I recently wrote my baseball autobiography, *The Pizza Guy Delivers*. Even when I was playing, people were telling me I should write a book about how I went from independent ball to the big leagues. I'd say one day I might, but it wasn't until many years later when Andrew Martin, a baseball historian, contacted me on Facebook and said he'd like to do a book with me. It started when he asked me a bunch of questions for a blog he has, but that got me started and the floodgates opened.

I wrote the entire book on my cellphone, if you can believe that. It wasn't until the very end that I got on a computer. Also, most of it was written while I was on the strike line at the mine. I had to serve time on the strike line, and didn't want to just sit there, wasting time.

It was therapeutic, a way to gain closure, and put certain things behind me. When you think back on stuff, you get emotional. It was

Following his playing career, Jim Rushford spent many years working at a copper mine driving large haul trucks. Here he poses in front of one of the trucks he drove (courtesy Jim Rushford).

almost like being in a chair at a psychiatrist's office going through all the emotions again. It was crazy. However, I was more motivated by wanting to leave a legacy through something that can be passed down through generations of the family. I am really glad I did it. I don't think I'll ever write anything else in my life, but I was determined to see that through and make it happen.

Scott Spiezio

Scott Spiezio played 16 seasons of affiliated baseball, including 12 seasons in the major leagues. His last year playing in affiliated baseball was 2008. Scott's father, Ed, also played in the majors. Overlapping with his

playing career, Scott struggled with drug and alcohol abuse for many years. Since gaining sobriety, he has started his own baseball instruction business and regularly serves as a motivational keynote speaker before schools, churches, and other organizations. At the time of the interview for this book, he was working and living in Illinois.

I had just come off some great years in Anaheim. I really wanted to stay with the Angels, but they had other plans. I signed a big deal with Seattle and got hurt in spring training.

In Anaheim, I had a great group of Christian guys, and we would hold each other accountable, but I hadn't established that yet with Seattle. I had doctors telling me I probably wouldn't play again and that I might end up paralyzed if I tried. I started getting depressed.

I was not a big drinker at the time. I didn't like the taste of beer and alcohol but started liking mixed drinks. They helped take away the depression, and my back wasn't feeling great either. I drank more and more because it was a temporary fix.

Every doctor I went to during that spring training kept telling me, "Don't play. You're going to need a major surgery for even the possibility of playing, and you should wait until June before having the surgery." Well, one doctor finally said my spinal column was thick enough, and that if I could withstand the pain, I could play. That was probably the worst thing he could have told me because then I did whatever I had to do to get on the field. There's no way I should have played that year. How I even hit .215 with 10 home runs and 49 RBIs, or even threw the ball across the infield, is beyond me.

I was drinking more and more for the temporary fix, and when I drank, I made bad decisions. Bad things happened, and they led to a divorce.

I thought Seattle would appreciate the fact that I went out on the field hurt, but they didn't. For 2005, they went out and got Richie Sexson and Adrian Beltre. I only had 40 something at bats that year, and many of those at bats would be two weeks apart. It was awful, and I ended up getting released. I just had the worst two seasons of my career, and I started thinking my career might be over.

I got remarried, and in addition to the drinking, I was introduced to drugs.

I didn't think I was going to play, but towards the middle of February in 2006, I got a call from my agent saying the Cardinals wanted to give me a shot. I got pumped up again. Not only was I getting a chance, but it was also with St. Louis. Because of my dad, I got to go down there for the reunion games as a kid, and it was one of the teams I loved growing up. It was like a revamp. They gave me number 26, which was my dad's old number, and I made the team on the last day of spring training.

Late that season, I started getting into drugs more. The night before a game in Phoenix I took some drugs and then hit two home runs the next day. It became a superstition that lasted the rest of the season. I still put up pretty good numbers and we won the World Series. However, I was a train wreck. I thought I'd stop, but it got worse in the offseason.

I hadn't talked to my parents in a year and a half or two years. When I got divorced, they were upset and could tell I was a different person. They didn't want to watch me destroy myself. Well, I started talking with my dad again around the time of the ring ceremony in 2007, and the Cardinals brought him in to give me my ring.

Eventually, I went to the Cardinals and told them what was happening with my alcohol and drug use, and that I didn't know how to stop it. They said they'd send me to rehab, nobody would know, and that they would put me on the disabled list. I had a finger infection earlier in the season and they were going to say it came back. Well, somehow things leaked and the next day it was all over the press. That really sucked because I hadn't told anybody in my family, and I had just started to talk to my dad again. When I went to rehab, my parents went there for two days, trying to understand ways they could help me. I thought after rehab things would be okay. I thought, "Okay, I'm done. I'm healed." However, it wasn't a healing experience. I went and played the night after my 28 days, against the Cubs.

I finished the 2007 season and was being tested regularly. I wasn't using drugs, but I was still drinking.

That winter I got in a wreck. I hit a fence and luckily didn't hurt anybody, but I ran from the scene. The Cardinals were like, "What are we supposed to do?" I said I'd go to rehab again and I was sent to Sierra Tucson in Tucson. Things started clicking and I was on track. I went to spring training, but the Irvine Police Department put warrants out for my arrest because I had left the scene of the wreck. At that time, the Cardinals released me and I just kind of lost it. I went off the deep end.

The Braves gave me a shot. I was doing well, and they were ready to bring me up. I started thinking about being in Atlanta and not seeing my kids like I was able to in St. Louis. I went on a bender and told them I was going to retire.

The next couple years I tried to play in independent ball. At the end of the 2009 season, I played for Phil Nevin in Orange County, and the first part of 2010 I played with the Newark Bears with Tim Raines as my manager. I came home over that Independence Day, saw my son play in a tournament, and thought about how much I was missing out. I went back and told Tim Raines I was done.

For quite a few years, I didn't really do anything work related other than a hand full of hitting lessons and letting a team rent my property briefly. I was spending a ton of my money, and it started dwindling down. I began selling stuff and eventually decided to turn everything over to my dad and give him power of attorney.

Between 2010 and 2018, I went to rehab eight or nine times. I got divorced a second time. There would be times where I was sober for eight or nine months, or even a year, and then I'd fall back.

There was one period for about a year where I was sober helping a church out. I became good friends with the pastors and would help work with the teen groups. I was volunteering to do just a bit of everything, then they hired me to work 10 hours a week. I wasn't making a lot of money, but I was in a good environment. However, the relationship I was in was unhealthy at the time, and I eventually went back to drinking.

I always had the attitude of never giving up. I was still reading the Bible and praying all the time, and I went to rehab a bunch of times. But it was still hard for me to kick alcohol.

I met a girl named Tonia Boyer, and we became great friends. She tried to help me. She'd come over and dilute my drinks. We'd have really good conversations about trying to kick drinking, my relationship with God, and things like that. She brought me to her church, which really clicked for me.

Then, in April of 2018, I turned yellow. Tonia called the doctor, and he said to go to the ER right away. Me being me, I said no. Well, I finally agreed to go about 24 hours later after she threatened to call everybody and have them drag me there.

I was told I had a 20 percent chance to live and that scared me. I remembered what a probation officer from one of my incidents had said. She said, "What do you want on your epitaph? Do you want your kids to read that you were the town drunk?" That flashed before my eyes.

I had always prayed to God to help me but afterwards I'd go back to drinking because I'd be like, "Okay, I've got it now." For the first time, I asked God to take away my cravings and that I'd do whatever he wanted. From that day on, I haven't had any cravings. When I had prior bouts of sobriety, I'd go past a liquor store and start thinking about vodka or go past a Mexican restaurant and start thinking about margaritas. My mouth would start salivating. I can't explain it any other way, but that God took those cravings away from me. To this day, if I see a bottle of alcohol, I feel like I'm going to throw up.

I was going to need a liver transplant. I had a special liver team telling me that after six months of no drinking they would try to find a match for me. Every few weeks I would have to go in and have two liters of fluid drained because my liver wasn't working. I had seen people like that in rehab and always thought to myself, "That'll never happen to me." Now, I was just hoping I could make it to six months.

Within a few months, my liver miraculously came back to health. The doctors said all my levels were normal and they didn't know how it happened, other than having somebody upstairs looking out for me.

I was very cautious about people, places, and things. I had Tonia stay with me because people would show up at my place, thinking it was for after hours. She would meet them at the door and chase them away. I started shutting my gates, and eventually people figured it out.

I wanted to share the message of my sobriety but was very reluctant at first. I knew in the past I got overly cocky at about a year and went back to drinking. I wanted my actions to speak because there were many times I had told people I was sober and done with drinking, and I think a lot of people got tired of hearing that only to see me fall again.

At a year of sobriety, I went and saw Brian "Head" Welch from Korn speak at a church nearby me. He spoke of having to put his daughter in a Christian rehab center, and she spoke as well. After that, I made my first social media post about my sobriety.

When Covid came, the local independent team, the Joliet Slammers, reached out and said they were going to put together a small four team league. If you remember, that year minor league affiliated teams didn't play. They had 120 guys on the draft list that included kids that just came out of college, were in independent ball, and even some in affiliated ball. They asked if I would be interested in being one of the managers. There wasn't much money in it, but it was an opportunity to test the waters of getting back into the game and seeing if I would like coaching. There was some really good talent, and I really liked it.

Well, I have a beautiful piece of property I bought right after the 2002 World Series. There's about 47 acres that sit mostly in the woods off a creek here. Because of the notoriety I had when playing, it was hard for me to hit at local places and lift weights because I would start talking with people. By the time I'd leave, I'd have spent way too much time talking and not enough hitting or lifting. I built a place on the property for me to hit, field, lift weights, and do cardio. I used it while I was playing, but after 2010 I didn't really use it anymore.

During that summer of 2020, my oldest son was home from college and coming over to my place, lifting weights and hitting BP. Sometimes I'd take him to games, and he would shag balls and take some swings. He started liking it and I had a lot of fun with him. Eventually, he went back to school, and we finished the season.

Some people knew about my property and because a lot of stuff was closed due to Covid, people started asking, "Would you work with my son?" I'd say sure. Word spread quickly in this town.

I have a buddy who helped me set up an LLC, and we named it Spiezio Baseball. I set up a Facebook page and while I'm not great at posting stuff, it grew to where I have become incredibly busy. Things have grown every year. I've also started doing team lessons.

A great thing is that I didn't have a lot of overhead to get started. The facility was already there. I've just had some minor expenses. However, I throw so many pitches in a day my arm's about to fall off, so I'm about ready to purchase a pitching machine.

It's been really cool. I've had kids as young as six and probably as old as about 26 in here hitting. Some of the kids I started working with are now playing in college. I get texts from kids and parents, and I find it very rewarding.

I've also helped out some of the kids with drug and alcohol issues, and often share my story with them. Just yesterday I was working with a kid for the first time, telling him about my career, and letting him know I probably missed out on four or five years because I was drinking, doing drugs, and making bad decisions. I didn't know it, but his dad was a police officer, overheard it, and told me it was good for him to hear.

A few years ago, the Cardinals started inviting me back to do things. I figured they were still pissed at me. Even at the 10-year reunion for the 2006 team, I was still drinking and not myself. However, they reached out to me and invited me to a fantasy camp. I went and I loved it.

Scott Spiezio played in 12 big league seasons (courtesy Doug McWilliams).

Scott Spiezio regularly shares his redemption story as a keynote speaker before schools, churches, and other organizations (courtesy Scott Spiezio).

While there, I was talking with Joe Pfeiffer, who's one of the guys in charge of the alumni and fantasy camps. He's also a Christian and asked, "When you come back next year, will you lead chapel?"

It brought me back to one of the first times Tonia took me to church when I was still drinking. I was talking to the pastor, and he was smiling at me. I said, "What are you smiling at?" He goes, "You're broken. That's where you need to be so that God can heal you." He then started asking if I would go and speak to their teen group. I told him I wasn't a big speaker. He said, "Well, let the Holy Spirit do the work."

That planted the seed about speaking.

I went to fantasy camp the next year and shared my story. They recorded it and put it on YouTube. People started asking me to do podcasts and other speaking engagements to talk about my story. At first, I wasn't charging. Then I had to start asking people what I should charge. Often people will just reach out and say we'll pay you this or that. I'm often like, "Wow! Really? That's really good."

I've spoken before at least a hundred organizations over the last couple years. I share my story with schools, churches, baseball groups, and other organizations. It's more about the message than the money to me. The main reason I do it is because I don't want people to go through what my family went through.

People ask me all the time about regrets. The biggest regret I have is missing out on a big portion of my kids' lives. I regret the pain I put them, my family, friends, and community through. However, the one thing I can do now that I couldn't do before is show empathy towards people who are suffering. If I can help them turn their lives around or bring them closer to Christ, then all of it's been worth it.

I've learned you can't find your identity in what you do. For many years, I identified as a baseball player. My identity has become a Christian first, and then whatever else comes with that. I make sure I intentionally make room for God and his plan. That's a great thing about this property. I go outside, walk on the trail down to the creek, and just listen.

Lance Niekro

Lance Niekro played 10 seasons of affiliated baseball, including four seasons in the major leagues. His last year playing in affiliated baseball was 2009. Lance's dad, Joe, and uncle, Phil, also played in the majors. Following his playing career, Lance has worked in real estate, coaching, and sales. At the time of the interview for this book, he was coaching at the colleigate level and living in Florida.

When I was playing, I thought when I was this age, I'd be retired, playing golf every day, and living the vacation life. That's what everybody thinks when they're playing.

I was released by the Giants, signed with Houston, and then released by them. I didn't want to go to independent ball, and I didn't have any teams calling. My mind was already kind of out of it. I could just tell at that point of my life. My dad had died recently and so much of baseball for me was connected with my dad. I felt that when he died, part of my baseball career died also.

My dad died before my last season in San Francisco. At the time of his death, it looked like I was at the beginning or middle of my career, so I never really had a conversation with him about what's after playing.

After my time with the Astros in 2008, I worked for a telecommunications company. I had worked a fantasy camp in Cooperstown with my uncle Phil, and one of the guys I met there called me and asked if I was interested in the job. I said I'd try it.

I was in charge of purchasing. We had crews in four different cities throughout Florida and Alabama. They did the cables for cell phone towers, and also assisted with disaster recovery for hurricane areas, and things like that. Anytime anything needed to be purchased from nuts and bolts, to 300-foot cell phone cables, it went through me. I was not qualified for it at all. I did that for about nine months. It was a great job, and I could have made a career out of it. However, I was sitting at a desk all day and I'd never done that. It wasn't what I was used to, and it wore on me.

Then, an opportunity came up with the Braves. I approached the guy who helped me get on with the company and told him about it. He was like, "Oh my gosh. You've got to do it."

In late 2008, I was here in Lakeland. I had a buddy who had this barn and big outdoor area where everybody would congregate, watch football games, and stuff. There was a guy there one night named Brian Bridges who at the time was scouting for the Braves. He asked, "Do you still throw a knuckleball." I said, "Yeah." I had a couple of gloves and a ball in my car. We got them out, I threw him two knuckleballs, and he called the Braves about me getting a shot at pitching.

That year the Rays were in the World Series against the Phillies. I was at one of the games and saw my agent there. I said, "I think I want to give pitching a try." He said, "All right, let's do it."

I called my uncle, he called the Braves, and he pulled some strings to get me into the organization. Before I knew it, they called me, asking if I wanted to come to minor league spring training.

I had a buddy that was able to set his own schedule. Every day, I'd work half a day at my telecommunications job, come home, and then we'd go to the Little League fields to throw. We flew up to Atlanta to work with my uncle for about a week, and that was it.

I was fortunate I had the connections to get into it. If I didn't have those connections, obviously it never would have happened. I just told myself I would give it a try if the opportunity presented itself, and the opportunity presented itself.

I had a lot of fun doing it, and who knows where it would have gone. It was a two-year plan for me. The first year they said they could send me to Low-A, short season, or stay at the spring training complex that was 45 minutes from my home. I chose to do that. They told me the next year they'd probably send me to High-A.

When I was with the Braves working on the knuckleball, I obviously wanted to try to get back up to the majors. It was one of those things I told myself I'd give a try if my career as a hitter ended early.

Towards the end of that first year my wife got pregnant, and I just had a moment. I remember we were in the locker room, and we were playing in Lakeland that night. They told me, "I know you're not scheduled to pitch, but since we're in Lakeland, I'm sure you'll have family and friends there. We'll throw you for an inning or two." Right then it just hit me like, "I'm done." I didn't even think about it that morning. It literally just hit me that day, and that was it.

It was my wife getting pregnant and realizing my age. Two years earlier I was hitting in front of Barry Bonds and now I'm sitting in the bullpen in extended spring training. I think everything just came to a head where things had gone backwards so much, I just felt like I was starting over. I was older than everyone and even though it was a unique pitch, I felt like I may have been doing it for the wrong reasons. Obviously, one reason was wanting to get back to the major leagues. However, I think a large part of it was that I was doing it in memory of my dad, and for my uncle. I just came to the realization that day that I just needed to move on.

Luckily, towards the end of my playing career as a position player, my wife, who I was engaged to at the time, really pushed me to get my degree. Against what I wanted to do, I went ahead and did that. Thankfully, she pushed me in that direction because it opened up more avenues for me.

There was guy named Roland Hemond, an old baseball guy that used to give out scholarships to people involved in baseball. I got wind of it from somebody and contacted Roland. I had to apply and write an essay, and was fortunate to get that scholarship. Global Business Management seemed like it had the most interesting courses, not that it necessarily was related to what I was thinking about doing at the time. I did it online through the University of Phoenix and it took me about a year and a half.

Some of the time I didn't have a job, and we didn't have kids at the time. Other than writing a lot of papers online every week, it was pretty easy. A lot of the people I was in groups with had families and full-time jobs. I couldn't imagine doing it at that stage in life.

It was a humbling experience because when you're in the major leagues, you think that's going to be it. You're going to play, have your career, make your money, and you're not going to have to do anything else unless you want to. Although it was virtual, it was still a school environment, and it made me wish I had paid a little more attention when I first was in school so I wouldn't have had to take so many classes later. However, you can't go back and change the past.

Some of that time overlapped when I was pitching with the Braves. There were a lot of late nights staying up and trying to finish schoolwork after being at the field. I was at the field in the mornings and afternoons. I'd get home, chill out for a little bit, eat dinner and stuff, and then focus on school.

I wanted to make sure I wasn't working in an office.

The assistant coaching job opened up at Florida Southern, right here in Lakeland. It just kind of fell into my lap really, but after doing it for a little bit, I realized it was something that I really wanted to do.

I'm now the head coach at Florida Southern and it's my 13th year there. I also have my real estate license so in the summers and falls when the schedule's a little lighter, I do some real estate work around town. However, in general, coaching college baseball keeps you going a lot of the time. Between the regular season with practices and games, there's also the recruiting. We're a smaller school, so we don't have a huge support staff. When it comes to budgets, orders, compliance, and all that, a lot of that falls on me and the other coaches as well.

I think my experience as a former professional player definitely helps just for the fact that I've been there. Everyone in the locker room has aspirations of at least getting a shot in the minor leagues. I've been through the minor leagues. I've been to the big leagues. I have advice, stories, realizations, and expectations that I can relay to them. We've had guys drafted and I've tried to help them through the process of agents calling them, questions from scouts, and things like that.

A lot of the time I think these 18- to 22-year-olds know more than they do. Being in professional baseball, there's a lot of stuff you're just expected to know and do on your own. I have to separate myself from that and remember these are young men in a huge transition phase of their lives. I can't expect them to know all the things I know right now from my experiences.

I had worked with Phil a lot on throwing the knuckleball and know he wasn't extremely happy that I gave it up after a year. However, he was always supportive with everything I did.

Neither my dad nor Phil ever put pressure on me to play baseball. There are certain pressures that come along when you have a family member or two that played that long in the big leagues, and that starts when you're little. I even see it now with my kids. My older one doesn't play baseball. My younger one does. There's a certain expectation just because I played professionally, as well as his granddad and great-uncle. They expect him to be at a certain talent level, and it's an unfair judgment.

I try to take the same approach as my dad and Phil. I figure, "If you guys don't want to play, don't play. If you want to play, I'll support you and be there to help you, but I'm never going to put pressure on you to feel like if you don't play Major League Baseball that your career was a disappointment. Just go out there, have fun, and be a good teammate. That's all I'm going to ask."

It took me a long time, even after I got done pitching with the Braves, to really enjoy watching professional baseball again. I wasn't bitter. I was just kind of over it. My boys are nine and 13, and they've taken a love of the Phillies. Last year was probably the first time I've really gotten behind a team and started following them. I've always followed the Giants, but it was the first time I really got back into it and was excited to watch. It may sound weird after 15 years.

I think there are a lot of people who don't have careers that end on their terms, and struggle to get back into watching baseball. Some people do, some people don't. I was one that took a while. Maybe inside I thought

I could still play. Now I'm 45 and know I couldn't play if I wanted to, so maybe that's made it a little easier. I've always loved baseball. It just took a while.

There are a lot of things former players must address.

There's a fulfillment issue you can supplement with other things. You can play golf, or now pickleball. You can find things to somewhat replace the competition you thrive upon and that you're used to. For me, coaching is the competition.

The financial part is a huge piece. When you're going from making a major league salary to what you'd consider nothing in comparison, there's a huge culture shock.

Your identity is also a big one. I was known throughout Lakeland as a baseball player. People heard my name, and they associated me with baseball because of what my family and I did. Once you're done with that, especially when it's not on your terms, you have to try and figure out who you are without playing baseball.

The Major League Baseball Players Alumni Association has done a great job in recent years. They have great resources and do a ton of stuff like webinars and seminars on how to deal with it, because a lot of guys do struggle. They do interviews with people who have moved onto different jobs, they help with resumes, and they even help with college. Alumni have done a great thing by looking out for each other and being a resource to assist with what's next.

I've realized if you can try and be a better person every day, then you're going to be successful no matter what it is. That doesn't matter if you're playing professional baseball, coaching college baseball, or whatever you're doing. If you can learn to be happy with it, then you're going to have a better life.

Since 2010

Since 2010, statistical analysis has continued to grow and influence affiliated rosters. Player movement has increased, and teams have become more reluctant to invest in veterans, in favor of unproven players, according to predictive metrics. Minor leagues have been restructured. Rules relating to the injured list, previously known as the disabled list, have changed, and roster moves have become more frequent. International talent continues to develop.

In 2018, the Major League Baseball Players Alumni Association, in collaboration with the Major League Baseball Players Association, created the annual Career Development Summit. The forum serves current or recently retired players looking to explore careers, both in and out of the game, and gain professional development beyond their playing days.

There are six stories that follow from players whose careers have ended since 2010.

Jonathan Van Every

Jonathan Van Every played 10 seasons of affiliated baseball, including three seasons in the major leagues. His last year playing in affiliated baseball was 2010. Following his playing career, he worked in numerous fields before entering the pool industry. At the time of the interview for this book, he was working and living in Tennessee.

In 2011 I was in big league camp with the Nationals. I got sent down out of big league camp and then was one of the last cuts before going into the season.

I joined on with St. Paul. Going into St. Paul, I kind of knew that could be it. I had known guys who had been picked up by big league organizations and gone straight to either Triple-A or the big leagues out of indie ball. However, I had already endured my time in the minor leagues and that was not the lifestyle I wanted to continue to live. The goal was to get to the big league level and stay there. I knew I couldn't play baseball forever.

I went into St. Paul just to have fun. Indie ball doesn't pay nearly anything; just enough to get by and survive. I had a good year but got no calls. By that point I had already made the decision mentally that I was pretty much done.

I enrolled in school that fall to finish my education. After a year and a half at Southern Miss, I got my degree.

I had no idea what I was going to do. I was going through the decision process at 34 years old that a lot of people go through when they're 21 or 22, trying to figure out what they want to do. I bounced around a bit trying to see what might be interesting, what would light a fire under me, and what I could do for a long period of time.

The financial change wasn't big for me. I wasn't a big spender. During my last year in the big leagues, I was driving a vehicle that had already been paid off for seven years. I know finances are a big one for a lot of guys because they have no income and the bills keep coming in. But for me, I had built up retirement in an IRA while I was playing. When I was done playing and had zero income as a student, I converted the traditional IRA to a Roth IRA, so I didn't get hit as hard on the tax burden.

The biggest challenge for me was finding that new identity. You work your entire life to get to the pinnacle of a profession. You are the elite of the elite, and then suddenly you're not in that profession anymore and it has nothing to do with your decision. When that time comes, you basically must start over from scratch. That was mentally challenging at times because you've put a lot of stock and energy into being the best in a single profession. Now, that time has come and gone. You have to recharge and refocus in a different industry.

Originally, I would have loved to have been front office personnel and stay in the game within an administrative role, whether it had been in player development or assistant to a GM, and follow those ranks. I made efforts to do that through attending winter meetings and rekindling connections I made on the field. However, nothing ever materialized. I wasn't going to keep spinning my wheels. I had to pivot and go a different route.

I entered the corporate world in banking, then went into property management. I also sold lighting for large scale commercial hospitality projects, so I learned a little bit about looking at plans, construction documents, electrical guidelines, specs, and those sorts of things.

Somehow, I landed in the pool world.

I had a buddy I played with in college who was a home builder. We had lunch one day and he was starting a pool company in the middle of Covid. He needed somebody to run it. I told him, "I know how to swim. That's about it." He said, "We're going to figure it out." I took some classes to get the basics down, and there's nothing better than on-the-job training. We learned a lot and started building some pretty cool stuff. However, that also ran its course. It just got to be too much to handle.

I had made a lot of friends and connections with POOLCORP because we bought a lot of our materials from them. They had a sales opening, it turned out to be a good fit, and I moved into swimming pool equipment distribution as a sales guy. That also ran its course.

I've been with Riverstone Pools for about seven months now and am back to building pools for residential housing. We do fiberglass and gunite install. I'm on the sales side but I'm also a project manager on a number of jobs.

My baseball experience has definitely provided both benefits and challenges.

First, in terms of benefits, if you can endure minor league baseball for a couple years, you definitely have determination. In my case, it was eight years before I reached the big leagues. You encounter roadblocks, whether they are organizationally, politically, or through injuries. You're always going to have trials and tribulations. They teach you to be mentally tough. If I have a homeowner screaming at me about why their fancy pool is not getting done timely, well, I've worn a Red Sox jersey in Yankee Stadium. I can endure that and put up with it in a calm manner.

Also, in baseball, you're interacting with front office staff, coaches, fans, and others, all on a daily basis. I translate that to the business world. I can converse with homeowners with endless pockets who want you to bow down and do everything they want you to do. I'm also able to converse with the subcontractors and workers on site. I often must converse with different layers of the construction process all within a 10-minute period and they all require a different way of being spoken to. Baseball teaches adaptability and the ability to pivot.

On the flip side, the downfall I still struggle with, is that baseball's a very structured environment. Your schedule is created and tells you when you need to show up to the field, what time BP is, and what time the game is. In business, especially in my world, I must create the schedule.

You can't be afraid to fail. Baseball's a game built on failure. You're going to encounter failure in the real world. You must embrace it, learn from it, and use the resources around you to try and pave your way to success.

Freddy Sandoval

Freddy Sandoval played seven seasons of affiliated baseball, including two seasons in the major leagues. His last year playing in affiliated baseball was 2011. Since his playing career, he has worked in mental skills coaching. At the time of the interview for this book, he was working and living in Oregon.

I was hurt my last three years. I made my big league debut, got hurt, got to the big leagues again, then got hurt and was out of the big leagues the entire year. My three years on a big league roster were pretty much on the DL, which is now the IL, the injured list.

The Angels were nice to me in a way. The date when you become a free agent is November 15. Within a few games of the season ending in Triple-A, they called me into the office and said, "Freddy, it's been a pleasure having you in our organization for seven years, but there are no plans for you moving forward. We have two options. We can wait until November 15, and you can become a free agent, or we can let you go at the end of the season to give you more time to find another team. Talk it over with your agent and let us know what works best for you."

At that time, I talked to my agent and he's like, "Get released at the end of the season. That way it gives us more time. Freddy, you've got a guaranteed job. You're a recent big leaguer and near career .300 hitter in the minor leagues. This is a no brainer. We're going to have a job. No problem." Well, that's what we thought.

Months go by, teams are calling, and my agent does his work, but "medical liability" are the words we hear. We keep hearing, "Is he healthy? He's been hurt for three years. We don't want to sign someone that is going to get hurt again." I had three contracts get voided because they didn't like my medical history. Next thing you know, nobody wants me. I'm talking about not even a minor league job. Nothing at all.

Luckily during those three years I was hurt, I went back to school. I had signed as a junior out of college in 2004, and after 2008, I picked up my schooling again. I completed my degree, and then I finished a master's. School was always important for me. I come from a family where my dad had multiple degrees, and all my siblings have degrees, including master's degrees. It was very important to have a backup plan, so I used my downtime in a sense to get better in other areas. I knew the baseball playing window was small.

I'm a person that believes in God and I remember thinking, "Put me where you want me to go. Open doors for me where you want me to go and close those doors where you don't want me to go."

I gave it one last push. I went to independent ball with Somerset in New Jersey in the Atlantic League. I put up good numbers the first month, and was calling my agent, but there were still no opportunities. Ultimately, somewhere around May I told myself I was going to look for a job and move forward. I went back to Phoenix, Arizona, where I was living at the time, and started looking for jobs and opportunities.

About two months later, I got a call from the winter ball team I had previously played on in the Mexican Pacific League, Mazatlan. I thought, "Maybe a door is opening up." I was in shape, but I started training harder.

We had winter ball training in Tucson. It was a short drive. I'd go practice with the team and thought maybe it was another opportunity.

One of the days while I'm walking out, I see an old friend of mine, Gene Watson, who at the time was a scout for the Royals. I see him in the stands, go up, and say hello. He was more than a scout. He was a friend and someone I had talked to all the time. I say, "I'm so happy to see you. It's been a long time. What are you doing now?" He says he's the scouting director for the Royals. Jokingly, I said, "Are you guys hiring? I have a master's in psychology." He looked at me and he's like, "Are you serious?" I said, "Hey, why not?" Literally, right in front of me, he gets on a call, then says, "All right. Next Monday you have an interview." Granted, I'm still playing. I'm thinking, "Oh my gosh. What am I going to do?"

Two days later, I got called into the office, and Mazatlan let me know they planned to trade me. They let me know I didn't have to travel back with the team. I think this is now Saturday. Now I can go to the interview on Monday without any issues.

I went to the interview, and everything went awesome with the Royals. I got to know them a little bit and what they were all about. They asked, "What do you want to do?" I had no idea. I was still playing. At the end of the day, we didn't come to terms.

Three or four days later I got traded to Guasave. I went there and played my last year of winter ball. At that time, I retired.

I always said, "I'm going to stop playing the game once the butterflies are gone." I was always the player that showed up at 12:30 to get ready. I just loved the feeling of being at the stadium. When I was in winter ball that last year, the feeling started to go away, and I started to notice it. It was very obvious to me. I was like, "Oh my gosh. I don't even want to go to the field today." I would go to the field, and it was hard to work out. It was almost like my heart wasn't in it anymore. It wasn't that I didn't love the game. My playing days were just done.

Somewhere around December, I called the Royals again. They had left the door open, and I wanted to revisit where we were. I still didn't know what I wanted to do. They hired me as a player-coach, knowing I wasn't going to play while I figured things out. I was fully dressed. I threw batting practice, hit fungos, worked with hitters, worked with infielders, worked on baserunning.... I was just helping around.

During that time, something clicked. I'd call it a "God thing." It came out of nowhere. I woke up one day with an idea of talking to players, advising them, and giving them my opinions through my psychology background. I presented the idea to the assistant general manager at the time, J.J. Picollo. He loved the idea, and we started venturing in that direction. He said, "Why don't you stay here in Arizona for the entire season and put a plan together. If you need anything, we are willing to help." I got a hold of some mentors that showed me some things, and five months later, I became the Kansas City Royals mental skills coordinator.

When I started with the Royals, mental skills development wasn't very well known. It wasn't very well accepted either. There were a lot of old school mentalities that thought the game had always functioned well without people that deal with the mental side. The first couple of years with the Royals were a little tough getting the player's confidence, trust, and buy-in.

However, being a former player played a huge role in terms of credibility. I played the game. I know what it's like and how it feels. I got to the highest level. I know the lifestyle, travel, and how difficult it is. I get to skip a lot of the questions. Without any disrespect to any of my colleagues that work in the same area who didn't play, it's just easier for me to connect because I was there.

Working on mental skills was a beautiful process. There was a lot of learning and trial and error. I didn't know how to do what I do now. I started working with one player. Then, it grew to three, to five, and then to 10. The next thing I knew, I was working with half the team. It was very overwhelming in terms of calls, text messages, traveling, and all that.

I did that for four years with the Royals, while also working with people outside the Royals organization, with their permission. I was so fresh out of the game that a lot of players I had played with started finding out I was a mental skills coach and helping people with the mental side of baseball. I started that business while still with the Royals.

After four years, I was a little bit overwhelmed with a lot of work. A decision came to whether I wanted to continue to be a Royal full-time or if I wanted to go out on my own completely. A dream of mine was to be my own boss and dictate my own destiny, so I went that route.

I've been independent about 10 years now and I absolutely love what I do; helping people change their lives, and the way they think. In 2020, during the pandemic, I wrote a book, *Mentally Strong*, that became a bestseller. Last year I wrote another book, *Mentally Stronger*, and it became a bestseller as well. Right now, I'm writing another book that will hopefully come out next year. Life's been good.

My sole focus is 100 percent on allowing and helping people to improve their faults, problems, tensions, stresses, addictions, and all that stuff. It's such a rewarding job and I feel like I've been blessed with the ability to connect with people. I don't think it came from me. I genuinely believe this is a "God thing" and that maybe my playing days were just a steppingstone to be where I am right now.

Like I said earlier, at first, there was a lot of trial and error. I didn't know what I was doing. Little by little, I started growing within what I was doing. It's easy now, but during the first few years there were a lot of sleepless nights. I didn't know if the players would be receptive. There were a lot of people that didn't believe in this.

Again, as the type of person I am, I am always going to get better at whatever I do. I started getting certifications on relaxation, breathing techniques, hypnosis, neuro-linguistic programming, and all those things, and tools I could use to help whoever I was working with.

Even today, I'm still taking certifications, and learning more about how the brain works, human behavior, and things like that. At the end of the day, people come to me with problems, and I have to find a way to help them. You can never learn enough.

A lot of people think that mental coaching is like magic, like you can just talk to me, solve your problems, and play well. It doesn't work like that. It's a process. It takes time to build rapport, get to know players, and build their trust. There are things you need to do. There's a program to follow. You have to put in time. It's not just showing up and talking. You actually have to put in some work.

Most of my clients are baseball players, but I also work with people that have nothing to do with the game. Over the last 10 years, I've worked with pretty much every sport. It's also not only sports. I've worked with business owners, CEOs, CFOs, and others.

I was blessed with my career transition. At first, it was difficult dealing with the feeling that nobody wants you. However, I'm a very "in the present" type of person. It was a "God thing" being led in the direction I went, being put in front of the right people. I prayed, "Put me wherever you want me to be and take me away from where you don't want me to go." So, when those playing doors closed, I realized it wasn't for me anymore. For the transition, I was blessed because I was still in baseball, and I got picked up really fast.

There was no struggle with the transition. If anything, it was kind of overwhelming in the other direction. I was done playing winter ball by the middle to end of January, and I was already working with the

Royals in February. It happened fast. That was a blessing by itself because I didn't have time to overthink about what I was going to do. I turned the page fast.

A lot of people think if you're a professional athlete, you make millions of dollars, and that's not true. That's only the case for very few. I knew that. I got to the big leagues, but I didn't make enough money to not work the rest of my life. I'm so glad I was able to finish my playing career and already have a master's degree to face the world, and real life.

You can never learn enough. You have a lot of free time as a professional athlete. You should pick up a book, take some classes, and learn something outside of baseball. Life after baseball gets real. It gets hard, really quick. I think the more knowledge and information you acquire, the more you're able to put that into practice. Don't get me wrong, you must actually apply it.

I do miss the camaraderie and the clubhouse. You spend so much time with the guys you really get to know them, and it's like a second home.

As far as the game itself, this might sound weird, but I miss turning a double play. Baseball's different now but back then people would slide at you hard to knock you down. The adrenaline of having your back against the runner, getting that throw from the third baseman or shortstop, and jumping over the guy sliding, is one of the things I miss most about the game.

It's important to get that adrenaline. As a professional athlete, you often put all your time and life into one thing and when you don't have it anymore, that's when struggles, issues, and problems happen. I became a recreational golfer years ago, and that provides some of the adrenaline I was missing. I also found it in school, and now I find it in my job.

I've been privileged. I feel so blessed.

Jason Bergmann

Jason Bergmann played 12 seasons of affiliated baseball, including six seasons in the major leagues. His last year playing in affiliated baseball was 2013. Since his playing career, he has worked in the insurance industry. At the time of the interview for this book, he was working and living in Texas.

Everyone tries to stay in as long as possible. It's what we've been doing since we were kids. Every year baseball's been the focus—through high school, college, the minor leagues, and the major leagues.

It's hard to relinquish that. That's what you are. That's what you're trained to be. Then, suddenly, it's not there anymore. Teams don't want to sign you. You're not good enough to hack it at that level. That's fine. Part of the game is moving on.

I tried holding on for so long because I didn't really want to think about life after baseball. For me, those last couple of years in the minors, I wasn't as dominant as I had been in previous years. I was 32 years old and not getting out of Double-A. I knew it wasn't happening anymore.

I also didn't want to be away from my kids starting school and miss those years of my kids' lives. I wanted to be a little more settled.

I can recall when I was playing in the Dominican Winter League towards the end of my career. My daughter was still young but was getting more aware of the situation. She was like, "I don't think daddy's coming home." I'm like, "Oh, this isn't good."

I could have gone into coaching, but I would have been in the same boat, being gone all the time. I wanted to be more settled, and the insurance business was calling me.

My insurance agent was an ex-athlete as well. He asked me what I was doing after baseball, and I said I didn't really know. He said, "Well, you can obviously talk to people. What about sales and insurance?" I didn't have anything else going on, so I gave it a go.

It was the only opportunity I had at the time and something I could jump into very easily. It just made sense for me. For whatever reason, the insurance field works very well with my mind. It just fell into place. I studied up, took the test, got certified, and was off to the races.

The good thing about insurance is that everyone needs it. It's not a niche business. For everyone you talk to, it's something you can sell. So, it fell into place pretty easily.

State Farm was the first place I hung my hat. I was just a salesperson, but I learned a lot of things there. I learned how an agency runs, how to engage with clients, how to provide services, and how to sell policies and products. It provided me with my first steppingstone.

From there, I was able to see the landscape. Just like with baseball or other jobs, you get to find yourself within your industry and gain an understanding of whether it's where you'd like to be or move onto a different place. Once I got my feet wet with State Farm, I saw a different path for myself and took it.

I founded my own insurance agency in 2019. I'm a one man show and don't have any employees. I like everything going through me. I like being engaged with all my clients and speaking with them directly, knowing what's going on in their lives, and helping assist them with their insurance needs and any changes that may need to be made. I can market out to several different companies, and I think there's beauty in that by not being boxed into one corner. I have the ability to mix and match, and service my clients in any way deemed the best fit for them.

I like what I do, and I like the fact that I work for myself.

I was fortunate to have the time that I played. However, I think it was shortsighted of me that I was just focused on baseball. There's only so many hours in a day you can work out and so many throws you have in your arm. You have to fill your time with something else. I should have been more productive with my time. There was time I could have dedicated to finding a post-playing career. I spent 12 years in the minors and majors and could have looked for an opportunity to have something in place for later on.

I think players should be actively working on something post-playing career from the very beginning. Nothing's given and everything can be taken away. You could be the best ballplayer ever and with one injury you're done. Maybe you're just not good enough anymore. That's a fact a lot of people don't want to see. Just because you've reached that top level doesn't mean you're going to stick around for a while. Whether you don't want to admit it or don't want to see it, it's going to happen. There has to be an avenue after you're done playing to set yourself up. You shouldn't be waiting until the last second to jump on something because it may not be something you want to do.

If I had started working in the offseasons on a career path early on, I probably could have set myself up a little better. I was 32 years old, had played 12 years, and my life was starting again all over. Most people are taking entry level positions out of college, and I was 10 years older than them, trying to find my own path.

Major League Baseball is getting a lot better with providing resources to help players transition into the real world. It's almost like playing baseball was a fantasy. Nothing about it was normal. People wake up, go to their jobs, come home, eat dinner, watch television, and go to bed. I was playing a game. I was on the television, traveling around, and doing all that fun stuff. It was fantastic, but it's not like everyone's life. It was great while it lasted but when it ends it is very difficult to swallow.

As a kid you grow up loving the sport and wanting to make it big. You get there and it's everything you wanted it to be and more. Then, it's gone. I tell people it's very hard to live out your dream at such an early age and then have the rest of your life to live knowing that you've already seen the top of the mountain.

Personally, I couldn't watch baseball for many years. It was so real for me for so long. You wake up one day and you're no longer a baseball player. However, the sport's still there. It took my son being involved in sports, and him getting excited about baseball, for me to get back into it.

It's funny living in Austin. So many baseball players live here. I run into them and it's crazy how we don't talk baseball. We just hang out, which is kind of cool. It's like we're in a clubhouse of sorts. There are less than 24,000 baseball players that ever played in the majors, and I'm just lucky to be one of them.

Casper Wells

Casper Wells played 11 seasons of affiliated baseball, including four seasons in the major leagues. His last year playing in affiliated baseball was 2015. After his playing career, he worked in sales for multiple industries before entering the insurance industry. At the time of the interview for this book, he was working and living in Arizona.

I had LASIK troubles the entire 2013 season. During my time with the Phillies that year, I had LASIK redone because it wasn't originally corrected to the full extent to see a 100 MPH fastball and slow it down.

Going into 2014, I didn't have a team. Teams were waiting to see how things played out.

The Cubs saw me down in Venezuela, figured I was hitting well enough, and offered me an opportunity at big league camp in 2014.

I really wanted to build something with the Cubs. I was on that team with a bunch of guys that ended up winning the World Series. I was probably slated to be the fourth or fifth outfielder there, but I hurt my back pretty significantly in one of the spring training games. I couldn't even walk.

It was just a freak situation, but it set me back. Ultimately, I didn't break camp and got sent down. I went to Iowa and even months later, I felt like I was behind the ball. Obviously, if my numbers and production started flourishing, I would have had an opportunity to go to the big leagues with the club because they needed outfield help. However, I just wasn't performing to where I was before the injury or before my second LASIK.

I kind of knew the writing was on the wall.

I remember one time specifically sitting at a bar when I was with the Iowa Cubs. I was going to the bar solo quite a bit, eating dinner, and just chatting with the bartender or whomever. There was a lady that asked, "What are you going to do when you're done? You're in Triple-A, what do you have planned?"

I didn't even want to address it. I actually took offense to the question and was like, "Why are you asking this question? I'm going to make it back." She's like, "Well, what if you don't? What's your plan?" I never wanted to even think about it.

Shortly after, Manny Ramirez wanted to come back and be a player-coach. I grew up a Yankees fan and hated the guy. I remember Marty Pevey was the Iowa manager and he said, "I tried to fight for you. It's kind of beyond my control. I know you work hard, and I think you'd be valuable for this club, but Manny Ramirez has taken your spot." I'm like, "God, this guy." But he was a good player. I wish he had just coached and didn't take my spot, but I could have had my spot taken by worse people, I guess.

I went to play independent ball when I got released from the Cubs in Iowa. When I was in independent ball, it was tough to think about crawling out of those conditions with where I'd come from. Being in the big leagues a year before, I wouldn't say it was humbling as much as just disappointing in my mind. It was also emotional for my family. They're watching you play in the big leagues, and now you're in independent ball the next year. It was a tough pill to swallow.

After that, I trained the whole offseason at Exos here in Arizona to put myself in the best position possible to try and make it back to the big leagues, but I couldn't get a job with any club.

I called Al Avila with the Tigers and asked, "Can you just get me to spring training and let me compete?" He said, "We might not have a spot for you in Triple-A." I said, "I'll go anywhere. I don't care. I just want to continue to play."

I was on the Triple-A roster throughout spring training and then ended up going to Double-A in Erie. I got released a couple months into it. However, I stayed in Erie and was planning to try to come back and pitch. I was working with Mike Henneman, their pitching coach, and he thought I had some stuff. However, I was getting some elbow issues in the Tommy John area so I thought it would be best to go back to my childhood home in Schenectady, New York, to regroup.

Upon my journey back home, as fate would have it, my parents' house got hit by lightning. I was like, "All right, that's God giving me a sign that I need to be at home with my family right now."

I was naive to think I'd be playing baseball forever. I didn't want to think about something else because it would take my focus away from what I needed to be doing. In hindsight, I should have had some things in mind that I might've wanted to pursue or at least had a few of those conversations. There isn't a quick transition. I hear it's a lot like leaving the military. It was like, "See you. Good luck."

There's a mourning period.

It's something you've loved and pursued your entire life. I had baseball posters and baseball wallpaper in my room from the time I can even remember. Watching the Yankees growing up, I'd stare at the posters on my walls every night before going to bed, dreaming of hitting home runs at Yankee Stadium.

I had those dreams and aspirations from the time I can remember, and they manifested themselves into reality. You think about those dreams, and how much they've been on your mind.

Then, it just stops. It's done.

There's going to be a mourning much like the death of a loved one. You've loved them every day of your entire life, and they're gone one day.

I was mourning the game of baseball, and I was upset I wasn't still playing.

I'm sure most ballplayers go through a phase where they don't even want to watch baseball. Then, you have a period of identity. You realize you're more than a baseball player.

However, businesses don't see the value in you or any transferable skills, even though there's a lot of intangible aspects—team camaraderie, competitiveness, hard work, determination. There's a bunch of intangibles. But those aren't tangible in terms of sales numbers and business experience, so they don't translate into the business world. So, you're learning the business world after you're done with baseball.

I'm 39 years old and I played 10 years of professional baseball. So, I really view myself as a business professional that's 29 years old. That helps me, especially when I see buddies that are much further along.

It's tough. A lot of my buddies who I played with are still going through it. You've got to alter your priorities and focus. I try to focus on my family and my wife. In baseball, I was just focused on myself.

Meeting my wife afterwards helped. I don't know how guys do it. A lot of guys, if they meet their wife when they're playing, they're known as the ballplayer. There's a certain persona and lifestyle. Not only do you have to deal with that yourself, but when your significant other has a certain perception of you as the athlete and that's not you anymore, it can have a strain on the relationship.

It's tough to get rid of that lifestyle because it is awesome. You're in private jets flying to different cities, you're eating the best food at the best restaurants, you're meeting celebrities, and you're getting invited to the best things. Then, suddenly, it's gone. It's like, "You don't like me anymore? I'm not cool anymore because I'm no longer on TV?"

There's an adjustment. It's not only tough for the athlete but it's tough for their significant other and family as well.

I never wanted to even think about it. I probably should have at least had conversations with some people about what they were doing after baseball. I didn't have anything set up. I didn't have a family business. I didn't have an idea outside of my major what I wanted to do once I went back to school. If I had conversations with other people about what they were doing, it might've been a little easier transition for me. However, I've learned a heck of a lot in a bunch of different industries, and we are where we are right now, so I have no real regrets.

I didn't have a job in baseball and needed to do something, so I went back to school. I wanted to keep moving. I went back to get my degree at Towson University in Maryland, and bounced around a couple careers when I got out of school.

I was a film major and before I met my wife. I was either going to Georgia or California to pursue film, either on the production side or acting side, or a little bit of both. I was fully committed to doing that and taking that chance. I figured, "I've already played in the big leagues so I might as well take a chance doing this too." That was my mindset.

However, I met my wife and I'm very fortunate for that. I'm not regretful that I'm not in Hollywood by any means. I have two beautiful children and an amazing wife, and that's really brought more fulfillment to me than anything film or baseball could have ever provided.

I'm glad for the situation I'm in now. Everything happened for a reason.

From the recommendation of my old roommate when I first went to school at Towson, I went into medical sales. He's an orthopedic doctor. I figured, "He's smarter than me so I'll listen to him." I took his advice and did some 1099 orthopedic sales for a while. It was tough getting doctors to meet with you on post operative devices but with my experience there, it allowed me the opportunity to get a job selling in the hospital systems back in Arizona.

One of the other reasons I moved out to Arizona as quickly as I did was to form a recruiting company. My partner and I started it in Maryland and branded it Major League Consulting. We tried to help athletes transition out and find jobs once they got done playing, because there's a need for it.

We found a lot of challenges within that. As previously referenced, a lot of employers didn't see tangible assets. We'd get a resume from a ballplayer, and they'd say, "Well, he has no sales experience, so we can't hire him."

We were getting a lot of positive feedback from the players. I was getting resumes from people that needed help, but there weren't a lot of companies that were willing to invest in ballplayers and see the value that ballplayers can bring.

We got linked up with a large insurance company and were moving pretty well. I got a couple of guys jobs with them. We were doing it on a retainer basis and were hoping to reach the point where we could talk about some amount of money that would be fair to bring certain numbers of athletes over to the company. However, when we pitched it, it just never came to fruition.

We thought we'd have more opportunities here in Arizona. However, I had a falling out with my partner, and it became too difficult. Then, Covid happened, and everything got put on the backburner.

I worked on that for a couple years, but it was a side job. It couldn't be my main job because it wasn't bringing in any revenue. There are a couple other guys here doing it, which is great to see because there is a need for it.

As far as my job in medical sales, I linked up with a company based out of California and my territory was Vegas and Arizona. However, when Covid happened, I couldn't get into hospitals at all, so I had to transition from there.

I did some residential outdoor landscape design, but I'd only get paid when the jobs were complete. I'd sell the jobs, no problem. I had sold over a million dollars' worth of residential construction projects over 18 months. However, with supply chain issues and subcontracted work, most of them weren't going to be completed for two years. It was a tough situation.

Then, a recruiter reached out about insurance.

I think the common joke amongst the industry is that insurance finds you, you don't really find insurance. My dad owned an insurance agency in upstate New York growing up. I recall him having flexibility and maintaining a good lifestyle for us. He didn't miss any of my baseball games, and our quality of life was there for our family. I talked to my dad, and he thought it would be great for me.

Insurance affords me the opportunity to provide for my family and get where I want to be. Also, it's recession proof to a certain degree. When things are bad, from inflation to Covid, things are actually good for insurance from a producer and brokerage firm standpoint.

I also like establishing relationships and being able to build on those relationships. From annuities to renewals on insurance programs to protect a business' risk, I like maintaining those relationships. It's not just a one-time transactional job, but more of a consultative job in which I'm acting as an extension of their business.

You caught me at an interesting time because I just accepted a new job offer and gave two weeks' notice to my boss. I'm still in the same field of commercial insurance, but I'm leaving to go to another insurance company where I'll be calling on larger commercial accounts.

I think the last company I was with was like the minor leagues and I was in Triple-A. Now, with this opportunity at my new company, especially with the size of accounts I'm going to be calling on, it's kind of like going to the big leagues. I'm going to relish the opportunity and not take it for granted, especially with the state I'm in. It's time to see what I've got.

I think the confidence I gained through baseball has helped my business experience most. During the interview process for the position I'm entering, the CEO asked, "Are you going to be comfortable in front of CFOs and heads of companies?" I said I've been in locker rooms with A-list celebrities and athletes. Heck, I sang karaoke in front of Kid Rock, Sean Penn, and Uncle Cracker in Detroit. I don't really get intimidated by people because I've been around a lot of really famous people that you see on TV all the time. I think baseball instilled confidence that I can go into a room and have a conversation with anyone.

Baseball also brought me validation. I was a 14th round draft pick and then made it to the top 1 percent of the industry. They can't fill a major league stadium with how many major leaguers there have been in history. I'm in elite company and carry that, knowing I've done something that I strived my entire life to do, and had some success doing it. It was short lived in my mind, but I don't discredit anything I've done.

I try to bring that same mindset and confidence into my current career. I'm looking to try and be on the top of the leaderboard in this profession as well.

Being a former major leaguer makes me feel like if you dream it and believe it, you can achieve it. I always wanted to be a baseball player, and I did everything to put myself in a position to make it to the big leagues. I think having some success throughout my baseball career gave me the confidence to feel like I can do anything.

I think it's a good thing to instill in my kids too.

My family and I are in a good mental, physical, and spiritual spot. We're really blessed for this time.

I want to be conscious of the work-life balance in relation to what career opportunities I have. I also want to be able to balance and support my wife's career. She's in medical sales and super motivated with her career, so we can kind of push each other.

However, goal-wise, family is always first for me. If I'm ever putting my career before my family, then I'm not doing it right in my mind. Not being there for my kids and seeing them grow would tear me apart. I don't want to miss my kids' events. I think it's important for me to be there.

I follow a lot of social media accounts that talk about the importance of early child development, being there, and being present. I've seen posts about people's regrets on their deathbeds. They're usually about not spending more time with family, and dedicating their life to work. For older generations, that was kind of it. You worked to provide. You didn't always

Casper Wells played in four major league seasons (courtesy Casper Wells).

see the full value of being there for your kids because you had to work first. I'm glad that society's changing in that regard.

I get asked all the time, "Why aren't you involved with baseball as a coach?" I think I would be a great coach and mentor but it's the lifestyle. I want to be there for my family. With the schedule and all the travel, I couldn't be away for that long. It was fine when I was playing, and even fun. With a family, I don't want to do that again. My son and daughter are where my time's going to be allocated most.

However, baseball is still an important part of my life.

I've tried to get involved with the Major League Baseball Players Alumni Association and help that grow here in Phoenix, especially with some of the younger players. There are a lot of older players who want to be involved and give back. But some of the younger players are still going through that mourning period. They think, "I'm not alumni, I'm still getting over baseball." It often takes a few years before they're right with baseball again.

I also got involved with the Miracle League of Arizona when I first moved here. It's for kids, and even adults, with special needs. They get to play on a baseball field and they're just so happy in that moment playing baseball. There's so much fulfillment for them.

One of the representatives for the organization reached out to me when she saw I was in town and asked me to come over and volunteer. My wife and I went over there, and we got to chaperone one of the players for a day. After that experience, I vividly remember my wife and I

Following his playing career, Casper Wells returned to Towson University to obtain his degree and has since entered the insurance industry (courtesy Casper Wells).

just sitting in a car and having some tears for probably a good 10 to 15 minutes.

It's still really emotional for me when I see the players because there's such joy there. In the back of my mind, I know they're not going to be afforded the same opportunities from an athletic standpoint, and it just makes me emotional thinking about that. I said if I ever have an opportunity in my career to be able to be part of a nonprofit, this would be it.

I've been a board member there for a couple years and I just love it. They have them around the country, so you might have heard of them. It's a phenomenal organization and they continue to grow. We're really excited about the future of the organization.

A.J. Achter

A.J. Achter played eight seasons of affiliated baseball, including three seasons in the major leagues. His last year playing in affiliated baseball was 2017. Following his playing career, he coached at the collegiate level before entering medical device sales. At the time of the interview for this book, he was working and living in Michigan.

I had a great year in 2016 with the Angels. I was up and down between Triple-A and the big leagues and had a ton of success in the big leagues. I had just over a three ERA. Going into that offseason, I was taken off the 40-man roster. I figured I'd sign a minor league deal somewhere with a big league invite, go to Triple-A, and keep doing what I'd been doing.

I signed with the Tigers, which I thought was a great opportunity. I grew up as a Tigers fan and their Triple-A team was in my hometown. I figured it was a perfect fit. Well, out of camp, they sent me to Double-A to start 2017. I was a bit shocked having come off such a great year. I thought, "In a year did I lose it somehow?" I had some ups and downs in Double-A that season, got released, and went to independent ball.

My goal was to keep playing and get back to affiliated ball.

I made some tweaks to my mechanics, but I felt good about myself going into that offseason. November and December came, and a couple teams put out feelers, but there were no offers. That's when I started to think, "I'm married now. I don't know if going back to independent ball is going to cut it."

Once mid- to late December started rolling around, and I didn't have any offers, I was like, "Maybe it's time to start thinking about what's next."

I didn't have my degree yet, but I did have three and a half years at Michigan State under my belt. I knew I had options. I just had to figure out what that was going to be.

I was still training to play and then, suddenly, at the end of December, I got a call from one of my former college teammates, Eric Roof. He was an assistant coach at Eastern Michigan at the time, and we're really close. He said, "The head coach just left and I'm going to be the interim head coach. Do you have any interest in being my pitching coach?" I initially told him I was training to go back and play. I said I appreciated it, but no thanks.

I thought about it for a couple days, called him back, and said, "Okay. That sounds kind of interesting." I figured it would be a good transition from playing. It's a common theme for when players get done playing. Coaching is a way to give back and stay in the game. Additionally, I'd step right into a Division I pitching coach job with no previous coaching experience, working with one of my best friends.

I took Eric calling me as a sign. It was perfect timing.

What's funny about transitioning to Eastern Michigan is that I actually worked out there in the offseason of 2014. In my wildest dreams, I never thought the strength coach that helped me train there would be someone I would work with three years later. It shows you how important it is to always network and make friends. When it came time for Eric to hire a pitching coach, he could say, "This guy knows the strength coach, facility, and program."

It was a really cool transition and great opportunity. Thankfully, I was able to work on finishing my degree online while coaching. I was just married and had no kids. It was great to step in and work with a great group, and I really enjoyed it.

We had my daughter in 2019, and the ups and downs around recruiting, and travel during the season, made it pretty hard to sustain a family.

Thankfully, after four years of coaching at Eastern Michigan, I was able to land a job with Stryker in medical sales. Some of my former college teammates work for Stryker in the same field division that I'm in now. It all comes back to the relationships I made in the game while I was playing. The Michigan State Spartan family has helped me with every step of the way, both with playing and post-playing, to get where I'm at right now.

For my transition after playing, I think there was an advantage with not being a high round pick. You're always on the edge of your seat and because they don't have much invested in you, in the back of your mind you're always thinking, "I'm one bad outing or one signing away." That's why I was probably a little more prepared or had an idea of what I wanted to do than others.

I played with guys who were high draft picks and signed for more money who were lost when they got out of baseball. When you're a high pick, you're told, and you assume, you're going to make it to the big leagues and play for a long time. Then, injuries and other things can happen.

I was also brought up in a home where education was really important. My dad's a high school football coach, and as a son of a coach, coaching is what I always envisioned myself doing. I always wanted to give back, especially as someone who wasn't a high round pick. I had to learn different tips and tricks, and felt coaching was the easy transition for me, at the time especially.

I was going to be a teacher. My goal was always teaching and coaching. I got drafted and put things on hold for a little bit. I always felt I would chase the dream of playing baseball and when the time came, finish up the degree and get into teaching and coaching. Obviously, it didn't go exactly as I planned, but there was a similar trajectory with getting right into coaching.

My experience as a player has helped a lot in my transition post-playing.

I think back to my time coaching. I could tell them I walked the walk, especially with my pitchers that first year when I was building relationships. I could say, "I was in your shoes six months ago. I've had failures like you've had. I've had days when my slider isn't breaking." The experience helps.

I think about what I do now in sales. I'm in the capital process, which is a lot longer sales process. It feels like you're doing a lot of busy work sometimes and don't see the fruit day to day. But I think about the off-seasons when I was training and thinking, "It's November 25! What am I doing waking up at 7 a.m. and working out?" Well, when it's March and cut day at spring training, that's when it shows up. That translates a lot into the way the sales process works with my job. From day to day, you may not think you're making an impact, but when it comes time for the customer to make the decision on what they're going to buy, they're going to remember those little moments. That correlates to weightlifting days or playing catch days you didn't think mattered. I think that's why a lot of sales companies like to hire athletes.

Athletes don't need to be told what to do. They know what work ethic is and can find their way, knowing their careers are in their hands. I think there are a lot of transferables from playing. Obviously, coaching was an easier transition, but being in sales has been a lot less complex than I thought it would be.

For eight years baseball was what I did every single day. Even in the offseason when you're training, it's your whole world. As much as we may want to say it's just a job and it's not who we are, it really is who we are. You're living it every day, especially in the minor leagues when you're grinding and chasing the goal of playing in the big leagues. I was fortunate to obtain that goal and play three seasons. I think what made it a little bit easier for me is that I tried to have an identity outside of baseball and made sure I always networked.

You miss the locker room and your buddies. One of the cool things about coming up with the Twins was that there was a solid group of us that played five or six years together level by level. That's pretty cool and we stay in touch. You miss that day-to-day with guys you spend five or six months with every year.

One of the things I miss most, and I missed it especially when I was coaching, was the competition. When you're coaching, you have no control when you see a guy out on the mound struggling, and it's the worst feeling ever. I miss it being me versus the guy in the batter's box and seeing who wins. I miss those one-on-one matchups probably the most. Now, being in sales, there's that competition with competitor products.

I have a few buddies that still play, and try to follow the Twins and Angels, having played for them. However, with young kids now, I can't tell you the last time I watched a full major league game. My son's about to turn two and he's starting to play catch, so I'll get into it more. But for now, I don't miss it as much as I thought I would.

I would never change anything that I did or any of the summers I spent playing, but as I get further and further away from playing, I just think there's so much more to life outside of playing baseball. I'm grateful for what I did and glad I did it, but now it's good to enjoy life and the things I missed.

Nick Kingham

Nick Kingham played 10 seasons of affiliated baseball, including two seasons in the major leagues. His last year playing in affiliated baseball was 2019. Following his playing career, he took over his father's pool cleaning business. At the time of the interview for this book, he was working and living in Nevada.

Even in 2018, when I made my big league debut, I knew I was on borrowed time. I had a lot of ups and downs, both injury wise, and with performance. I just wasn't the same pitcher I once was.

My last year in affiliated ball was 2019, and I was not playing well. I knew I was on the back nine, you could say. I just said, "I'm going to play as long as I can. It's a kid's game. If I walk away now, I might regret it."

I went to Korea for three years. Then, going into 2023, I knew it was probably my last year. I went to Mexico. I figured I'd use that as a steppingstone to get back into affiliated ball, since it was close and scouts could come down to see me play there, or I'd head back to Asia. I ended up going back to Asia. I went to Taiwan, started getting some more injuries, and wasn't pitching well.

I had a kid and one on the way. It was time to hang it up, be a dad, and enter the real world. My wife was about six months pregnant. I told myself, "Let me get ahead of it, try to get my life in order, and be more stable to help her through the second pregnancy and set things up for the rest of our lives."

It wasn't an abrupt thing for me. I had no regrets and no one to blame. I'm happy I played that additional year, got that clarity, and knew I gave it my all. There was nothing I didn't try, and I'm happy with it.

My dad had a pool cleaning service I knew I could fall back on. I delayed the real world as long as I could but knew that was probably the direction I was going to take. Nothing else really stood out to me. It was all baseball, until it wasn't. I do like finance and economics, but I don't think I would like a job that entails going to an office from nine to five. I also didn't go to college, so I don't know if something like that would've worked out anyway.

My dad had actually wanted to retire in 2020 when Covid happened, but he knew I was getting close to being done with baseball, so he held onto it for another three years. I'm super thankful he did that. He had a route with about 50 pools in the southwest area of Vegas that I took over.

I'd helped my dad with pools since I was 14 years old in the eighth grade and did that for a job during my offseasons. I was familiar with it and knew it would give me the freedom I wanted. It's not a sexy job, especially coming from baseball. It's not glamorous by any means.

If I'm being honest, I did not want to clean pools. However, when push came to shove, I figured I'd try it for a little bit. I have a much different perspective on it now. It's my own gig and I'm my own boss. I take pride in it and I'm very fortunate. I get the freedom to come and go as I please and make my own hours. Now that I have two kids, it's better than I could have asked for. It's been the perfect transition.

Like I said previously, I have a route of about 50 pools. I do each pool once a week. I usually do 18 pools on Mondays, 12 on Tuesdays, and so on, throughout the week. It's the same order and sequence every week. I often don't see a soul all day, but it is nice.

It's just me. Maybe I'll expand eventually, but it's only my second full year doing it on my own as far as bookkeeping, customer relations, and all that stuff. I don't want to get too big too fast and lose the reputation my dad built up with these customers. All of them stayed with me and they expect a certain caliber of quality. I answer the phone and if I have too many pools, I might not be able to do that. I'll keep it small for now and will see what direction I can go.

Baseball is a team sport, but as a pitcher, you're on your own a little out there. You're more in control of your results. If you give up three or four homers, you're the one who threw the pitches. There's nobody really to blame but yourself. I think that it translates into the real world and business too. It gives you the motivation to say, "If I'm failing at this, it's my fault." On the flip side, it also gives you the motivation to say, "If I bust my ass and market well, I'm the one that's going to succeed the most." You can use that to your advantage and be real with yourself when evaluating. It's being a competitor, and I think that part of being an athlete translates well into the real world.

Identity after baseball can be really hard for a lot of people. Fortunately, it wasn't that difficult for me. When you're a baseball player, that can be your identity. But it's important to separate things. In my early days of pro ball, I was taught it's just something you happen to do right now, it's not who you are. I'm a son and brother, and now I'm also a husband and father. Those things will always be more important than what I do.

As far as transitioning, eventually you're going to have to accept the reality that you're going to be a former baseball player longer than you were a baseball player. The day comes, whether it's tomorrow, or whether it's in 20 years. I knew the day was coming, so I was mentally preparing for it five or six years into my playing career. It was an early realization that helped a lot when the time actually came.

However, if I didn't have this job and opportunity, I don't know what I would be doing. I don't know if I'd still be searching for who I am. I guess I'm a pool guy and there's nothing sexy about that. However, it puts food on the table for my kids and pays the bills. I'm happy I can provide and be a good dad and husband. That's all that matters to me right now.

Index